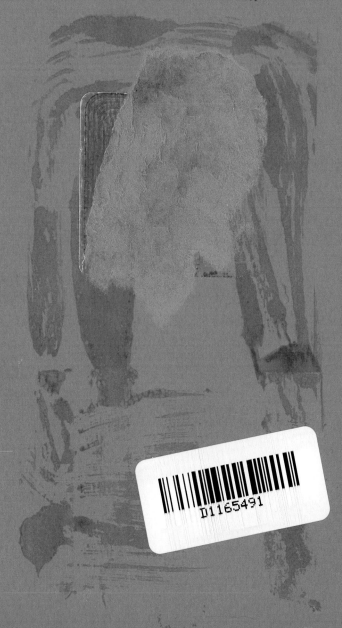

Englishmen
Frenchmen
Spaniards

Englishmen Frenchmen Spaniards

by Salvador de Madariaga

SECOND EDITION

HILL AND WANG
New York

PREFACE
TO THE SECOND EDITION

Early in January 1928, just after I resigned as head of the Disarmament Section of the League of Nations, and before I took over as Professor of Spanish Studies at Oxford, I boarded the steamship *Dresden* in Cherbourg for a visit to the United States. It was 8 P.M. and the passengers had already dined. A special dinner was offered to those of us who had come on board in Cherbourg and I was asked to sit at the Captain's table. I had just begun my soup when I saw a gigantic man enter the dining room; skillfully navigating between the tables, he came over and sat down at my right and began to address me in swift, voluble, and extremely incorrect Spanish.

"Count Keyserling, I didn't know you spoke Spanish."

"Neither did I," he retorted. "I am trying it on."

And he proceeded to explain to me confidentially that he had with him the proofs of his coming book *Spectrum Europas*, an analysis of the characters of the European peoples, for which he expected to win the literary prize founded by the Paris review *L'Europe Nouvelle.* So, at least, he had been given to understand.

This took some thinking on my part. For, as a matter of fact, I had recently exchanged letters with Louise Weiss, the editor of *L'Europe Nouvelle*, to the effect that she had read the manuscript of the French draft of the present book and wanted me to stand as a candidate for the prize, assuring me that the jury would select me; to which I had answered that it seemed to me rather ridiculous to stand as a candidate for a literary prize, but that if she would accept my letter as an act of candidacy, well, there it was.

I had written the book in three languages; I got the prize; and Keyserling wrote to me one of the most generous letters I have ever received.

I bring these memories to life again as a new edition of my book is being prepared, and the question naturally arises how far I stand by what I wrote forty years ago. Every now and then I have had to intervene in a debate on whether national characters exist at all. The opposition nearly always springs from the camp of scientific rationalism, unaware of the fact that the world can only be perceived by the mere intellect in those parts of it which admit of concrete measurement. A man may be extremely intelligent and yet lack the intuition to understand without thinking, to penetrate to the core of such a living fact as national character. Everything that has happened since I published this essay has confirmed my belief not only in the existence of national characters but in the analyses of the three western-European peoples here described. There is one point, however, on which I should be inclined slightly to correct this book. It is a mere matter of vocabulary. I find I speak of English race, French race, Spanish race, and that I have developed a definite dislike for the word race in connexion with human beings; for I hold that these national characters in which I believe so firmly are in fact the outcome more of history than of biology. Other minor semantic adjustments will easily be made by the reader; such as, for instance, references to the British Empire, which remain true in essence even though recent political events would have led the author to draft them in a different form today.

I should not like to waste this opportunity to point out how neatly a modern technological development confirms my analysis of the contrast between the abstract form preferred by the French and the concrete form which the English will naturally adopt. The *avion à géométrie variable* becomes in English the *swing-wing aircraft*.

S. de M.

Oxford, 1969

Contents

PART TWO

FOREWORD

======

This essay was planned and carried out while the author was engaged in international work as Director of the Disarmament Section of the League of Nations. While fulfilling his official duties the author was led to realize the importance of the psychological factor in politics. Since politics is the art of organizing men and things, it may be understood in two main ways, according to whether stress is laid on the personal or on the real element. The first may be defined as the politics of people, the second as the politics of things.

Far be it from me to suggest that the study of things should be neglected. Yet its importance should not make us forget that ultimately the solution of political problems depends on the human element. It is in men that we shall find the true resistance; it is in men that we shall find the power to overcome it. Men, and not things, are the soul of politics, and if things must be studied in order to show the way out of political labyrinths, men must be studied in order to move actually out of them.

Now, in national politics, the primary factor is individual psychology, and the actual elements with which the statesman must deal are the psychologies of class, occupation, and region. He must endeavour to play on the several sub-characters which he finds in the several categories of his countrymen in order to bring them to a state of happy co-operation and mutual trust. In international psychology, by far the most important factor is national character.

Strange as it may seem, national character is not universally accepted as a fact of nature. The time-honoured argument is still heard that, if a Chinese new-born baby were brought to London and educated at Eton and Balliol, the result would be undistinguishable from Sir Austen Chamberlain (to quote, with all respect, a typical Englishman). Yet, even if we admitted this preposterous suggestion, the fact would remain that the Chinese baby in question, if left in China, would make a typical China-man, and that is surely the crux of the matter. It may be argued that, in this example, racial differences are so considerable as to amount to a difference in species. Yet, even within the same race, even within the same continent, the existence of distinct national characters is one of the obvious facts of nature. It leaps to the mind's eye. It is keenly felt by our intuition.

This subject, however, is so open to misconception that, in order to make clear my point of view on the matter, I may perhaps be allowed to quote here an opinion I have published elsewhere, on the fundamental ideas bearing on national and international character.

"If you were to ask a Frenchman (before the War) what his idea of Englishmen was he would probably answer: They are hypocrites with practical sense. It is a curious thing that national character is usually summed up by the voice of universal opinion as a pair of features, one a quality, the other a defect. Thus, to the pair *hypocrisy-practical sense* which represents the Englishman, correspond *clearness-licentiousness* for the Frenchman, *thoroughness-clumsiness* for the German, *dignity-cruelty* for the Spaniard, *vulgarity-vitality* for the American. It is as if, in this big village of the world, each individual nation had been sketched down by its neighbours to its fundamental features—more or less accurately understood—and in this operation a good and a bad quality had remained, witnesses to the double origin of the human soul.

"However hasty these sketches of national types may be, they have the merit of establishing beyond doubt the great fact which many a dogmatic internationalist would have us forget: There *is* such a thing as national character. Opinions may differ as to the influences which create or alter it. Race, climate, economic conditions may enter for a greater or a lesser part in its inception and development. But the fact is there and stares us in the face. History, geography, religion, language, even the common will are not enough to define a nation. A nation is a fact of psychology. It is that which is *nat*ural or *nat*ive in it which gives its force to the word *nat*ion. A nation is a character.

"And what is a character? The first answer that suggests itself is 'a combination of qualities and defects.' Yet, it is doubtful whether this splitting up of human ways into defects and qualities is sound psychology. It savours too much of the old suzerainty which the science of Morals exercised over all the sciences of the spirit. The facts of psychology are human acts. If we look at them with open eyes we shall come to the conclusion that acts are the fruit of the whole of the human being which performs them. To attribute them to a particular faculty, quality, or defect of the agent may be a convenient form of language, but nothing more. All my body and all my soul co-operate in all my acts. More or less consciously present, all my faculties are responsible for them, as all the Cabinet Ministers for the Government.

"The faculties in fact are nothing but abstract names given to the life-power considered in its capacity for performing certain acts. They are different names of the same object, attributes of the same essence. Our kindness, thoroughness, fairness, sincerity, hypocrisy, what are they but names given to the waves of the sea of the spirit? Who can tell where sincerity merges into humility, and where it folds itself over and becomes hypocrisy, and where it touches self-righteousness? When does generosity become ostentatiousness, or kindness weakness, or weakness heroism, or heroism love of display? And how often do modesty's eyelids fall over the glowing eyes of pride?

"Our acts are the flowers of our character. Qualities and defects are the colour, the scent, the shape of our acts. We speak of a brave act as we speak of a red rose, and the combination of causes and circumstances—both internal and external —which brings forth the act, flower of character, is not less complex than that which produces the flower, act of the plant. Nature and culture co-operate in both. Change some of the conditions, and the plant will change the colour of its flowers and the man the quality of his acts. Thus, all we can say is that under certain conditions the plant evinces a tendency towards producing red roses, and the man a tendency towards performing brave acts.

"Now, a tendency is a spontaneous force, blind and undiscriminating. Its only business is to *tend*—a bowstring ever taut— and to shoot forth to the limit of its possibilities. This limit is not rational but vital. Each tendency would act up to the limit of its vitality, but for the action of other tendencies which will partially or totally oppose it. It may enter into systems which will produce 'good' acts as well as into systems which will produce 'bad' acts. But it will always be the same tendency. Thus when we say of a man that he has the defects of his qualities we really mean that he has both the defects and qualities of his tendencies. For tendencies are anterior to all moral law.

"Originally, at least, or in its essence, a character is a given set of tendencies, and one character differs from another not so much in the tendencies it contains as in their relative strength and mutual interplay. For, stronger or weaker, all tendencies are probably in all men—thence the unity of the human race. Yet, when composed in one living total, all these differences in the *quantity* of the particular tendencies produce that distinctive difference in *quality* which we call character; just as quantitative differences in hardness, yellowness, weight, sensitiveness to acids make up the qualitative difference between copper and gold.

"This fact explains not only the underlying unity of the human race but also the inconsequence of individual character. There is a curious assumption—much resorted to by literary critics—that a character must be consequent. The principle is most useful for writing novels of the 'distinguished talent' as opposed to the 'genius' type. It is all like a mathematical calculation. You start with a given number of equations; you shuffle them according to the rules and you find yourself conveniently carried on by a ready-made logical mechanism which safely deposits you at your conclusions. Characters thus *calculated* are to the great creations of art what automatons are to men. Hamlet, Don Quixote, Sancho Panza, Tom Jones are not consequent, because they are living. Hamlet is full of filial love and respect and reverence for his father, yet humorous at the expense of the Ghost. He is tender and cruel, procrastinating and determined, courteous and rude, refined and barbaric. Sancho's love and reverence for his master are genuine and sincere, yet he is always ready to mock him and take advantage of his frailties. Sancho's real attitude towards the profession of his master, the power of magicians, his governorship of the Island of Barataria, the exalted rank of Dulcinea has been the object of numerous commentaries. Did he believe? Did he not believe? In fact, he at the same time believed and disbelieved, which is a state of mind much more complex than mere doubt. And as for Don Quixote, the depth and sincerity of his faith are above suspicion. Yet, when Sancho, alighting from the wooden horse, tells an imaginary version of his excursion among the stars, Don Quixote, drawing him aside, whispers in his ear these pregnant words: 'Sancho, since you will be believed as to what you saw in the sky, I will have you believe me as to what I saw in Montesinos Cave. And I will say no more.'

"For inconsequence may not satisfy the mind but it is good enough for life. Two tendencies may be contrary without being incompatible. Man is not a mere system of qualities, but a complex of all the human tendencies, more or less developed, a kind of microcosm which reflects mankind as a convex mirror, the world—condensing it and deforming it. But the simile is too static. For the dominant fact is that this microcosm is alive and the forces within it are ever in a state of becoming. Each moment of life brings a wholly original set of circumstances, and therefore gives rise to a wholly original act.

"Yet, for all its inconsequence, there is unity, a *coherence* in human character without which it would vanish into the cloudy realm of the undefined. All these tendencies live and work together. Some among them predominate; certain plays of combination and opposition will recur in a given way. A moral physiognomy will result, and this will permit the drawing of portraits or sketches sufficiently accurate for everyday life. For this, a purely scientific or intellectual work will never be sufficient. There are elements in character which can only be defined by instinct and felt by intuition, and which require for their expression words which it is easier to understand than to define, such as rhythm, atmosphere, grace.

"The territorial setting of nations determines that other microcosm, national character. Here, the difficulties of observation are increased by the fact that the character of the whole must be induced from the acts of individuals or groups of individuals. Inconsequence is raised to the second power. History, i.e. the record of the facts of the collective being, is only an element of study, less useful than might at first appear, and not without its pitfalls; for it is either told by contemporaries, who are biased, or by writers too far removed from the facts to be able to render their inner meaning. Then, again, perhaps the deepest and most effective tendencies of national character are the most difficult to observe, for they are, as it were, diffused in the national atmosphere, and like light and air are not seen. Here, more perhaps than with individual character, divination is more useful than observation, and feeling than logic. Through the poetical faculty it is possible to guess some of those mysterious relations within nature which give their value to metaphors—for were they not the symbols of the secret sympathy of things, metaphors would be but mere intellectual toys."

In the above pages will be seen the criteria here adopted as regards national character. First and foremost, an earnest endeavour to conquer the obstacles which stand in the way of all useful work. Nor are they all easily overcome. We must resign ourselves to consider as inevitable the most important of them, i.e. the inherent relativity of our knowledge, a law of practical psychology as it is of rational mechanics. Whatever we may say or feel about other people's characters is bound to be governed by our own character, and therefore resembles estimates of movement made from moving bases, such as the measuring of the speed of a boat from another moving boat. Other difficulties are not insuperable, yet are seriously to be watched and guarded against: thus national prejudices, inborn or cultivated, and ethical estimates, both of which inevitably tend to warp the impartiality of our observation. To this category would also belong pseudo-scientific ideas, in particular that pest of international psychology—the belief that language kinship implies likeness in character through race kinship. No unnecessary hypotheses have been made. Race has been relegated to very few (one or two) footnotes. Language has been treated as an important sign of national psychology, after due elimination of the error just mentioned. An earnest effort has been made to secure national and also ethical serenity and impartiality in the estimate of the facts observed—an attitude rendered relatively easy by the author's deep conviction that qualities and defects are intimately intertwined, as outlined above. The author earnestly hopes that, in the development of his ideas on national character, not one single word has been written which could be interpreted so as to give offence to the most susceptible. He expects the reader, however, to read with the same detachment with which he himself has endeavoured to write.

It is obvious that an essay of this kind must be based on first-hand knowledge and on intuition. This is no "scientific" work, based on statistics, comparative study of sources and "facts." It is, on the contrary, an attempt at utilizing the method of the *living witness* for purposes of knowledge. Strictly speaking, this method is not without scientific interest. We may consider the living witness as a re-agent plunged successively into various national environments in order that he may report his reactions. A strong personal factor, a possible source of error, is to be expected, but the estimate of this error can always be made by the reader—of course with his own personal and inevitable source of error as well.

For these reasons, the choice of characters to be studied has been limited to three: England, France, Spain, the three peoples of which the author can claim to possess some intuitional knowledge. For the same reasons, these peoples are considered mainly as they are today. Some illustrations and arguments are drawn from history, but only from relatively recent times. All allowances are made for possibilities of change and evolution. No causes of national character have been investigated.[1]

The starting-point is the observation of the three peoples in order to note their instinctive attitudes towards everyday life; hence, a law or hypothesis has been drawn, the development of which occupies the first half of the book; the second half is devoted to a series of parallel studies in which the three peoples are watched in the several aspects of life, in order to justify by experience the conclusions arrived at in the first part.

1. Such so-called causes are more often than not effects of national character. Thus, for instance, the Reformation and the Roman Catholic Church, so often quoted against each other as the respective causes of national characteristics in various European peoples, should be more reasonably considered as the effects of these different characteristics: their effects, not their causes.

Though written through the sheer fascination of the subject itself, and with a detachment which he fancies not unworthy of science, the author hopes that this essay may contribute in its small way to better international relations by strengthening the feeling of relativity in matters of national psychology. When we realize that we are all more or less the same, we are more likely to agree.

The substance of this work was the subject of two courses of lectures delivered at the Geneva School of International Studies, so ably conducted by Professor Alfred Zimmern, to whose stimulating friendship I am much indebted. Acknowledgements are due also to my wife (Constance Archibald, M.A.) for the patience and ingenuity which she devoted to the revision of the manuscript, and for many a suggestion for its improvement.

S. DE M.

GENEVA, *September 1927.*

PART ONE

PART ONE

Introduction

A FIRST OBSERVATION OF THE DAILY LIFE OF THESE PEOPLES LEAVES us with an impression of unity, an apparent and superficial unity due to the influence of a system of general ideas and customs common to all white—or at least European—civilization. But if, delving under the crust of conscious ideas, we try to penetrate into the subconscious underworld of instincts and tendencies, we shall observe in each of these three peoples a distinctive attitude which determines their natural and spontaneous reactions towards life. These reactions spring in each case from a characteristic impulse, manifesting itself in a complex psychological entity, an idea-sentiment-force peculiar to each of the three peoples, and constituting for each of them the standard of its behaviour, the key to its emotions, and the spring of its pure thoughts.

These three systems are:

in the Englishman: *fair play*.
in the Frenchman: *le droit*.
in the Spaniard: *el honor*.

We will notice at the outset that the three terms which represent our three systems are untranslatable. *Fair play* has no equivalent either in French or in Spanish. The English translate *le droit* into *law*, which is admittedly a solution of despair; the Spaniards possess a word, *derecho*, which more or less represents in their legal texts the *idea* of *droit* which is handled in the Law Faculties, but the vital *droit* of the Frenchman who has not studied law is unknown in Spain; the average Spaniard, in fact, does not easily discriminate between the words *derecho* and *obligación*. As for *honor* it is the more untranslatable for the existence of French and English words physically related to it. For *honour* and *honneur* differ profoundly from *el honor*, particularly when these words are accompanied by such epithets as Spanish and Castillian.

These three terms therefore cannot be translated, as was to be expected, since they represent not abstract ideas, but psychological species as clearly defined to the intuition as the horse, the birch, or galena.

Fair play is a term of sport. Let us note this: sport; pure action. Fair play means the perfect adaptation of the player to the game as a whole. It regulates the player's relations with his team-partners but also with his adversaries. This is already wisdom. For good relations with our allies are but reason. Now wisdom is something more than reason. It is a vision of the whole, an intuition of all as one single game, and of opposition as a form of co-operation. Fair play implies an effacing of the individual before the team, and even of the team before the game. But this effacing does not mean annihilation. Far from it. It provides better conditions for the efficiency of the individual, since it makes his actions fit in with the actions of others in a perfect system of co-operation. This intuitive and instantaneous sense of balance between the individual and the community is the true essence of fair play.

Fair play cannot be put into formulas. It soars over all regulations, a living spirit. Elusive, yet precise; supple, yet exacting; it fits the mobile forms of life as closely as the glove the hand. As a living spirit, it manifests itself in concrete actions. It is inseparable from action, undefinable without action. It is a way of doing things. In fact, *fair play is action*.

Le droit is an idea. It is the solution which calculating Mind has contrived to the problem of the balance between the individual and the community. *Le droit* is a geometric line which, on the map of the intellect, marks the frontiers between individual liberties. While fair play fits itself to action at every moment in a perfect empirical way, *le droit* draws beforehand a scheme of rules to which it forces action to conform. While fair play occurs at the same time with action, *le droit* precedes it. *Le droit* is not, like fair play, a spontaneous and ever-renewed alliance between reason and nature, but a system in which nature bows to reason. And while fair play unites object and subject in the act, and, active, is neither subjective nor objective, being both simultaneously, *le droit* is coldly objective. To life's rebellions its answer is that the intellect is infallible. *Le droit is intellect*.

El honor is a psychological species upon which a number of preconceived errors prevail. Let us therefore, for its sake, break the balance of this discourse, and, in order the better to understand the facts of daily life connected with it, let us begin by examining a few texts. We shall choose three particularly clear: first, the quatrain which, in forceful and commanding tones, falls from the lips of the famous Mayor of Zalamea, immortalized by Calderón:

> Al Rey la hacienda y la vida
> Se ha de dar; pero el honor
> Es patrimonio del alma,
> Y el alma sólo es de Dios.

(To the King we owe life and fortune, but *el honor* is patrimony of the soul, and the soul belongs to God alone.)

Our second text shall be a celebrated episode in the life of Spain's greatest legendary hero. The Cid, in exile, needs money. He borrows it from two Jews in Burgos, leaving them as security two coffers full of sand, which he assures them are full of gold. Victorious and rich anon, he sends the money back, together with a touching message of explanation:

> You will beg them in my name
> To be so good as to forgive me,
> For I did it with great reluctance
> Under pressure of necessity;
> And though it is true nothing but sand
> Had I left in the two coffers,
> I had buried in that sand
> The gold of my veracity.

Our third text is the curious "romance," or ballad, of the Count of León. Courtiers and ladies are whiling away time in the rooms and galleries of the Royal Palace. From an elevated gallery they can see a cage with four ferocious African lions. Doña Ana lets her glove fall into the cage in order to test the gallantry of the courtiers. The Count of León walks into the cage, rescues the glove, and before giving it back to Doña Ana he slaps her across the face, saying, "Take this, and henceforward do not, for a mere glove, stake *el honor* of so many well-born men. If there is any one who does not approve of what I have done, let him come forward to the field of *el honor* to uphold his opinion according to the laws of chivalry."

These three examples show in actual life *el honor*, of which a somewhat high-flown and grandiloquent idea often prevails under the name of Spanish honour. Let us observe its matter-of-factness, a feature never to be overlooked in connexion with Spain. This feature is apparent in the episode of the Cid's life, the utilitarian character of which is evident. But the ballad of the Count of León is perhaps even more instructive, for it shows a knight, famous for his courage, reproaching a lady for having played with *el honor* of his equals and his own. This eminently reasonable and practical nature of *el honor* must be emphasized, for, under the influence of the type of Don Quixote (not, perhaps, very correctly understood), *el honor* has come to be considered as a kind of extravagant idealism of no practical value.

El honor consists in the setting up of a subjective law of conduct above all objective laws, whether spontaneous and natural (fair play) or calculated and intellectual (*droit*). This subjective law is an imperative sense which the well-born man feels pointing clearly to what he must do in each case. But this absolute emancipation from all social law can only be justified in the case of well-born men, i.e. men who would not take advantage of their freedom for any mean end. As a guarantee, the well-born man gives his own blood. The limit of his liberty is his life. The sword answers for the action.

We have just seen examples of this way of living. The Cid leaves two coffers of sand as a pledge for a loan, but he does so in order to go to fight, and the true guarantee of the loan is not this sand, but "the gold of [his] veracity." Gold, because the veracity is that of the Cid, a well-born man. The Count of León feels free to do this unheard-of thing, to strike a woman, but he comes from the lions' cage and is ready to sign with his blood the sentence which he has just pronounced against the too light lady who would play with *el honor*.

For *el honor*, as the Mayor of Zalamea eloquently says, is the patrimony of the soul and the soul belongs to God. The King, i.e. society, the team, have no rights on our soul, therefore on our honour. In every case our soul remains free to reach a direct understanding with God and to act accordingly.

Society gives way before the individual, save for a test *a posteriori:* the offer of the individual's life (physical life, or, in the case of the dishonoured man, moral life).

We saw fair play coincide with action, *le droit* precede it; *el honor* follows it. In the English standard, rule and action are one; in the French standard, the rule binds action to it; in the Spanish standard, the action binds the rule to it. Nature, allied with reason in the Englishman, bowing to reason in the Frenchman, triumphs here over reason. *El honor* is therefore subjective, ineffable. *El honor is passion.*

The group: fair play—*droit*—*honor* leads us therefore to the group: action—intellect—passion. It would be childish to claim that each of the three peoples is, as it were, specialized so as to be entirely devoid of two-thirds of the faculties which belong to all men. Our general hypothesis goes no farther than this: that the psychological centre of gravity of each of our three peoples is placed respectively:

> for the English people, in the body-will;
> for the French people, in the intellect;
> for the Spanish people, in the soul;

and that the natural reaction towards life in each of these three peoples is:

> for the Englishman, action;
> for the Frenchman, thought;
> for the Spaniard, passion.

2

Any state, whether active or passive, in which a man may be is of a complex nature. When analysed it will be found to contain three orders of tendencies: the first, associated with the idea of mechanical force, and which we understand as the struggle between a principle of power in us and a principle of resistance in the outer world; the second, associated with the idea of vision, and which we understand as an attentive observation of the world with a view to connecting all its parts with each other and with ourselves into an harmonious whole; the third, associated with the idea of union, and which we understand as the assimilation of life by our own being, the circulation in our own being of the life-stream. The first tendency we call will; the second, intellect; the third, passion.

This analysis should not be taken too literally. It is perhaps already too bold to cut the river of life into sections which we call *states*. But even if that is granted, it would be obviously venturesome to dissociate the state itself into component parts on the ground that the different aspects which it presents are connected with the will, the intellect, or the soul. There is no doubt, however, that the complexity of human states can be better understood if an effort is made to separate in them the elements which belong to each of the three orders of tendencies under which our vitality becomes manifest. There are, moreover, extreme cases in which one or other of these three orders of tendencies predominates. We are then in the presence of an act, a thought, or a moment of passion. But it is possible to carry still farther this distinction between the tendency and the state. We may consider, on the one hand, the group of tendencies—will, intellect, passion—and on the other the group of states—act, thought, moment of passion. Each of the elements of the first generates one of the elements of the second. This observation allows us to penetrate more deeply into the internal constitution of a state. A man is acting while feeling a passion; this state may be due to an action (generating factor) which gives rise to a passion (resulting factor), or, inversely, to a passion (generating factor) which drives the man to action (resulting factor). Here is a state which may be analysed as a mixture of thought and action: it may be due to an action which stimulates thought or to a thought which provokes an action. A similar remark applies to a state composed of thought and passion, which may be explained in two different ways according to the element in it which fulfils the generating role.

Normal psychological types, i.e. those which present a perfect balance of the three tendencies, are rare. In the current type one of the tendencies predominates. In all these types, therefore, the predominant tendency becomes the generating element of most states. This factor would constitute a kind of psychological "key" giving the general tone to the symphony of each individual life. Some lives are lived in the key of action; others, in the key of thought; others, in the key of passion. The key or tone of each individual life must, of course, be discriminated from the actual substance of the life in question. Gifts pertaining to the other two tendencies are perfectly compatible with a life lived in the key of any one of them. Thus Cromwell was certainly a highly intelligent man and a passionate man, yet he lived his life in the key of action. Voltaire was far from inactive and certainly knew what passion was, yet his life was lived in the key of thought. St. Theresa, though a most active individual and an intelligent woman, is a perfect example of a life lived in the key of passion.

For we are here in the domain of natural and spontaneous tendencies independent of all opinion or standard. These primary manifestations of nature cannot be submitted to any judgement, whether moral, intellectual, or aesthetic. Each type obeys its specific tendency, wholly ignorant of the fact, with the same blind fatality with which rain obeys the law of gravity, the tiger the law of the strongest, and the rose the law of beauty. We are men of action, of thought, of passion, as we have black hair, a small mouth, or an aquiline nose. There is no question here of a conscious choice but of an idiosyncrasy which implies as many gifts as incapacities. The tendency thus dictated by nature becomes the true law of the psychological type which it defines.

It follows that each psychological type subordinates everything to the service of the law which it incarnates. The man of action harnesses to the chariot of his acts his intellect and his heart; the man of thought gives his acts and his passions as food to his intellect; the man of passion burns in his ardent soul his acts and thoughts. In each case the type gives himself to his tendency with all disinterestedness. Action for the one, thought for the other, passion for the third is life. And life is the flame in which we all burn for nothing, for the sake of burning.

If the hypothesis which is at the basis of the present work is accurate, each of the three Western peoples will correspond more especially to each of the three types here enumerated. The predominant tendency will point towards will in the Englishman, thought in the Frenchman, passion in the Spaniard. In each of them, moreover, it is possible to observe action, thought, and passion as resultant states. We are thus led to the following table:

Predominant tendencies providing the active element

Resultant states	ACTION	THOUGHT	PASSION
ACTION	Action in the man of action	Action in the man of thought	Action in the man of passion
THOUGHT	Thought in the man of action	Thought in the man of thought	Thought in the man of passion
PASSION	Passion in the man of action	Passion in the man of thought	Passion in the man of passion

The detailed study of the nine cases thus defined should constitute, on our hypothesis, a parallel of the three peoples in question. This study might be undertaken either down the columns or along the horizontal lines of the table above. In the first case we should be led to a division of the matter into three main chapters which might respectively bear the titles England, France, Spain. It seems preferable to follow a method along horizontal lines which will allow a more closely intertwined comparison of the three peoples in the several aspects of their life.

I

Action in the Man of Action

THE MAN OF ACTION IN ACTION IS IN HIS ELEMENT. WE MUST therefore expect to find here the Englishman at his best. The English people in effect excel in all aspects of action whether individual or collective.

The superiority of the Englishman in action is well known. It has often been explained by the education which he gets. But, who gives the Englishman his education but the Englishman? It is not English education which explains the Englishman, but the Englishman English education. Let us watch therefore the Englishman himself. We shall see how everything in him instinctively points to action. His main preoccupation consists in being wholly at the disposal of his will at the moment when it must apply itself to the world. With this end in view, the Englishman organizes himself, disciplines himself, *controls* himself. Self-control is essentially a requirement of action. It may have evolved its philosophy and its ethics, but originally it is an instinctive and empirical tendency, the natural development of the human type specialized in action.

Man is a microcosm much less unified than the outward appearance of his physical embodiment might lead us to believe. On the impact with reality it often happens that the extreme variety hidden under the apparent unity of the human being manifests itself by shattering the aims of the will, weakening the means of action, provoking internal rebellions against the decision taken. These are cases when the little people called man is under the orders of a weak Government. The Englishman sees to it that the Government of his being is solidly established. Self-control is therefore but a sound method of individual Government. In making self-control his main preoccupation, the Englishman reveals his primary tendency towards action.

This same tendency is also the origin of the Englishman's empiricism, for the man of action is naturally led to keep in constant touch with experience. Thinking implies a separation from the things thought, a distance which enables us to dwell on the ideas of things and not on the things themselves. Experience, on the contrary, is a stream of life which bathes us at every moment. In this stream the Englishman swims with the same pleasure wherewith he bathes in the cool waters of his rivers and shores. Empiricism is but the instantaneous and continuous mixture of thought and action, or rather, the blending of each instant of action with the minimum amount of thought needed for carrying it into effect. This feature of the English character accounts for the Englishman's neutrality towards theories and for his indifference towards everything that cannot immediately be translated into terms of action. Hence two consequences: the first is that feature which passes for lack of logic in the Englishman. Others reproach him with it. He glories in it. As a matter of fact, logic regulates English thought as it does all human thought. How could it be otherwise? It regulates even English actions, i.e. each action in itself. For a human act must contain the three elements of man's vitality—will, thought, passion. And inasmuch as it contains thought, it contains logic.

But the *allogic* of the Englishman (a necessary neologism in this case, more exact than *illogic*) means that from one action to another the basis of English thought may have changed. Why? Simply because the Englishman subordinates thought to action, so that, when the course of his will changes, his thought is bound to follow in what may be, for it, a broken line, yet is for the will a continuous one. For—and we find here one of the typical features of the man of action—the line of conduct of the man of action is winding because the topography of action, like that of physical nature, avoids the straight line. At every moment, the man of action instinctively seeks and finds the line of least resistance which skirts round the obstacles and adapts itself to them. Hence the continuous and winding rhythm of action.

A second consequence of the indifference of the English towards theoretical thought must be found in utilitarianism. What is utilitarianism? The question is not, of course, raised here from an abstract and general point of view, but in direct connexion with the concrete problem which is being discussed. We are concerned with utilitarianism, not as a philosophical doctrine, but as an instinctive and "innocent" feature of English psychology which manifests itself in many ways and among them in utilitarian philosophy.

Thus understood, utilitarianism is a tendency to exact from every moment of life a positive yield in action. This feature of English psychology has often been misinterpreted. It is therefore necessary to insist on the difference between utilitarianism and selfishness. The two are only connected by fortuitous and circumstantial relations, so that utilitarianism is perfectly compatible with a certain disinterestedness. The business man who gives a sum of money to a hospital on condition that guarantees be given that the money will be spent with the utmost efficiency for the aim in view is both utilitarian and disinterested. Utilitarianism is in reality a tendency wholly different from selfishness; for selfishness aims at enjoyment, while utilitarianism aims at results. Utilitarianism is but an instinct which demands that action should be fruitful. There it stops; if the man of action happens to be altruistic it adds: "for my neighbour"; if selfish it adds: "for myself."

For, as we have seen, the *specific* function of each of our three human types is distinterested. Action is disinterested in a man of action. Thought and passion, as we shall see anon, are not, for they are subordinate to action, and it is this feature, the tendency to demand results in terms of action from any other form of life—thought or passion—which constitutes the utilitarianism of the man of action, therefore of the Englishman.

Hence the misunderstanding mentioned above as to the real character of utilitarianism; for, action being of an immediate, tangible, and material character, the tendency to demand results in terms of action may seem tainted with selfishness, with a certain materialism, with a kind of shortsightedness. And, in fact, these are the defects most frequently attributed to the Englishman. It cannot be denied that he is liable to them. Utilitarianism does not necessarily imply them, though it constitutes a ground favourable for their development. We have therefore on the one hand a certain psychological relationship between two sets of features, and on the other a relatively frequent coincidence of these two orders of features in individual Englishmen; and this double fact explains the all too frequent confusion between the shortsightedness, the materialism, and the selfishness which may be circumstantial defects of certain Englishmen and the utilitarian tendency inherent in the Englishman as a man of action and compatible with the most generous disinterestedness.

There is, however, a sense in which the word *materialism* can be applied to English psychology, for this kind of materialism necessarily goes with a tendency to action. Just as a lever cannot act without a fulcrum, action needs tangible and material objects on which to exert itself. This tendency to action therefore leads the Englishman to concentrate on matter. When the Englishman says "That does not matter," he means "that has no importance." *Immaterial* means *without interest.*

The Englishman has in him a strong tendency towards solid, massive, weighty things. Instinctively he moves in the world of forces and masses. And there is no doubt that this tendency to the solid, so closely allied to his main tendency to action, is deeply felt in all the aspects of his character.

Yet this sense of matter, again, does not necessarily imply materialism in the bad sense of the word. It does not exclude disinterestedness. Supreme disinterestedness is supreme liberty. A faithful knight of action, wholly devoted to its service, the Englishman refuses to divert his activity to the benefit of other no less exacting Goddesses. To thought he opposes the barrier of empiricism; to passion the iron gates of self-control. The Goddesses of the spirit know how to reward their faithful worshippers. The Englishman succeeds in action because he devotes himself wholly to it. His thought, slow when his will is at rest, wakes up in order to act and just enough for action; his passion, normally repressed, manifests itself in action just enough to lend the act its vital warmth. The intellect and the heart are therefore in him the seconds of the will over whom the will retains full authority. We shall have occasion to dwell on the consequences of this fact when we come to comment on thought and passion in the man of action, but this may be said here, that the entire subordination of all other vital forces to the will explains the supreme liberty of action in the Englishman and is undoubtedly one of the most important factors of his success as a man of action.

This is in reality what is commonly meant by *practical sense.* The phrase is not very happy. It suggests a simplifying tendency which is far from being a typical English feature. Simplification is an operation of the mind. It is closely allied to abstraction. It follows the act as criticism and precedes it as a method. Now, the Englishman avoids abstract and intellectual operations and thinks only in connexion with action. What is meant, more or less obscurely, by practical sense is precisely this attitude of the bee that goes straight to the flower, which is the attitude of the Englishman when, on his way to action, he comes up against ideas or sentiments across his path. He brushes them aside, surmounts all obstacles without hesitation, and goes straight towards his goal without worrying about preconceived plans. *Practical sense* is therefore the negative aspect of the tendency to subordinate all to action, which has been considered here as the typical feature of the Englishman. On its positive side, this feature of English psychology implies a severe discipline of the intellect and of the heart.

Just as a chord contains more sounds than the sum-total of the notes which compose it, so the combination of the psychological notes of individual characters in collective life is richer than the sum-total of the individual characters combined. Collective life manifests itself mainly in action. It is therefore in the domain of action that we may expect to find the greatest number of such psychological repercussions. We know that the man of action instinctively expects a yield in terms of action from all he does. In the sphere of collective life, this instinct at once detects the value of co-operation. Through co-operation man does more than merely add his worth to that of his partners. Endowed with the faculty of co-ordination, he organizes all individual efforts, thereby multiplying, instead of merely adding, them. The genius for co-operation is, therefore, one of the typical features which distinguish the communities composed of men of action and must accordingly be found amongst the characteristics of the English people.

The instinctive nature of this quality should be adequately emphasized. Nothing in our general hypothesis justifies the view that the world owes to the English people the *idea* of co-operation. Everything, on the other hand, leads us to the conclusion that the English people, composed of men of action, is endowed with the *instinct* of co-operation in the highest possible degree. This conclusion is confirmed by experience. A wag of unsure taste once said: "One Englishman, a fool; two Englishmen, a football match; three Englishmen, the British Empire." Well observed though deplorably said. The first term of the epigram is not merely discourteous; it is absurd. But its absurdity is but a twisted view of a truth which in due time we are to find on our path. The second term is better: a match is perhaps one of the social phenomena which most clearly reveal English character. As for the third it is admirable and sins only on the side of modesty. Contrary to what the author of the epigram seems to think, in order to make up the British Empire it is not necessary to bring together three Englishmen: one is enough.

For the individual instinct of co-operation manifests itself collectively in that genius for spontaneous organization which is the most admirable feature of this people of action. Now, this feature implies the existence of a group. An abstract and universal instinct of co-operation would be a mere theoretical creation of the intellect and not a vital force. In actual life, co-operation implies action and action always has a clearly defined scope. The English instinct of co-operation operates therefore within a well-defined group which is no other than the race. This is, at bottom, the true meaning of the expression *British Empire*. Hence it is literally accurate to say that wherever there is an Englishman there is the British Empire.

It seems then that the limitation of the instinct of co-operation to the frontiers of the race must be considered as a direct consequence of the tendency to action suggested as the typical feature of the Englishman. In other words, the tendency to action in each Englishman recognizes itself in his fellow-countrymen, and this recognition constitutes the criterion by which every Englishman chooses his co-operators, since it is in the nature of things that a man of action should seek his co-workers so as to ensure the greatest efficiency, i.e. amongst men of action. The choice ceases where the tendency ceases, and therefore, the instinct of co-operation stops at the frontiers of the race.

The group once defined, it acquires its own self-control. This follows from the genius for spontaneous organization, which is the collective form of the individual instinct of co-operation. A community endowed with the genius for spontaneous organization is like a healthy body in which each cell goes of itself to its place to fulfil its function. Such is the case with the English community. The group self-control manifests itself in two ways. The first is a strong tendency toward a social discipline. If attentively observed, this tendency will be found to be, in England, a wholly spontaneous force, issuing from the collective mass without any intervention from the social, established, and, so to say, external order. In actual fact, indeed, this social order is due to the tendency toward social discipline, and not the tendency to the order. Without wishing at this moment to discuss English ideas on conduct, we may note here as a feature of the people of action in action, the vigour of English reactions in matters of conduct. This vigour shows itself in two ways which do great honour to English collective life: the Englishman is *true* and he has a deep sense of social service. He is true, i.e. he is faithful to the axis round which he must turn as a wheel of the social mechanism. Each Englishman is his own regulator. He sees to it that all his faculties and individual tendencies are subordinated to the action which is expected of him in the social whole and that they develop in it their maximum efficiency. It should be noted that the good work of each individual piece in the social whole is, in England, ensured from within the individual piece itself. It is the individual soul that is endowed with the sense which makes it keep true to its social axis. The need of outside safeguard or guarantees of any kind is therefore less urgently felt than in other countries. The average level of honesty in English civil life is singularly high, as is shown in the usual disregard for detailed precautions against fraud or deceit.[1] This precious social

1. As an example of a humble but telling nature, we may recall the fact that no vouchers are delivered in English railways for travellers' luggage, yet no trouble arises, though at the end of the journey anybody can pick up as his own the luggage for which he may on inspection feel a particular attachment.

quality is made still more fertile by a strong sense of social service. Each of these *true* individual pieces would waste its well-adjusted movements if all these movements were not co-ordinated in view of a common aim by a common sense of social service. The vitality of this sense in England is the first fact which claims the attention and forces the admiration of the observant visitor. All functions—not merely official functions, more especially spoken of in England under the name of *service*, but all social functions, in the widest sense of this word —are held in a spirit of social utility which most happily combines the utilitarian and the group tendencies of the race. We shall dwell later on the relations between the sense of service and the religious sense in the Englishman. It is sufficient to point out for the present that the sense of social service is the outcome of a tendency as vigorous as spontaneous in the English character, and that this tendency along with that for *true* conduct explains the admirable working of the English social machine without the intervention of the State.

Apart from this ethical tendency, the genius for co-operation can also be seen at work in two other ways in which individual forces are co-ordinated and turned to account. The first of these ways may be understood as the co-ordination of these individual forces between themselves; the second as the co-ordination of these forces with nature.

We refer in the first place to a remarkable and typically English phenomenon which might be described as collaboration in opposition and can best be observed in games and in the parliamentary system. The discourteous wag quoted above, who coined as the second term of his epigram on England, "two Englishmen, a football match," said more than he meant, for a football match is perhaps the purest expression of this profoundly English characteristic. The opposition between the two camps is certain. Their collaboration is no less certain. Both camps fight in co-operation under a complicated system of four groups of tendencies: first, the rivalry between the members of each camp to serve as well as or better than any one else in the team; second, the co-operation within the team; third, the fight

with the adversary team for victory; fourth, the collaboration
with the adversary team for the success of the game as a whole.
This delicate adjustment of demands, which at first sight might
seem irreconcilable, is attained in England by the simple virtue
of instinct and is therefore considered as a usual and natural
thing; in fact it is taken for granted. It is no less admirable for
that. It results from a happy combination of social and individual tendencies, among them the tendencies here called: practical sense, utilitarianism, self-control. This sense of collaboration in opposition will be found to be as keen in the field of
politics as in the field of sports. It may even be said that it
constitutes the very essence of the parliamentary system. And
the fact that the tendency is missing in other peoples less gifted
for action explains, better than any other reason, how the
parliamentary system has given its best results in countries
populated by Anglo-Saxons. The parliamentary system was
born in a people of action and is therefore inseparably associated with, and explained by, the qualities of the peoples of
action, particularly by utilitarianism. For utilitarianism demands
that all activities—even those activities which are inherent in
opposition—should lead to "practical" results, i.e. to results meas-
urable in terms of action. A people of action such as the English
cannot tolerate that the opposition should limit itself to "felling
the Government" or merely to putting spokes in the wheel of
its politics. The utilitarian sense of the people manifests itself in
this connexion by means of well-known phrases which can be
read in every leading article of the country wherever the opposition becomes restive: "The criticism of the opposition must be
constructive," "The opposition must say whether it has any
practical proposals to offer as an alternative to those of the
Government." But these phrases are but the growlings of zeal-
ous dogs. The English opposition is too English to forget the
utilitarian tendency of its co-operation which it feels within
itself and any Government may rely on the collaboration of its
opposition if only because, being the Government, it holds the
means of action.

The second of the ways in which the genius of co-operation

co-ordinates individual tendencies for the general good is what might be called the spontaneous adaptation of these tendencies to the natural laws of collective action. A community of men presents some of the attributes of matter. A crowd flows, can be diluted or concentrated, can undergo vibrating movements; a crowd is in fact something akin to a liquid. The movements of men have their laws independent of caprice or imagination— laws which, therefore, are up to a point as inevitable as physical or biological laws. The English people, composed of men of action, know and respect these laws by instinct. In this way they manifest their genius for spontaneous organization en- riched with certain individual tendencies such as their empiri- cism and their sense for matter. This combination explains the English sensitiveness to the "laws of things"—the law of the road, the law of the sea, the law of the hunting field. In all the spheres of pure action, the English are the teachers of the world, not merely in their quickness to perceive these natural laws, but in their cordial and sincere obedience to the restric- tions which they impose upon each individual for the good of the whole.

We are now in a position to assign a place to the tendency to fair play in this sketch of the psychology of the English in action. We may now analyse it as a synthetic instinct in which can be found the tendency to collaboration in opposition, the sense for the laws of things, and the limitation of the group. For fair play is a tendency which acts within a well-defined group. This fact can be explained in more than one way. First, fair play is thoroughly empirical and therefore implies a con- crete aim. The fair play of a football match is not quite the same as that of a parliamentary election. The limitation of the group is thus an indispensable condition for the appearance of fair play. Moreover, fair play fails if it does not act in a homo- geneous element. Its characteristics are vital and irrational and cannot be reduced to a formula allowing forethought and pre- calculation. It cannot be generalized. It must permeate the whole group and enter all its members in a uniform, better still, in an amorphous way. If fair play is to produce all its effects, it is necessary that the whole action, so to say, should be saturated with it. It follows that fair play ceases to act in all its vitality when the group goes beyond the maximum limits which it may attain, namely, beyond its national frontiers. In this case, a certain sense, a certain habit of fair play remains active, but the practical results of it will depend essentially on the environment on which it is called to act.

There is an important manifestation of English social life closely related to the instinct for spontaneous organization here dealt with: we refer to the hierarchical sense. *The right man in the right place.* But let us immediately point out that English hierarchy does not follow from a theoretically established order. That is rather the French way. A theoretically established order would be in direct opposition to the instinctive nature of the tendency which explains English hierarchy. In England the hierarchical sense is the result of a combination of a number of race characteristics in which the genius for spontaneous organization is intimately associated with empiricism and with the sense of continuity which is so typical of English life. That is why in England the hierarchical organization of society results from a slow and continuous evolution carried out under the aegis of tradition—a kind of living archives of past deeds always open to present actions.

Hence the aristocratic bent of the English nation. *Aristocratism* is in fact neither more nor less than the sense of hierarchy spontaneously organized through the slow, continuous, and empirical action of tradition. The English aristocracy does not rest on military force; it does not maintain its privileges by means of a political system unfairly or fraudulently applied; nor can it be said to subsist owing to the ignorance of the masses. The English aristocracy is solidly established on the consent of the people; better still, one cannot speak of England as an aristocracy with a people under it, but as a people which has an aristocracy of which it is proud. The English people have their aristocracy as the wealthy banker his motor-car de luxe. The aristocracy is therefore in England the manifestation and not the cause of a tendency which is general to the whole

English people, for aristocratism is as strong in the man of the people (and especially in his wife) as in the courtier (or perhaps stronger). Every man is in England the aristocrat of another man. The nation is divided into horizontal layers of which the aristocracy is the highest, so that it does not differ essentially from the rest of the nation and can only be distinguished by the particular rank in which it is placed. It should, however, be noticed that, through the crossing of this social tendency, aristocratism, with an individual tendency, the sense of matter, the criterion by which aristocracy is estimated in England tends to become material. Too often the aristocrat is the man who can spend money and knows how to do it; but even here the Englishman demands that the wealthy should know how to spend their money, so that pure aristocratism quickly regains its rights.

The combination of the aristocratic tendency and the tendency to the limitation of the group explains in its turn the well-known feature which goes by the name of insularity. The Englishman's insularity is self-evident. The sense of clear separation between himself and others (i.e. other than English people), which every Englishman feels in him, springs perhaps in the last resort from animal sources, or is perhaps due to geographical causes. Our purpose, however, is not to explain the facts but merely to present them in a co-ordinate form on the basis of our main hypothesis. The word *insularity* seems to prejudice the case in favour of geographical causes since it would seem to explain this well-known feature of the English people by the fact that they inhabit an island. But the presence of a similar feature in the inhabitants of other islands would have to be proved. The word is, however, graphic and accurate as the metaphorical representation of the feature in question. We need not go farther than observe that this feature can be easily explained, as stated above, by the combination of aristocratism and the limitation of the group, two tendencies which we have deduced from the main tendency to action detected in the Englishman. The insularity of the Englishman may easily become a foible inasmuch as it tends to foster in him a prejudice of superiority. Thus the word *foreigner* takes on English lips a shade of contempt from which it is usually free in other languages. In combination with the tendency to erect moral-social standards of life, the insularity of the English produces, in the psychology of the English people at large, a kind of collective self-contentment due to the comparison of their national moral-social level with that of other countries. The Englishman is well aware of this feature of his character, against which he often reacts. It is known as *self-righteousness*.

We see here at work the English tendency to live under the watching eye of the self. This tendency is due to a combination of individual and collective forces. The most important of the former is self-control, which we know to be one of the best taut springs of the psychological mechanism of the Englishman; while the most important of the latter might well be considered as a kind of group self-control. It is a sort of mutual vigilance which keeps ever alive the complicated system of collective tendencies of the Englishman. The individual lives in an atmosphere which is not free and diaphanous, but on the contrary crossed by a network of tendencies, divided into zones of different densities, ruled by laws and obligations which, owing to their natural and vital character, attain a most absolute efficiency. The individual thus closely watched by his own self and by the social self becomes obsessed by a continuous *presence*. This feeling the Englishman describes with an untranslatable word: *self-consciousness*.

Self-consciousness in its turn explains another feature of the English character, at first sight almost paradoxical, which moreover, for reasons we shall examine later, is little known outside of England. The Englishman is *shy*. Here again the language warns us that we are in the presence of something typically national, for the word *shy* has no exact translation. *Timide* corresponds to the English *timid* and contains a strong proportion of pusillanimity. *Shy* describes the vacillation which seizes the Englishman who feels insecure on the social soil he is treading at the moment. It is a feeling which can only arise in the presence of the group. Put the Englishman outside his group, for instance abroad, and his shyness disappears. Plunge him again amongst the social classes of his country and he will think of nothing but to get out, if the class is inferior to his own, or, if it is equal or superior, to pass unnoticed.

We are in the psychological zone in which another typical feature of the Englishman must be described, also with an untranslatable name; for *snobbery* has not been translated by *snobisme*. Snobbery might well be defined as the tendency to judge things and people by the social criteria generally accepted in higher classes. It contains a fair share of another tendency referred to when dealing with aristocratism, the tendency to value men and things according to a criterion of wealth.

Finally, we must consider here as the safety-valve of the individual under the pressure of social oppression the often discussed hypocrisy of the Englishman. Too much importance has been granted to it, for, to a certain extent, this reputation for hypocrisy is undoubtedly due to the difficulty which other people less gifted with moral-social tendencies find in accepting at its face value the high ethical level of English collective life. "There is certainly a trick somewhere," they will say. The fact remains, however, that hypocrisy is an indispensable condition in the existence of a man of action, for it allows the necessary play for individual weakness in the face of rigid moral-social demands. We shall find later an opportunity for noting that, provided the idea is generalized on right lines, hypocrisy is a feature common to all psychological types.

II

Action in the Man of Thought

"YOU MUST NOT CROSS THE BRIDGE BEFORE YOU COME TO IT," says the English proverb. Under its apparent truism this proverb means that we should not seek to solve our problems until actually before us. It is evidently a proverb for men of action who think while acting and in order to act. The man of thought, on the contrary, thinks for the pleasure of thinking, so that while the Englishman reflects at the very moment when he acts and in order to act, the Frenchman sees in prospective action an excellent opportunity for setting problems before his mind. The man of thought "forethinks" action. He considers the action of tomorrow coldly and abstractly as a problem of today. He theorizes.

In order the better to see, he limits his field of vision. For the intellectual guards himself against the complexity of nature by carefully marking out the frontiers of every one of the problems which prospective action raises. This explains the frequency in France of such expressions as "Il faut sérier les questions," "Il faut procéder par étapes" ("It is necessary to put the questions in order," "It is necessary to proceed by steps"). In order to make this method easier, the intellectual endeavours always to define the problems and the elements which compose them. *Definition* and *limitation*—at bottom two different aspects of the same tendency—are then as the two tentacles which the intellectual puts forward towards life in an attempt to seize it. This limitation of his field of vision leads him to sacrifice certain aspects of active reality. The intellectual in action instinctively suppresses all that does not fit his theory of the situation. We must see in this feature the equivalent of the inhibitions to which the man of action submits his thought in order to prevent it from interfering with his activity. The man of thought tends, therefore, to force nature to fit the categories pre-established by his intelligence. His attitude in action is one continuous protest against the illogical behaviour of life. The man of thought draws out plans. From him come always the studied schemes, the ordered principles, the complete provisions. Foresight is one of the characteristics of the scientific spirit, perhaps indeed its touchstone, for if, as the saying goes, "to govern is to foresee," one might say with perhaps greater accuracy that "to know is to be able to foresee." Foresight is a requirement of the intellectual tendency which dominates the man of thought—it is, therefore, disinterested and finds in itself its own satisfaction. Yet it is accompanied by other less disinterested preoccupations; for the man of thought, having, like everybody else, the defects of his qualities, tends to give free rein to his intellectual tendency, and therefore is apt to pre-establish so-called "laws" which nature does not always feel bound to obey. Such a situation usually fosters in the man of thought a kind of war psychology. Foresight is self-defensive. The man of thought seeks to make the net of his logic finer and finer so that nature may not escape him. In this way foresight leads to mistrust. The intellect distrusts the complexity of nature and dislikes it for being so refractory to the order of the mind. Each of these crises in which nature rebels against the laws which the intellect tries to impose on her is followed by a critical study in which the intellect judges guilty nature, examines the circumstances, draws its conclusions, and ... prepares a new crisis by establishing new laws. Thus it is that the curve of action of the man of thought is a broken line composed of logical straight lines tangent to the winding curve of nature.

We have seen that the man of action expects that his acts should produce fruits of action and we have understood in that sense the word *utilitarianism*. The man of thought expects from action something far more difficult, for he wishes it to produce *order*. Order is the intellectual category of action. It is the ideal projection of the world on the plane of the intellect. However utilitarian he may happen to be for personal or other circumstances, the man of thought is, as a psychological type, indifferent to the fruits of action. What he wants is that action should obey the laws of reason, i.e. that it should fall into a clear order of things.

This explains why the Frenchman should excel in the preliminary stages of action, when situations have to be analysed, an ideal order designed, and a scheme of action established; as well as in the stages which follow action, when dead facts, having become ideas, no longer oppose any vital resistance to the critical intellect eager to handle them; while in the very moment of action, in that crest of the present in which ends the hill of the past and begins the slope of the future, the Frenchman is often seized with giddiness. For the intellect is a faculty which wants space and leisure, while the present is but a point and an instant.

The irritability of the Frenchman in action has no other origin. It presents a striking contrast with the calm of the Englishman often misunderstood as phlegm. No. The calm of the Englishman in action is due to lucidity, for every being is always lucid in his own element, while the Frenchman, more lucid than the Englishman before and after action, loses his lucidity at the moment when he feels overrun by the stream of instantaneous life. Embarrassed in his principles, in his plans, in his regulations, he sees chaotic life taking away everything in an unreasoned and torrential flow. His faculties are divided; a part of his being would prefer to rush to action; another part is drawn by his natural tendency towards understanding, connecting facts with principles and saving the structure of preconceived plans; and while he hesitates, the precious instant which cannot come back flows past between his fingers. This sensation of instantaneous impotence and incomprehension, at the moment when understanding and power are most precious, casts a dark shadow over his usually luminous intellect. And as, more than any other type of man, the Frenchman needs intellectual light, he becomes irritated and in his agitation he often loses control of the movements of his mind as a drowning man moves inordinately by mere instinct and desperation.

This psychological reaction reinforces the tendency of the intellectual to that distrustful foresight which we have already noticed in him. Sure of his intellect, he comes back to it in search of comfort after defeat, of reinforcement for the next fight. Hence it is that the Frenchman tends to prepare his actions by meticulous studies in tactics and strategy. The Frenchman is a chess-player. Life is for him a series of manœuvres and of General Staff work. His vocabulary of action is full of war metaphors: *attaque brusquée*, *mouvement tournant*, *surprise*, *guet-apens*, *stratagème*. This military psychology is quickened by an ardour for action which is peculiar to the Frenchman and which is also due, at least in part, to that previous vision which foresight implies. It is most instructive to compare the minute immediately preceding action in the Englishman and in the Frenchman. In the Englishman it hardly differs from the minutes that come before and after. They all belong to that firm and continuous state of dogged determination which is the natural state of a being whose essence consists in action. The Frenchman, on the contrary, comes to this moment at the end of a long period of intellectual and "visual" attention which gradually increases and even exasperates his appetite. He does not take action as it comes, but rather reaches to it with that *furia francesa* which has become proverbial both in war and in love. It is, at least in part, a psychological phenomenon analogous to that which precipitates the cyclist towards an obstacle he has watched too intensely. This *subjective speed* adds its momentum to the objective speed of the stream of life and contributes thereby to make even more chaotic in the eyes of the intellectual this life so regardless of intellectual categories. So that this appetite adds itself to the irritation which the irrationality of action awakens in the intellectual and makes it richer and more complex. For intelligence is the mother of desires and appetites, since it is the force which makes contemplation conscious and systematic. In rushing towards the object of action the intellectual seeks therefore possession of the object which has excited his appetite. Possession, therefore knowledge. While the Englishman seeks in action the satisfaction of a blind and spontaneous tendency, the Frenchman seeks in it the intimate union of his intellect with nature. Curiosity excites his appetite; intellectual experience is the supreme aim of his action. The Frenchman is therefore as utilitarian as the Englishman, but the yield which he exacts from his acts is, of course, of the order of knowledge. For it is knowledge and not action which is the food on which his main tendency feeds itself.

These non-rational elements of his conduct are the more important in him for the fact that by his very nature the Frenchman, i.e. the intellectual, has a very clear sense of the hierarchy of the faculties. For him reason is Queen, if not absolute Goddess, and just as she presides over his thoughts, she must have the free disposal of his actions. Such a tendency leads him to under-estimate the importance of instincts and of animic impulses as well as of the force of intuition. The driving wheel of his acts is in the full light of his intellect and it is in this light that every other vital force must justify itself.

The collective life of the Frenchman in action is controlled by this fact: the Frenchman regulates his conduct and judges that of others by means of intellectual standards.

Hence his lack of that genius for spontaneous organization which we have noted as the main characteristic of English collective life. This was to be expected. For the genius for spontaneous organization is due to the fact that the individual Englishman, bent on action, sacrifices without difficulty every other personal tendency in favour of collective action, i.e. of co-operation. The Frenchman cannot take this line. An intellectual, he owes absolute fidelity to his thought; he could not therefore sacrifice it to co-operation. Even assuming he were willing to make this effort, it would be impossible for him to contradict himself, for let us remember that the Frenchman governs his conduct by intellectual standards, and therefore submits his actions to his opinions. This opinion that you ask him to sacrifice in order to ensure the success of co-operation is precisely the opinion which he thinks indispensable to that very success. How can we reproach him with his intellectual honesty which is but one with his moral honesty? The fact remains, however, that, in French collective life, rich in opinions precisely because composed of intellectuals, the co-ordination of efforts and wills towards a common aim by means of common methods is particularly difficult.

But the intellect, cause of the evil, defines it instantly and seeks to provide a remedy for it. A community cannot live without some organization. The intellectual, in view of the failure of spontaneous organization, brings to the community that other kind of organization: order. We have already observed this tendency towards intellectual order in the individual. Social necessity, recognized by the *reasonable* individual, leads to the placing of society under a pre-studied order. There is a distinction, as essential as evident, between French order and English spontaneous organization. English spontaneous organization is free, instinctive, vital, omnipresent, natural, simultaneous with action, unwritten. French order is official, imposed from above though accepted below, intellectual, artificial, regulated, preceding action by a complicated system of written laws which aim at foreseeing all possible cases. The intellectualistic tendency gets hold of the field of action, limits and defines it, and throws over it a network of principles to which all future action must conform. This network of principles is *le droit*. These principles of course remain, in their perfect regularity, too far from the irregularities of life. In order to hold to things in action more closely, the intellectual inserts within the network of *le droit* another network finer still: *les règlements*.

We are therefore in the realm of *les règlements* dictated by foresight and inspired by distrust. While in England the anonymous citizen is supposed to be innocent until the contrary be proved, in France the anonymous citizen is considered as a hypothetical being in whom all evil intentions conspire and against whose machiavellian plans the State must be ever on guard. We are no longer in that English atmosphere of peace and co-operation between all citizens, grouped in a healthy and active collective being, working without coercion for a common aim; but on the contrary, in a kind of war atmosphere in which officials, solidly entrenched behind their desks, assiduously prepare battle plans against X with all the military genius of real Napoleons. French bureaucracy is therefore but the natural consequence in the collective world of the feature which we consider as fundamental in French psychology, i.e. the predominance of intellectual standards.

This regulation of collective life implies an order established by authority. A Frenchman it was, and a typical one, who said: "Authority must come from above and trust from below." Collective life, a *social* structure in England, is therefore in France a *political* structure, and instead of the internal and spontaneous discipline which freely circulates in England as the very blood of the social body, we see in France an external and established discipline which tends to crystallize into formulas.

There is then between the English and the French community a difference similar to that which distinguishes organisms from mechanisms. While in English collective life, questions are solved at the very moment when they arise and by virtue of the very vital instinct which makes them arise, in France, the whole collective life is regulated beforehand and all cases are foreseen. This watch must naturally have a watchmaker. The State is in France the watchmaker-in-chief of the social mechanism. Thus it is that the tendency so typically French towards centralizing all public functions in the State appears as a natural consequence of French intellectualism. Let us remember in passing that it was an intellectual class which initiated and completed in France the centralization of authority. The type of legal expert known to French historians by the name of *légiste* was the intellectual of the collective life, the definer of *le droit*. The *légiste* may also be considered as the precursor and even the creator of bureaucracy. For bureaucracy is to the State what *les règlements* are to *le droit*; and the two lines of development, the one in the abstract, the other in the functions, which go from order to *les règlements* by way of *le droit* and from order to bureaucracy by way of the State, come both from the same origin: the necessity of an order intellectually conceived and established by authority.

If we return now to the root tendency, that which seeks to impose an intellectual order, we shall again be able to observe that, by combination with another French tendency to limitation, this intellectual order is limited to the strictly indispensable. What is it after all that is at stake? The possibility of living in common. To secure this, the regulation of the political relations between citizens seems sufficient. Nothing in man that is not citizen concerns the State. Such is the origin of the strong French tendency towards the political specialization of the State, which is at bottom what is understood in France by *laïcité*. It should be added that the citizen generously gives back to the bureaucrat the distrust which the bureaucrat feels towards him. Hence a tendency antagonistic to the statist tendency, which keeps statism within the strict limits assigned to it by reason.

From such a limitation of intellectual order in collective life, two consequences result: the first is moral tolerance; the second, political intolerance. The moral tolerance of the French people can be easily explained. We have seen that the intellect solves the problem of co-operation between individuals by establishing a political intellectual order within the network of *le droit* and *les règlements*. There is no need to interfere with the conduct of the private individual so long as he moves within the zone of freedom which does not affect the social organization.

The social spring in favour of an ethical standard, which we have seen in England as particularly strong, is therefore absent. Moreover, the intellect of itself is unable to provide a sufficiently solid basis for a system of morals universal enough to impose itself on all as a kind of geometry. The intellectual standard is therefore here in default, or at any rate, it leads to what mathematicians might call an indeterminate solution of the problem. Therefore the standard of action of the Frenchman results from two tendencies, one of which, *le droit*, is extremely rigid, while the other, *morality*, is extremely flexible. This moral tolerance results in an atmosphere particularly favourable to frankness. The intimate connexion which exists between the words *frankness*, *France*, and *French* is not a mere linguistic caprice. Frankness is the quality of the Frenchman, as straightforwardness is that of the Englishman. Frankness declares its actions. Straightforwardness endeavours to keep them on the right road. There is in frankness an element of intellectual honesty and also an element of affirmation of the individual right to interpret the moral law, both fitting to a people of intellectuals. Individual frankness works with particular ease in a collectivity always ready to recognize individual liberty in all matters not affecting the political established order. It gives to non-political relations a clearness and a definiteness which are, no doubt, amongst the most attractive features of the French character.

The combination of this tendency to moral tolerance with the rationalistic tendency of French thought naturally leads to hedonism.

> Jeunes fillettes,
> Profitez du temps,
> La violette
> Se cueille au printemps,[1]

says the French song. Hedonism, fertilized and polished by the intellect, leads to refinement. For the Frenchman, the body is an instrument of the intellect, and all pleasures, even those of the body, are for him intellectual pleasures. Moreover, so soon as we penetrate into the zone of action ruled by the intellectual tendencies—spontaneous in the Frenchman—we notice the appearance of spontaneous order. The refined hedonism of France provides a *special* atmosphere favourable to spontaneous organization, in the same way as the tendency to action provides a *general* atmosphere favourable to spontaneous organization in England. Thus it is that the spontaneous organization of French refinement presents many characteristics similar to those of the spontaneous organization of English social life. It has a collective standard, taste, i.e. a tradition, half intellectual, half active, which regulates everybody and is respected by everybody, without imposing itself on anyone. It has its discipline, fashion, a discipline continuously rejuvenated in order that it may be tolerated; it even has the two features which seemed so exclusively typical of English life when we noted them in connexion with moral-social standards: hypocrisy and self-consciousness. For, since the atmosphere of refinement implies a certain number of obligations established by taste and fashion, it follows that there must be in it a certain hypocrisy and a certain self-consciousness. The hypocrisy of people who have violated the laws of taste or of fashion and who dare not confess it; the

1. Young ladies,
     Make use of your time,
     Violets
     Are gathered in spring,

self-consciousness of those who keep watch on themselves for fear of committing mistakes condemned by the laws of fashion or of taste. These are psychological features which presuppose a social law recognized by all, even by those who feel themselves guilty of transgression or who fear to become guilty of it. There is no question of intolerance here, for intolerance implies the absence of unanimity, while the laws of taste and fashion, being the result of spontaneous organization due to the natural tendencies of an intellectual hedonistic people, are in this people universal laws, that is to say, laws respected by all.

Such is not the case in the world of politics, for politics are unable to impose on every citizen the same point of view. We come then to this result, that the requirements of collective order imply the existence of a scheme, a leading thought, in one word, unity; while on the other hand, intellectual honesty, that is to say the fidelity to absolute truth, which is the key-quality of the intellectual, tends to foster the multiplicity of points of view, at the same time preventing intellectual compromises which might ultimately produce unity. From this dilemma political intolerance results with all its consequences.

In such a people, it is but natural that social hierarchy should be based on the intellect. In France, intellectual distinction is in fact the true spring of individual progress up the social ladder. This is due in the first place to the fact that the intellectual man has, in the eyes of the Frenchman, a prestige which is inherent in his activity and independent of the utilitarian advantages which the collectivity may see in it. But it is also a result of the intellectual nature of the collective order established. Now, intellectual capacity comprises two elements: one, innate, talent; the other, artificial, culture, work, education. Talent being equal, intellectual capacity may be considered proportional to the second, artificial element. Hence the social importance of education and therefore of well-being, which is the primary condition of education. This first motive of the tendency towards well-being is strengthened by that which can be deduced from the natural hedonism of the French. Now, well-being implies money. Money, therefore, has in France (as everywhere else it must be owned, but perhaps more consciously so) a considerable importance. The tendency towards foresight—the strongest perhaps of all tendencies of action in the French character—combines with the tendency towards well-being, influencing each other in a way which adds their effects sometimes and sometimes makes them play against each other. Hence the tendency towards saving (with manifestations of parsimony). By combination with that tendency which we have already noted, towards establishing the intellect as the supreme controller of individual life, we arrive at the explanation of certain social phenomena typical of French private economy, and particularly the *mariage de raison*.

III

Action in the Man of Passion

LANGUAGE ITSELF DETECTS A CERTAIN OPPOSITION BETWEEN action and passion. If we tried to figure our ideas by means of a geometrical diagram, we might represent the *tendency* to action as a line OA; the *state* of action might then be figured as a line OA', coinciding with the line OA; the main *tendency* of the man of thought might then be represented as a line OT, perpendicular to OA, but the main *tendency* of the man of passion would be best symbolized as OP directly opposed to OA and OA'. So that while in the man of thought in action,

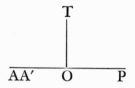

state and tendency merely diverge, in the man of passion in action, state and tendency are in direct opposition. Essentially, passion is a state of union with the life-stream which we let *pass* in us (for language has often strange coincidences). Passion is, therefore, the very negation of action, for in action our will acts on the life-stream in order to deflect it, forcing it to accept our own speed and direction, while in passion we let ourselves go with the speed and direction of the life-stream.

From this direct opposition between the *tendency to passion* and the *state of action* result the characteristics of the Spaniard in action.

The first of which is that when the man of passion acts, he enters into action with his whole person. We shall not find here that self-control which the man of action puts on like an armour, and for two reasons: first, the vitality of the man of passion flows, not in the channel which leads to the turbines of action, but free like a river; the second, because such a control would be contrary to his main tendency, since it would imply the sacrifice of passion to another aim. This free flowing of the river of life is what is known as spontaneity. The Spaniard is spontaneous. That is why he gives an impression of being an all-round man which we do not find either in the Englishman, entrenched behind the impassable barrier of his self-control, or in the Frenchman, limited within his intellect as within a laboratory. This all-roundness is the stranger from the fact that it may be accompanied by a veritable reserve. Reserve differs from self-control in that it is static, while self-control is dynamic. Reserve exists for itself, self-control exists for action. Self-control hides the natural man, while reserve is transparent like a veil which allows the whole man to be seen.

Wholeness. We are already in the realm of the absolute. For

the nature of passion is whole and absolute in a way which neither action nor intelligence can equal. In action as in thought, man becomes specialized. In both, he enters not with his whole person, but with a relatively small part of it. In passion he is in his entirety. This may well account for one of the most disconcerting features of Spanish psychology, a feature which excuses many a misconception. The Spanish character abounds in conflicting tendencies. It is hard and human, it is resigned and rebellious, it is energetic and indolent. For in reality it is both spontaneous and complete, and therefore it allows the manifestation of all the tendencies which are to be found in the human microcosm. The combination of this wholeness with the reserve which we have also observed in the Spanish character contributes to the richness and complexity of the famous Spanish indifference. Indifference, laziness, passivity are but various appearances of passionate life quietly flowing. For in reality, the man of passion is normally indifferent because the calls on his activity do not appeal to him as sufficiently universal to stimulate him to action. Actions and ideas are but the stones and the gleams of light on the road of life. The passionate life is the whole road, past, present, and future, apprehended and felt instantaneously. In the contemplation of this total spactacle, the will neglects actions which appear as details. Then, suddenly, all the sleeping energy slowly accumulated will discharge itself at once. It may be an impact, a psychological contact on an electrified point, a nothing or a great thing: the will leaps to action. In such cases, we are in the presence of another phenomenon well known in the man of passion, particularly in the Spaniard: the exceptional achievement. The man of passion surmounts unsurmountable obstacles. Action in the man of passion tends therefore to be unmeasured and discontinuous. The man of passion lacks continuity and perseverance, and his line of behaviour is a fitful line made of a series of new beginnings.

Hence, the third type of line of action: no longer the supple and continuous curve adapted to all the forms of nature, which we have observed in the man of action of England; nor the series of straight lines successively correcting each other by sudden turns, as in the intellectual of France; but a kind of rest followed by a sudden explosion of conquering will which, soon exhausted, falls back to its first indifference—a series of horizontal lines of action cut by abrupt peaks of over-activity.

This figure has one feature in common with that of the intellectual and in opposition to that of the man of action: it does not adapt itself closely to the profile of nature. It differs, however, profoundly from that of the intellectual in that the intervals between the successive actions of the intellectual in the field of action are filled in with mental activity, with that previous vision or foresight which, as we have observed, explains the appetite, the subjective speed in action which is typical of the Frenchman; while the man of passion lives in a state of imprevision. His spontaneity and his normal indifference are contrary to any previous vision; the intervals in the curve of his activity are therefore truly inactive, passive, so that the excess of activity which he evinces in a moment of action is due not to a subjective appetite or speed, but to a sudden discharge of accumulated energy. In the first case, that of the intellectual, we are in the presence of a desire seeking possession of the desired object; in the second case, that of the man of passion, we see a will which demands its own victory, its own triumph, indifferent, however, to the prize of victory.

This is one of the forms which disinterestedness takes in the passionate type. It will be noticed that it does not differ fundamentally from the disinterestedness of the other two types. In all three cases, what the type seeks is the satisfaction of its main tendency. In action, the man of action seeks results in terms of action; the intellectual, results in terms of knowledge; the man of passion, results in terms of passion. The first struggles in order to do things; the second in order to possess them in knowledge; the third in order to let off his surplus of energy.

By a combination of the two tendencies of the passionate type, indifference and wholeness, the man of passion tends to remain untouched by all that does not partake of the complete and absolute character of passion. We have seen that he does not enter into things by halves, that he is always with his whole self wherever he is. It is therefore natural that he should not enter into things unless he feels that they are worth while. This observation throws a new light on the habitual indifference of the man of passion. His indifference is only apparent. At bottom life circulates in his individual being, and it is this very sense of the life-stream ever present in his person which constitutes, as we have seen, the essential feature of his psychology. While the aim of the Englishman is to act and that of the Frenchman to understand, the aim of the Spaniard is to live and to let himself live. Inactivity for the man of passion is therefore fertilized by passion itself: it becomes contemplation.

The individual psychology of the man of passion implies a nature rebellious to the chains of collective life. Who says collective life says the connecting of individual lives into a system of gears. Now, in a gear only a small sector of each wheel is actually connected at every moment and playing an active role, while the man of passion, as we have just seen, is at every moment present with his whole self wherever he is. Therefore in the people of passion, each individual brings to the collective life an integral and subjective standard.

Three characteristics may be linked up with this initial observation: individualism, humanism, and amorality.

Individualism can easily be explained as the immediate consequence of the subjective standard which the individual brings to collective life. The man of passion does not possess the utilitarian standard of the man of action, neither does he find at his disposal the abstract and theoretic standard which guides the steps of the intellectual. He therefore relies on the intimate voice of his own self. The individual self acquires thus a first-rate importance and demands corresponding rights. The people of passion is therefore an out-and-out individualistic people.

Humanism is merely generalized individualism. The individual who sees himself in other men becomes humanistic. But it may be well to define this word, which is used here in a special and perhaps not quite legitimate sense. We understand here by humanism, the attitude which judges things and people from the point of view of the whole man as opposed to any more limited point of view (such as the moral, economic, religious, philosophical, technical point of view).

Amorality is in its turn a consequence of humanism, since the moral standard is one of the many limited standards which are only parts of the absolute and integral world in which the man of passion lives.

The combination of these three tendencies between themselves, and with the tendencies of the individual character of the man of passion as described above, will allow us to find, so to say, *a priori*, the most typical features of the Spanish people. Its humanism provides the root of that "personalism" which has been so often observed in Spain. The importance of personal contacts is well known wherever people of the Spanish race are concerned. Whether the question in debate is a trivial affair or the most important business, a relation from man to man is indispensable if results are to be obtained. In politics *personalism* is the main force which shapes not only, as we shall have occasion to show, the history of Spain, but also its political evolution as well as the evolution of the Spanish-American republics. When, moreover, this personalism is combined with the tendency to amorality noted above, we come to another typical feature of Spanish collective life, namely, the tendency to judge things and people by means of dramatic standards. A distinction must be made between the dramatic and the theatrical. The dramatic results from action; the theatrical aims at effect. The one is life, the other art. The one is spontaneous, the other is the fruit of premeditation. The Spaniard, in spite of many a misconception, is not theatrical but dramatic. He conceives life as a drama and judges things and people from the point of view of a spectator. This fact is full of political consequences. For the present, limited as we are to the more directly psychological features, we may observe that it explains why the Spanish people usually suffers from envy, which is, so to say, its specific defect. There is a famous saying often—one might say, always—quoted in Spain, in connexion with envy: "Envy"—said Quevedo—"is thin because it bites but does not eat"; a biting phrase which admirably conveys the impotence and ever-unsatisfied eagerness which consumes the soul of the envious man, yet a phrase which grants too much activity to this singular vice. No. Envy does not even bite. It would bite if it could. But it is contemplative. It may be worth while noting here how the three specific vices, observed respectively in each of the three peoples, truly correspond to the main tendency of each type: hypocrisy, a vice of action, always vigilant and self-attentive; parsimony, a vice of the intellect, connected with mistrust and foresight; envy, a passive and contemplative vice—thus, as we might expect, we find these vices to be as the wrong side of the soul stuff; yet the same stuff, the right side of which forms its qualities.

The dramatic standard which explains the deepest vice of Spanish psychology is also responsible, at least in part, for one of its typical qualities. Instinctively, the spectator wants to play a good part whenever he happens to be himself on the stage. If we put this tendency alongside of the imprevision which we have observed as the result of spontaneity and indifference in the Spaniard and add to it the sense of fraternity, which is a natural result of humanism, we shall come to the particularly rich type of generosity which goes by the Spanish name of *desprendimiento*, and contains no small proportion of detachment and indifference towards the future.

A similar mixture of psychological elements accounts for another Spanish characteristic: the adventurous spirit, composed of imprevision, the tendency to dramatize life, amorality, and individualism. The fitful curve of Spanish activity with its volcanic eruptions of energy lends itself admirably to the free and vagabond career of the adventurer. The tendency towards moral-social disorder allied to a remarkable facility for sudden discharges of energy explains why Spain is the typical country for personal achievements, in contradistinction to the country of collective enterprises. Cromwell is England, but Hernán Cortés is Hernán Cortés.

Let us stay for a moment before this picture. Here is a profoundly individualistic people, usually passive, but feeling within itself a high potential of energy, moreover a people given to contemplation. Are there not here all the elements of messianism? The Spanish people is deeply messianistic. It has a strong tendency to place itself—perhaps it is *always* placed—in a state of expectation, awaiting some providential event which is going to alter its life fundamentally, and of course for the better. There is a phrase, typically Spanish in its mixture of piety and irreverence, which describes this state of mind: *esperar el santo advenimiento*, "to hope for the holy event." We shall see later the consequences of this feature on the political life of Spain and of the countries of its race. For the present we may link up with it the Spanish attachment to lotteries. The official lottery is in Spain a national institution of an extremely popular character. In the economic field it plays the role of a messiah which is to bring to every individual the longed-for kingdom of well-being on earth.

The individualism of the Spaniard manifests itself with singular force in the form of a defensive attitude of individual personality against any invasions from the collectivity. Such is probably the secret of the instinctive hostility to association which has often been observed in the Spaniard. It is merely a feeling of opposition towards everything that may tend to regulate his personal liberty in advance. This is perhaps also the reason why the Spanish genius is hostile to technical work. Association binds men to men, technique binds men to things.

From the same individualistic root springs undoubtedly the Spanish tendency to invert the scale of social service usually accepted—at least in theory. Individualism does not necessarily mean egoism, and therefore, the self, in the narrowest sense of the word, will not necessarily occupy the highest place in the individualist's scale of social service. The self, nevertheless, dominates the scale, for it provides the standard by which the places occupied by other social entities are determined, so that those which are most intimately linked with the individual are nearest the top of the scale: his family first, then his friends, and the State last. And even within the State, the town, the province, the region have often a hold on the individual which is inversely proportionate to their real importance, but in direct proportion to the intimacy of the connexion which binds them to him.

To the combination of these features of Spanish character in action is due the tendency towards social, political, and moral disorder which has often been observed in societies of the Spanish race. For it is obvious that a race instinctively hostile to association, rebellious to discipline and to technique, and used to inverting the scale of social service in favour of such groups as are most closely related to the individual must find great obstacles in the setting up of some system of collective order; while at the same time, the very fact that these tendencies operate in the race weakens collective institutions and fosters an equalitarian instinct which acts as a powerful check against all hierarchy.

Thus the Spanish people are particularly defective in social qualities in the strict sense of the word, i.e. social qualities based on collective standards. Yet they show a certain number of qualities socially useful, but based on individual standards. We have already referred to *el honor*. We are now in a position to associate it, on the one hand with the resistance to association, which we know now to be a typical Spanish feature, and on the other to the humanistic and amoralistic tendencies which are, with individualism, the three fundamental tendencies of the Spanish character. *El honor* provides the Spaniard with a subjective standard of action. It accounts to no one save itself for its actions, and yet is profoundly sensitive to collective standards, for in the last resort it judges itself according to a standard which has been created and transmitted by the collectivity. Another similar quality, socially useful yet founded on an individual basis, is the spirit of equity, which is the form which the spirit of justice takes in Spain. Justice is somewhat specialized. It applies a written law. It is abstract, and, if not inhuman, at any rate *de-humanized*, if the word may be permitted. Equity reinstates in the idea of justice all the imponderabilia which turn it into a complex and living human sentiment. Equity is justice felt as a human passion. We should not therefore be surprised to find it amongst the features of Spanish people in action. The more so as it is closely allied to that generosity, or *desprendimiento*, which we have already noted in the Spaniard. Such breadth of feeling rather than of views, a kind of shame which prevents him from pursuing details with excessive care, from exacting his rights to the bitter end, are amongst the features which contribute to give its nobility to the Spanish people.

By his tendency to resist association the man of passion secures a certain liberty for developing his other individual tendencies free from social pressure. This circumstance contributes to explain the existence within the Spanish character of the most contradictory tendencies, a feature which has been observed, with his usual penetration, by Mr. Havelock Ellis. Thus, the warmest and sincerest human sense can be found in it, side by side with an utter indifference to pain, which would be cruelty, if it were less passive.[1] In this atmosphere of absolute freedom can also be best understood another Spanish feature, difficult to explain, and even to designate: the word *hombría* has no equivalent; the idea which it represents is perhaps inexplicable. It is a kind of synthetic quality embracing all the characteristics and faculties of man; it applies to the man who is, not perfect, but complete.

We thus come back to that preoccupation for wholeness which we have seen fertilizing the dramatic tendency of the Spanish people and fortifying its contemplative taste. Such are the elements which form its serenity. A people essentially synthetic and contemplative, it looks calmly on the continuous flowing of days and on the gradual dying out of struggles. In these deep sources it feeds that stoicism which from the time of Seneca (and probably long before him) has been the philosophy professed in Spain by all the philosophers who are not aware that they are philosophers—perhaps the most numerous and the best of the profession. This serenity implies also a

1. This disconcerting feature of Spanish psychology explains the great variety of opinions current on the subject. Good or bad, most of these opinions contain a certain element of truth.

certain type of Spanish empiricism which is content to observe and accept the facts of life—an empiricism which manifests itself most felicitously in popular poetry and proverbs. The serenity of the Spanish people is, finally, the basis of the static quality of this people, as resistant to the changes of history as are the rocks of its hard soil.

ACTION IS THE MAN OF PASSION

IV

Thought in the Man of Action

THE MAN OF ACTION IN THOUGHT IS, IN A WAY, THE REVERSE OF the intellectual in action. Between these two cases we may therefore expect to find a certain symmetry or, at any rate, to use a geometrical term, a certain homology, or correspondence of lines, not unlike that which may be observed between an object and its image in a mirror. In both cases the psychological situation is defined by the fact that life and thought do not coincide, for life is irregular, ever moving, unforeseen, ever renovated, while thought is regular, fixed, regulated in advance. In this dilemma the man of action takes the side of life, the intellectual, the side of thought. From this fact result the parallel and the contrasting features between the two types.

The law of thought is logic. If we consider thought as a vital phenomenon, and if we give ourselves as known any one moment of it, which we shall take as its initial state, the ensuing evolution of the phenomenon can be deduced from it by pre-established laws of logic, so that all the successive states of thought are implicitly given when its initial state is given.

Life has no law. It has laws, of which we know but a few, regulating a relatively small number of its aspects, but as for the totality of life, we are reduced to one or other of two alternatives: either there is no law for the whole, or else it is a synthesis of so great and so complex a number of partial laws, that it is equivalent to no law at all. Life in actual fact is unforeseeable.

The man of action therefore evinces a strong tendency to what we might term *allogicalism*. The word is necessary. Too often, particularly recently since they have begun to be better known, Englishmen have been reproached for their *illogicalism*, and, with their usual awkwardness in these matters, they have themselves accepted and commended this view. It seems a little exaggerated to lend them a tendency contrary to logic. If now and then they have manifested such a tendency, it must have been when they found the machine-guns of unreasonable logic aimed at them. But to attribute illogicalism as a normal feature to Englishmen would be tantamount to granting them a preoccupation with the world of thought, which is far from being a part of their constitution. The Englishman is not illogical, but allogical, for logic is a thing which he does not trouble about.

Which, by the way, allows him an attitude towards logic far more complex than mere illogicalism, for, after all, if he were merely illogical, there would be a certain method in his madness. But the Englishman is more complicated than that. He is both logical and illogical. And that is precisely what we might expect from a man of action. We have seen that English allogicalism is due to the fact that, faced with the dilemma *life—thought*, the Englishman, a man of action, stands by life. But the gravity of this dilemma should not be exaggerated. The lack of coincidence between life and thought might be compared to that between a flat map and a map in relief. There are zones in which the coincidence is absolute; others where but slight divergences appear; others again in which the difference is considerable. Moreover, the lack of coincidence between life and thought may bear on space or on time. In other words, life may differ from thought by its complexity at any given moment, or else by the complexity and the unforeseeable quality of its evolution. The Englishman's allogicalism is proportional to these divergences which he instinctively observes between nature and the intellect. Where the two are in agreement, the Englishman is logical.

We have therefore to consider the attitude of the Englishman towards thought according as he is influenced by the instantaneous complexity of life, or by its unforeseeable quality, or by the facts that life and thought happen to coincide. The sense of the instantaneous complexity of life inspires the Englishman with his mistrust of abstract ideas. An abstract idea is a form which tends to become universal. The man of action is too sensitive to accidents, nay, he is too deeply conscious of the personality of each individual object, as accidents define it, to admit easily the universality of ideas. Hence the concrete character of English thought. Ideas in English thought appear incarnated, materialized, borne by a tangible object. This tendency becomes a habit of the mind. The average Englishman thinks by means of material objects. The working of machines, which French students learn as a theory by means of formulae and mathematical curves, is explained in English schools by means of models which are miniature machines. This characteristic detail reveals the intimate working of the English mind, which, even for its imaginative work, must rest on material objects.

The sense of the complexity of life which tends to make English thought concrete, tends to make it also vague. This may seem at first paradoxical. Yet it is true. Though resting on tangible objects, English thought is generally blurred round its edge as if it melted gradually into the vital fog which surrounds it, prolongs it, and perhaps alters it. The Englishman is a master of periphrases and an artist of circumlocutions. Dickens immortalized the tortuous and labyrinthian style of English officials in his Circumlocution Office. Legal documents in England are verbal labyrinths which none but specialists can explore. In all this we see at work the instinct which leads the Englishman to connect his thought with the surrounding zones of life by links as elastic as possible. England no doubt it was that taught Verlaine to design mental lines:

Où l'imprécis au précis se joint.[1]

Thus can be solved the apparent paradox noted above. The Englishman is at the same time concrete and vague because he realizes that thought is flat and rigid, while life is mobile and therefore, since he wants to keep close to life, he feels it is better to reduce the surface of his thought to a minimum so that it may coincide with a corresponding surface of life (which amounts to making thought as concrete as possible) and to connect his thought with the rest of life by elastic links (which amounts to keeping the edges of his thought as vague as possible).

The unforeseeable quality of life inspires the man of action with a mistrust similar to that which he feels towards general principles. Principles tend to bind life beforehand. That is their nobility and their utility. Life seeks to evade their grasp. Hence the conflict between life and principles, and in this conflict the Englishman sides with life. The English language abounds in phrases which express this feeling: "we must not cross the bridge before we come to it"; the expressions "cut and dried plan," "hard and fast rule," which are always used as implicit arguments against methods which it is advisable to reject, describe precisely that tendency to foresee, or pre-establish, or catch life in advance which is typical of the intellectual. Born in the domain of action, where they certainly are at home,

---

1. Where the imprecise joins with the precise.

these English expressions often invade the domain of thought, which thus becomes hesitating and vague owing to an excessive mistrust of general laws.

The man of action is only really at home in thought when it happens to coincide with life. That is why English thought is never more vigorous than when it is empirical. The Englishman concentrates his intellectual effort on that spot of the intellectual plane which happens to touch at the time the moving sea of life. And whatever may be said of his mental forces in the rest of the intellectual plane, *on that spot* the Englishman is eminently intelligent. This faculty of thinking vitally and at the same time with life, is, in the profoundest sense, the true meaning of empiricism. But it is possible to discriminate between two kinds of empiricism: one which we might describe as instantaneous, corresponding to the habit of thought just described—an inborn and innocent tendency of a given psychological type; and another which we might call stored-up empiricism, a sort of treasure of accumulated experience which man applies subconsciously at the moment when it is required, in order to surmount the obstacle which happens to be before him. The first is an attitude; the second a method. Both are to be found in the Englishman: the first is a direct result of the feeling of the complexity of life; the second a substitute for the principles which the man of action rejects under the influence of the feeling that life is unforeseeable.

We may observe here a parallel and a contrast between the man of action in thought and the intellectual in action, i.e. between the Englishman thinking and the Frenchman acting. We have observed in its place the mistrust of the Frenchman towards life as rebellious to thought and his effort to regulate it, to imprison it within a network of principles. Similarly the Englishman mistrusts abstract thought, loyal to itself, rebellious to the caprices of life, and he is not happy as a thinking man unless he succeeds in catching thought at a vital moment by means of his empiricism. The Englishman, when thinking, meditates on action. The Frenchman, when acting, executes his thoughts.

Each one, then, remains faithful to the aim imposed on him by his own character and seeks to obtain the food on which his soul must feed. The Englishman feeds on action, the Frenchman on ideas, and therefore the one is disinterested only when he acts, the other only when he thinks. Just as the Frenchman exacts from actions a yield in ideas, the Englishman exacts from ideas a yield in actions. The Englishman considers as frivolous all activities which are purely intellectual. This intellectual utilitarianism of the Englishman manifests itself in his tendency to cultivate natural, physical, and economic sciences, as well as in the strong ethical bias which distinguishes his letters and his philosophy.

There is another most interesting aspect of English thought in which the vitalistic tendency of the man of action may be observed, namely, the numerous inhibitions whereby the Englishman spares himself from the corroding action of thought on certain notions or prejudices which life feels for the moment to be indispensable. There are plants which nourish the body, others which kill it. There are truths which feed the spirit, others which poison it. Some races, such as the Russian, for instance, evince an uncontrolled appetite for all kinds of knowledge and almost a tendency to seek the most enervating truths and subtle poisons which sap the will and weaken the wish to live. The English race, on the contrary, is gifted with a vigorous defensive instinct against all unhealthy intellectual curiosity and it rejects by strong inhibitory reactions any attempt of the spirit to bite into forbidden fruit. This phenomenon, well known to all who have frequented the English, will enable us later to explain a certain number of gaps and allogical ways in the intellectual life of England.

Here again we find a case of symmetry with the intellectual in action. For, while the man of action protects his life against the onslaught of thought by means of inhibitions, the intellectual protects his thoughts against the attack of life by means of abstractions.

Thus English thought endeavours to remain as close as possible to life. From life it borrows its complexity, its elasticity, its allogicalism, its delicate shading. A plant, not a crystal, it grows from inside and not by successive prolongations of dialectical planes as does French thought. It does not work on a preconceived plan. It does not worry beforehand about form. Or rather it does not conceive form as a category separate from substance of which it is necessary to think apart. Too often, perhaps, this indifference to form, to plan, to pre-established order leads the Englishman to present his ideas in the form of pure enumerations. The most frequent form of English composition consists in a mere enumeration of paragraphs, all placed on the same plane, all with the same relief, all in a purely statistical order. But when the work in hand is the outcome of inspiration, the neglect of form allows a greater freedom on the part of the creative spirit. A kind of internal inspiration seems then to guide the work, like the instinct which guides the root towards the rich layer of earth, or the stalk in a vertical line towards air and light. Like the root and like the stalk English thought knows how to turn round obstacles, how to avoid morbid zones. In this adaptation to the requirements of life, English thought no doubt loses in clearness, in width, in power of generalization. It remains in continuous contact with nature, but does not soar. Its progress is slow and hesitating, like that of the blind man who proceeds staff in hand with his ear open to the slightest sound, ready to alter his direction at every step. On the other hand, it is saved from the dangers of hasty generalizations and of abstractions. It never hardens into a system. It never engages the future. It refuses to shut itself into an intellectual orthodoxy of any kind, and, while affirming the truth of today, is always ready to give it up in favour of the truth of tomorrow. The curve of English thought is therefore—not unlike that of French action—a series of straight lines the direction of which changes now and then, the whole taking the aspect of a broken line. This feature enables us to understand an apparent contradiction in English thought: it is at the same time conservative and open to new ideas. Empirical, it does not lend itself easily to changes dictated by intellectual fashion; yet it is not sufficiently sure of established intellectual truths to oppose stray opinions, and that is why England is the ideal country for the development of minorities of opinion. The extreme limit of a minority is the unit. England is the country of minorities composed of one man. The *freak*, a typically English and untranslatable word, is not what the French call *un original*, but rather the individual whose opinion is like the discordant note heard the more stridently in a concert of perfect harmony.

For, as was to be expected, English thought is powerfully shaped by the vigorous social collectivity in which is is produced. Many of the vital inhibitions to which we have referred are imposed on it by social pressure. The group, the vigour of which we have observed when studying the English in action, is one of the most active elements amongst those which contribute to create the feeling of the complexity of life in the Englishman in thought. Nothing is more striking than the number of ideas the Englishman *takes for granted*. Many of them are racial and national ideas which constitute a kind of substratum for his consciousness and upon which he has never asked himself the slightest question—not even that of wondering whether there were any questions to be asked at all. His empiricism and his disinclination for gratuitous speculation are here allied with the instinct for inhibition undoubtedly prompted by the race in order to maintain in an unexplored condition a substratum of tacit ideas on which express ideas are built, just as buildings stand on lands of little solidity by the mere fact of their weight.

The group therefore provides English thought with a uniformity and a cohesion which it might otherwise have lacked in view of its mistrust of generalizations and principles. And it may be well to point out here again the symmetry between the Englishman in thought and the Frenchman in action. To the rebel in the intellectual collectivity in action corresponds the freak in the collectivity of men of action in thought, and just as the intellectual in action, lacking the spontaneous and intimate order which distinguishes the man of action, replaces it by the external pressure of a political order, so the man of action in thought, lacking the spontaneous order in thought provided by general principles, nevertheless attains a certain external uniformity through social pressure.

The action of the group in this sense is the more effective from the fact that English thought, like the rest of the civilization of the country, is under the leadership of an aristocracy (in the widest sense of this word). The people is frankly turned towards action and work, the middle classes towards commerce and activity. Only a select few evince an interest in the things of the spirit. Lamennais said that a minimum of well-being is indispensable for virtue. He might have said as much in connexion with culture. But this minimum differs with different countries and is certainly very high in England. Owing to a kind of marginal value of time, it is only after all other pleasures which leisure can procure have been satisfied that the Englishman thinks of cultivating his mind. It follows that culture, in England, centres in the well-to-do classes for whom time, which still is money, has nevertheless a smaller value like money itself since, like money itself, it is more abundant.

The combination of these tendencies explains the extreme complexity of English thought. The vitalism which typifies it seems to determine even the very organ in which it manifests itself. The Englishman does not seem to think with his brain. His ideas are not ideas properly speaking, but opinions, sentiments, sensations. He does not say "I think," but "I feel." His opinions do not seem to be emitted by his brain, but by his neck, chest, abdomen, elbows, or knees. His whole body emits vitalized thought as if the thinking function in him were not concentrated in the brain, but spread uniformly all over his nervous system. This explains in part the reputation for mediocre intelligence which he enjoys—enjoys is the word, for the Englishman does appreciate his position as a slow-thinking man. But is he such a man? The good-natured ease, with a touch of disdain, with which he accepts the universal opinion on the subject is, to say the least, suspect. It is, moreover, difficult to admit that the British Empire should be the work of a race of abnormally slow people. It is true that Englishmen, perhaps in order to enable other people to forgive them their successes, maintain that their empire is the result of a series of events which happened while they were in their usual state of absent-mindedness. But even if this were so, the absent-mindedness which allows such things to pass could hardly be that of a half-witted people. In fact we are in a position to know what to think about it. The English intellect is *potentially* of the very first quality. It yields its maximum efficiency in action and whenever results in terms of action are in view. For speculation *in vacuo*, it declines to set itself in motion. Hence one of the first origins of its bad reputation. But there is another one. We know that the intellect of the Englishman, less specialized than the mental vision of the Frenchman, is, as it were, diluted through his whole body. This explains that it should be slower to move. An external solicitation must mobilize, not only the brain, but all the nervous system of the Englishman in order that he may start thinking. In the same way, his perception is not merely the work of the brain, but of the whole nervous system. The English mental machine is therefore more compli-cated, heavier, slower to move, less easily unbalanced.

A parallel of language may illustrate this contrast between the French and the English intellects. The Frenchman says *avoir raison*. The Englishman says *to be right*. For the French-man, the fact of being right is a possession; he *has* reason, i.e. he *holds* the reason of the thing. For the Englishman, it is a vital state. He *is* right as he is well or as he is ill. The French phrase is limited to the intellect; the English phrase covers the whole person.

For indeed, the man of action in thought feels truth as some-thing more than a mere affair of logic. Truth for him must satisfy not only the tenets of logic, but also the requirements of life. The complex and vital character of English thought de-mands therefore a standard somewhat more complicated and at the same time more elastic than mere reason. This standard is wisdom. Wisdom is reason saturated with irrational knowledge and with stored-up experience, continually adapted to the moving waters of life, inseparable from action, which it guides and fertilizes, and so reasonable that it knows, whenever necessary, how to sacrifice reason.

V

Thought in the Man of Thought

WHEN HE IS THINKING THE INTELLECTUAL IS IN HIS ELEMENT.
The Frenchman excels therefore in intellectual work. He finds
within himself naturally and in their spontaneous vigour all the
tendencies which favour the exercise of thought. For instance,
the need for clearness which, in the intellectual, is like the
instinct which, in the plant, leads the stalk towards the light.
Place a Frenchman in the presence of an obscure subject explained in a confused way, and he will feel a kind of physical
uneasiness similar to that of a bird under the bell of a pneu-
matic machine, or of a child in the dark. He needs light.

"Faisons la lumière" is an expression more often heard in French than in any other language. The tendency towards clearness is perhaps the most profound, the most active of the French soul. Above all the Frenchman wants to know, to know exactly.

It is through no mere accident that this immaterial need typical of the French soul is usually expressed in terms borrowed from the physical phenomenon of light. Knowledge, as conceived by the Frenchman, is intellectual vision. For him, to know is to see. To understand is to see clearly. Let us observe at once the clear-cut separation, implied in this attitude, between the subject which sees and the object which is seen. This is a typical feature of pure intellectual knowledge, the kind of knowledge distinctive of French intellect. We have seen that English knowledge is blended with other than intellectual elements. It cannot be considered as pure vision. For the Englishman, to understand is, in a way, to mingle more or less with the object which is understood. The operation is more confused, though perhaps more intimate. We shall presently come to make a similar observation with regard to knowledge in the Spaniard—the man of passion. Though for different reasons, the Englishman and the Spaniard, the man of action and the man of passion, do not remain at a distance from the object of which they think. For the Frenchman, as we have just observed, to think is to look with the eyes of the mind. And for intellectual vision, as for physical vision, there is a given distance which is the best possible one between the eye and the object.

As a matter of fact, this separation between the subject and the object is but a direct consequence of the tendency to clearness which has been noted above as the main quality of the intellectual. Vision is in itself but a network of separations. Physicians are well aware of this, for they name *separating power* the limit of vision which an optical apparatus possesses. Now, it is obvious that, before trying to separate the elements which compose the object that is observed, we must begin by separating the object itself from that which it does not contain.

Thus the existence of a certain distance between the observer and the object observed is a condition of French thought which is implicit in the tendency to clearness which drives it.

The intellectual *separating power* is what is called *precision*. *Precision* is one of the typical qualities of French thought, and the need of precision is no less typical a feature of the Frenchman. The one and the other may be observed in varying degrees in other peoples, but nowhere but in France do they impose themselves as typical characteristics, a fact which proves again that the Frenchman must be considered as the intellectual *par excellence*.

Precision is, therefore, clear separation. It may be considered under three different aspects:

1. Separation from each other of the elements which compose the object.
2. Separation of the object from all that surrounds it.
3. Separation of the object from the subject.

1. *Separation of the elements which compose the object*

This is called *analysis*. French thought is strongly analytical. It likes to burrow into ideas in order to find out their elements, to classify them, and to build up with them a complete picture which may please the mind. Analysis is then a kind of dismounting of the machine which leaves all its pieces in their respective places, or a kind of drawing in which each piece of the machine is brought out and all connexions and mutual dependencies between the several pieces are clearly shown without destroying the good order and the beauty of the whole. Analysis *in fine* is detailed vision. It is therefore natural that we should find it in its place as one of the characteristics of French thought. We have here to note again the difference between French thought and English and Spanish thought. English thought works by enumeration or inventory. Spanish thought is synthetical and works as it were in a wholesale manner. The one takes from the object what it needs; the other what the object gives it. French thought does not take; it sees. It sees all there is to be seen and everything in its place. At bottom, this faculty of seeing everything and everything in its place constitutes what is called *the sense of measure*. And this explains why the French should rightly be considered as specially gifted in this respect. He who sees everything and everything in its place has the sense of right proportion, and right proportion means right measure.

2. *Separation of the object from all that surrounds it*

This is *definition*. We are here again in the presence of a contrast. While the Englishman seeks to safeguard the rights of life by surrounding his thought with a blurred outline, the Frenchman seeks to guarantee the clearness of his intellectual vision by defining the object with the neatest possible edge. Language here again remains faithful to the optical metaphor which so happily represents the feeling of the French soul in this connexion, and that is why we so often hear in French of *mise au point*. A *mise au point* is an optical operation which allows us to place the object we are observing in the exact plane which gives the neatest, most perfect, and most clearly edged image of it. A millimetre more or less and the image will become blurred and finally disappear. The *mise au point* is an operation which means exactitude.

3. *Separation of the object and the subject*

We have noted that this separation is indispensable to vision, namely, to knowledge as it is understood in France. This distance between the object and the subject, which is a guarantee of clearness, implies therefore the disjunction of all the extra-intellectual or vital elements which English knowledge contains. It follows that French knowledge is cold, scientific, and external. Clear, like vision, it is, like vision, geometrical. It partakes of the abstract character of science. And here we may observe once more that, while English thought is concrete and vague, French thought is abstract and precise. French thought delves under the object and reveals the general scheme which constitutes, so to say, the common factor between its structure and that of the other objects of its class. French thought is therefore essentially bent on classification. Through the individual object it seeks the species. It bears within itself the hierarchy of ideas, the intellectual order to which it adjusts the world.

This separation of the object and the subject, which allows clear abstraction, implies a severe discipline. French thought schematizes and simplifies objects and gives, not so much their coloured picture, their mass in relief, but their plan and their elevation. It represents nature in the manner in which an engineer or an architect does it. The French intellect suggests an excellent map of the world in which all the accidents of the ground are represented with a scrupulous care for accuracy by means of conventional signs which give an admirable illusion of reality. This clearness, this luminosity, this accuracy are happily combined in what is called the *nuance*, the sense of shades, a quality which the Frenchman possesses in a high degree. For the *nuance* is the separation of differences carried to its extreme limit of delicacy and the sense of the *nuance* is equivalent to a vision of the continuous shading of differences, a kind of differential calculus of qualities. This feature of French intellect naturally leads to a comparison with pure mathematics. French vision is essentially exact and scientific. This scientific vision is entrusted to pure intellect. In the Frenchman, therefore, the work of knowledge is entirely conscious. The Frenchman brings to it premeditation and initiative. He attacks the object to be known and does not wait in a passive attitude for the object to reveal itself to him (which is the Spanish way), or for the current of experience to force him to take a partial and conditioned knowledge of the object (which is the English way). It follows that knowledge in the Frenchman is prepared, organized, and regulated in advance. The Frenchman excels in all the qualities of the conscious intellectual worker. Thus he is eminently gifted in qualities of method. Method is the road that the intellect must follow in order to reach its aim. The French are acknowledged masters in the art of method, and it is not by a mere accident that their greatest philosopher gave to his main work the title, *Discours de la Méthode*. In point of fact method is but the application to knowledge of that need for clearness which constitutes the main tendency of the French. But the road once defined, it must be followed. The faculty of conceiving a method would be of little use without the faculty of remaining faithful to it. Here again the Frenchman is admirably gifted in that sense of continuity or *esprit de suite*, which constitutes one of the most fruitful forces of our conscious being. The *esprit de suite* plays, in the domain of the intellect, the same role that perseverance plays in that of the will. It ensures the continuous evolution of thought, just as perseverance ensures the continuous evolution of action. Here we may see in passing another of those significant symmetries between the man of action and the intellectual. The characteristic feature of thought in the intellectual, as that of action in the man of action, is continuity; while the line of development of thought in the man of action, like the line of development of action in the man of thought, is a broken line, a series of short continuous phases broken by crises of disagreement between life and the intellect.

Method, *esprit de suite*, and continuity, such are the qualities of a conscious and active intellect. French thought excels in its constant energy, its application, and a kind of genius for husbanding its forces, which is the reward of method and the true cause of elegance. The main virtue of French intellect is talent. No other people is better gifted for dealing with an idea, i.e. for drawing out on the plane of the spirit the map of its intellectual territory and that of the bordering ideas with all the dialectic roads and paths which connect them. The Frenchman is a past master in the art of composition. The sense of measure and the sense of construction, both typical of his mind, are here allied to his tendency for pre-established plans and for foresight. By means of composition the Frenchman draws a synthetic picture of all the objects which his luminous glance analyses and puts each in its place. All his qualities contribute to give him the sense of form, which is one of the manifestations of his instinct for clearness and a kind of discipline of his creative and representative mind. For form, in the eyes of the Frenchman, is not merely outward elegance, ornament, grace; it is rather a kind of inward elegance which results from the true balance of the parts, their harmonious arrangement, and the clearness and beauty of the whole.

Such an admirable capacity for knowledge is somewhat lacking in the understanding of irrational things. By placing himself at a distance from the object, chosen in the interests of the best intellectual vision, the Frenchman purifies his observation from all vital elements. All that he gains thereby in clearness, he loses in complexity and in intimacy with nature. The irrational elements of things can be perceived only through an observation more intimate, more complete, perhaps also more confused than mere vision; an observation which partakes, perhaps, of the nature of lived experience. All those elements in nature which cannot be projected geometrically on the plane of the intellect tend to escape the understanding of the intellectual. The Frenchman is, therefore, naturally rationalistic. He is apt to devitalize things, to pin them down like butterflies on the appropriate page of his collection. This same tendency to think in categories shows that what really interests him is the permanent scheme of the whole, the network of space and time, rather than the living instant under his eyes. And yet, along with this evident limitation of his intellectual perception, a somewhat paradoxical quality must be noted: the French rationalist is the most reasonable of all rationalists, the most open, the most capable of comprehension. The rationalist who is now and then to be met in non-rationalistic countries, like Spain and England, is generally limited and narrow, as if, deprived by his rationalism of the natural and vital sources of knowledge to be found amongst the men of his race, he were entirely cut off from nature. In the Frenchman, on the contrary, at whatever distance from nature he may place himself, the intellect is a natural source of knowledge, so that, even in the coldest and most abstract attitude, the French rationalist seems to keep a width and a comprehension peculiar to himself. He seems to benefit from a kind of vitalization of the intellect which compensates for the devitalizing effect which his intellect tends to have on things.

If the collective life of thought is examined in an intellectual people, several features will be observed not unlike those which distinguish the collective life of action in a people of action. We have seen how, in England, collective action develops through a natural instinct for spontaneous organization. Up to a point, it may also be said that collective thought in France develops in an atmosphere of spontaneous collaboration. Nothing, indeed, is more remarkable than the order of French intellectual society, an order, of course, neither established nor imposed by any outward authority, but issuing from the race and upheld by virtue of a natural instinct within it. There exists in France an intellectual society, a true Republic of Letters, Sciences, and Arts. This republic has its authorities, its statutes, its laws and regulations, its critical standards, its rewards, its punishments. The French Academy, the Goncourt Academy, the reviews, the critics (in France recognized as an order, under the abstract name of La Critique), the University, for literary life; the Academy of Sciences, the École Normale Supérieure, the Collège de France, the great technical schools, for scientific life; the Academy of Fine Arts, the School of Fine Arts, the salons, the Conservatoire, the concerts, for the fine arts—these constitute a kind of State within this society. (The political State itself plays a certain part in this republic of letters, particularly in the control of some of the theatres, such as the Opéra, and in the promotions in the Légion d'Honneur, a kind of hierarchy or literary Tchin more rigid than might be imagined.) But the real force of this republic of letters, sciences, and arts, that which gives the institutions which constitute its "State" their vigour and their authority, is the spontaneous collaboration of the whole country in intellectual life, the fact that an election to the French Academy, the award of a Goncourt prize, a first night at the Comédie-Française, or a *vernissage* in a picture exhibition are events which interest, and sometimes rouse, the passions of the whole public.

There is, moreover, an aspect of the spontaneous collaboration which distinguishes French intellectual life of perhaps greater significance than the existence of an intellectual republic. We refer to the fact that the ideas which circulate in the country are apt to move and evolve in a collective way. The abstract, geometrical, and precise nature of French thought implies a tendency to crystallize, to become solidified in clear forms, pleasing to the mind, but set, and so to say, final. From time to time the whole of intellectual France finds itself so caught, as it were frozen into a mould of thought. Then a renovating movement begins and grows slowly in momentum; the crystal crust which had held the spirit of the country is broken, liberating it for a new phase of life under a new light. The collective, spontaneous, and harmonious character of such intellectual movements in France is as worthy of admiration as the collective, spontaneous, and harmonious character of the movements of collective action in England.

For in France intellectualism is general. The taste for things of the mind resides especially, and in a more conscious fashion, in the middle class, which, by the way, is particularly numerous and forms the most vigorous and most typically French class in the nation. In the *lycée*, or secondary school, French boys, we shall not say *acquire*, for they have it from birth, but *learn to cultivate* the taste for culture, so that the basis of the republic of letters, sciences, and arts is, in the last resort, not a mere *cénacle*, or expert body of people, but the whole middle class of France.

Thus French intellectual life develops with a collective spirit and under the protection of collective institutions which constitute a kind of intellectual State. The history of this intellectual State, like that of the political State, is made of phases of quiet development followed by crises or intellectual revolutions which provide the transition between two different and successive evolutions. Classicism, romanticism, symbolism, naturalism are but literary examples of this tendency. Other similar examples might be quoted for the other arts. We find here again the broken line of evolution which we noted as characteristic of the intellectual in action. For, in observing the development of intellectual life in the French, we can no longer consider thought strictly in itself, but as a phenomenon of collective life which must present characteristics similar to those of action in the intellectual people.

VI

Thought in the Man of Passion

ALL THE FEATURES GENERALLY RECOGNIZED AS TYPICAL OF Spanish thought may be explained if the natural attitude of the man of passion towards life is taken into account. We have seen the Englishman in thought taking from the object of which he thinks all that he considers useful to him at the moment; and the Frenchman in thought looking at the object systematically with intitiative and premeditation; the Spaniard thinks by contemplation. He waits in an apparent passivity for the object to reveal itself to him. He lets the continuous stream of life pass through him, until chance, a happy coincidence, a secret sympathy, will suddenly illumine it with a new light. The Spaniard thinks by intuition.

Intuition is the passion of the intellect. For in it, the intellect remains passive and it is from life that the spark of comprehension springs. But such comparisons, borrowed from the vocabulary of light, are not so satisfactory here as they were in the case of the French intellect; for intuition is more and less than intellectual vision, or rather is quite a different psychological fact. There is a moment in the search for truth in which our mind feels that it has come to the end of its labours. Even if the road that has been followed is coldly logical, the final moment which we call certitude is vital, and takes place in a region of our being where the mind no doubt is present, but where also the waves produced in the mind by the little shock of certitude prolong themselves into bodily sensations. The moment in which our being touches this vital certitude (a moment which the intellectual reaches along mental roads) is called intuition. We should observe its integral character from a twofold point of view: subject and object.

The whole being is present in intuition. There can be no question here of an intellectual observation carried on by means of the "optical apparatus" of analysis. Neither can we say that we are in the presence of an operation by which we take hold of an object empirically, with a view to utilizing it. Intuition is rather an instantaneous and spontaneous contact of the life of the object and the life of the subject, and, therefore, intuition *involves the whole subject at once*. Thus the opinions of the Spaniard are not mere ideas carried in his head, but convictions which he breathes and which circulate in his blood. We find here a certain similarity between knowledge in the Spaniard and knowledge in the Englishman. For the Englishman also, as we have observed, participates with his whole body in the *feeling* of knowledge. In his case, however, the presence of the body in knowledge means that, as a man of action, he takes material hold of a known object through the instrument of the will, i.e. the body—a kind of empirical guarantee which he takes in order to prevent thought from straying away from matter.

That is why the body of the Englishman gives the impression that it participates actively in thought, while in the case of the man of passion, the participation of his body in intuition is as passive as that of his mind. Both his mind and his body are as the bed of the river of life on which life itself lets fall the rich deposit of truth.

Hence a feature sometimes observed in Spanish psychology: Spanish thought is born at the moment when it manifests itself. The Englishman thinks while acting, the Spaniard while speaking. There is no doubt a close relationship between this feature of the Spanish character and the spontaneity which we noted as characteristic of the man of passion in action. Such a feature may, moreover, be connected with the tendency of the man of passion towards improvisation, a tendency of which more will be said hereafter. But there is no doubt that in any case it can be deduced from the integral character of intuition considered from the point of view of the subject, namely, from the fact that intuition takes place in the presence of the whole thinking subject as an all-round person.

This observation may be confirmed by watching Spaniards speak. It often happens in ordinary Spanish conversation that remarks of a most abstract nature begin with an energetical *yo* (I), which is afterwards connected with the rest of the abstract argument by a more or less tortuous line of grammar. The process is obviously one of a vigorous incarnation of abstract thought in the person who happens to think it.

Integral from the point of view of the subject, the moment of intuition is no less so from the point of view of the object. This follows from the vital character which we have observed in it. In intuition the object contemplated reveals itself all at once in its essence, with all its relations and all the connexions which attach it to the rest of life. Hence the final character which is often found in Spanish thought, as well as the insep-arability of body and spirit which is one of its deepest features, a kind of material spirituality, or spiritual materiality, peculiar to it.

It is at this moment, when it emerges from the depths of the subconscious, that Spanish thought is strongest, most vigorous. It has all the vital freshness of natural facts, not to be disputed since they are themselves their own demonstration. Free from all preparatory argument, independent of all dialectical plan, Spanish thought appears on the surface of the intellect still warm from the innermost folds of the soul in which it is formed. We saw English thought limit itself to that spot on the plane of the intellect which coincides with the vital moment of action and take on a blurred outline—in one word, manifest itself as concrete and vague; we saw on the other hand French thought seize the general characteristics of the object and draw them out with the greatest accuracy in the form of a well-defined scheme—that is to say, show itself abstract and precise. Spanish thought springs, such as it is, from the moment of intuition which gives it birth; it is entire but localized, synthetic but substantial. True, it is situated at the point where the moving and undulating surface of life touches the plane of the intellect, but it is not limited to the vision or idea of this point; rather does it there receive the whole vital impulse with which life acts there; and that is why, though individual in its incarnation, it is universal in its essence. Thus, while English thought is concrete and vague, and French thought is abstract and precise, Spanish thought is concrete and precise.

Spanish thought, then, proceeds by a series of intuitional revelations. Now it is evident that while the conscious working of the intellect is reversible, the moment of intuition is irreversible. Nature's act of grace, it cannot be repeated at will. Knowledge by intuition is therefore as irreversible as it is spontaneous, as final as it is integral. It can be neither verified nor begun again. This observation explains a phenomenon often observed in the Spaniard. He improvises almost always. This improvisation may be immediate, namely the outcome of an instantaneous intuition, or it may be the expression of a long chain of accumulated intuitions; but, in either case, the Spaniard works without a plan, and, his work once finished, he is incapable of correcting it. For in his case, composition, which is not always defective, is also the fruit of intuition. Though he works without any explicit plan, yet he feels a kind of design which guides him at the moment of writing. But as this design is not conscious, once the work is finished, correction becomes impossible.

Intuition also excludes any possibility of establishing a method beforehand. And in fact, method is far from being a typical feature of Spanish thought. A method, we have said, is a road for the mind. It is difficult to imagine how a road towards knowledge could be traced by people who find themselves in knowledge before they set foot on the road. Yet it may be necessary to go more closely into this question. Intuition acts somewhat like the sun which little by little lifts the mist which covers a landscape: a peak will first appear and emerge out of the grey; then another one, then two near-by; then a valley will begin to suggest itself behind the grey veils of the mist; little by little, the whole landscape will spread before the eyes of the spectator, who will have arrived at the knowledge of the total view by a series of revelations succeeding each other in apparent disorder. Something similar happens in intuition. Spanish thought has a method of its own which is certainly not the road-schedule which the General Staff of the Mind prepares for the Frenchman on his way to truth. For the Spaniard does not get on the way at all. He does not budge. He contemplates. And his method consists in watching the peaks of the landscape appear each in its place and in connecting them by means of his imagination. Nevertheless, it cannot be doubted that Spanish thought, though rich in finds, is weak in method. Accustomed to following the caprice of intuition, it lacks that continuity which is but the habit of an intellect trained to follow up the roads of method.

This weakness of Spanish thought in all the conscious intellectual virtues deprives it of much efficiency and effectiveness. The raw-material of Spanish thought is generally much superior to the complete product. But the weakness does sometimes affect the raw-material itself, for there is no doubt that, by relying too frequently on intuition, Spanish thought is apt to indulge in arbitrary ways. This unfortunate tendency becomes the stronger from the fact that, as the sources of intuition flow from nature herself, Spaniards prefer to contemplate nature directly, rather than to seek food for their thought in the thought of others. Hence they are able to indulge their tendency to arbitrary ways of thinking unshackled by the experience, the tradition, and the intellectual discipline of those who have thought before them. With this feature must be connected the typically Spanish tendency towards building intellectual edifices on foundations of clouds. An instinctive creative urge, a certain sense of form leads the Spaniard to seek to complete his thoughts even when his intuition does not furnish him with a natural basis for them. Then, not sufficiently accustomed to discipline and method, still less so to experience, he builds *in vacuo*. Such is the shortcoming of an otherwise real quality of the Spanish mind—*el ingenio*, that is to say, creative intuition.

Left to itself, intuition would probably bring back from the depths of the subconscious nothing but pearls of truth. Unfortunately, there is in the psychology of the man of passion an inherent element of error. The very essence of his psychology sets passion, and not knowledge, as his ultimate aim. It follows that if and when the fire of a particular passion deforms his intuition, knowledge in the Spaniard becomes irretrievably warped. The subordination of thought to passion is therefore a typical feature of the Spaniard in thought. It fosters his tendency to arbitrariness and further curtails the efficiency and effectiveness of his intellectual work on the rich intuitive raw material wherewith he is endowed by nature.

A general observation may be deduced from all that precedes. Spanish thought is as rich in subconscious elements as poor in conscious elements. Now, in the work of the spirit, the subconscious provides the seed, while the conscious cultivates it and makes it fructify. From the subconscious comes the creative impulse; the conscious utilizes it to make it yield its maximum efficiency. The one is creative, the other critical. In the conscious, talent works; from the subconscious, genius springs.

Spanish thought is therefore more closely connected with the essence of genius. Here, a word of explanation. Too often the words *genius* and *talent* are used to suggest ideas which differ only in degree, so that genius would be a kind of superlative talent. Whatever reasons there may be in support of this use, *genius* and *talent* will in these pages signify two ideas differing, not in degree, but in kind. There may be great or small talents, great or small geniuses. Genius is not great talent, nor talent small genius. Genius and talent are different types of the human spirit which may be distinguished in that talent is mostly conscious, continuous, methodical, analytical, critical, skilled in matters of form, while genius is above all subconscious, discontinuous, free from all method, synthetic, creative, fertile in matters of substance.

This admitted, Spanish thought is rich in genius, but poor in talent. Now, genius being equal, the greater the talent, the better the work; for it is evident that the efficiency of a genius depends on the talent which it has at its disposal. This observation will enable us to understand a fair number of facts of Spanish intellectual life, in particular, artistic life: thus, the evident superiority of the arts in which genius may more easily pass for talent (literature, painting) and its weakness in science as well as in those arts in which talent plays a more important role (architecture, music).

A similar remark applies to the place which form takes in Spanish thought. We saw the Englishman neglect form, the Frenchman cultivate it and excel in it. The Spaniard occupies a somewhat intermediary position. Concrete and precise, he certainly has a sense of form, but he is rarely capable of applying it successfully if such an application implies an effort of perseverance and critical judgement. He may attain to great excellence in form if the work is happily conceived in a flow of inspiration. But if the inspiration happens to be defective, he will find it most difficult to refashion it. In one word the Spaniard, whether in form or in substance, is unequal, and this inequality is the permanent witness of the, so to say, volcanic nature of his intellectual production.

A Frenchman said that genius is a long patience—a typically French saying, for it assimilates genius to a talent indefinitely prolonged. Another Frenchman, with a genius-like talent, has wittily corrected Buffon's saying:

Génie, oh longue impatience!

—genius, oh long impatience—and provided they are adequately interpreted, both these sayings might be accepted. Rather than a long patience, the Spanish genius would appear to be a long passivity. The river of intuition flows continually in our being, and even though none of its waves may waken undulations of thought in our intellect, there is a kind of continuity of touch between the world and our being, a kind of subconscious certainty, a kind of subterranean knowledge the sense of which never stops. This latent intuition gives the Spaniard, even when not particularly gifted from the strictly intellectual point of view, a philosophical serenity which acts in him as an intellect. We find here again the participation of the whole being in passive thought which we noticed as the typical feature of the man of passion in thought. This philosophical serenity is not unlike the wisdom of the Englishman, which we mentioned when dealing with the man of action in thought. It has the same width of view, the same calm. Yet it differs from wisdom in that, faithful to the type of the man of passion in which we have observed it, it is disinterested from the practical point of view. It is not wise with a view to action. It is, and that is all. It is not, like English wisdom, a potential rule of conduct, but merely a state of the soul which is in itself its own aim and its own justification.

Just as the finds which intuition throws up to the surface of conscious intelligence succeed each other without continuity in time, so the intuitional finds of a people take place independently in different individuals and without continuity in space. This fact explains why the intellectual life of the people of passion should be particularly weak in conscious tradition, i.e. in cohesion along the line of time, as well as in unity at any given time, that is to say in cohesion within a given epoch. This double phenomenon may be observed in the intellectual life of

Spain. Every individual seeks the sources of intuition in nature herself. Social intellectual raw-materials, scarcely solicited by the individual, cannot reach a sufficient density and therefore cannot take shape—for in social life creation and consumption are intimately blended together. Such a rarefaction of intellectual collective life strengthens, in its turn, the individualistic tendency which is its cause. And thus it is that the life of thought in Spain evinces an uncompromising individualism and a true anarchy of ideas.

We do not find, therefore, in Spain the beautiful uniformity which French thought attains spontaneously by virtue of an inner rhythm which is able to manifest itself precisely because it finds in the pure intellectual plane the possibility for general and collective movements; neither do we find in her the cohesion which English thought can reach under the pressure of social forces. In truth, Spanish collective thought does not exist otherwise than as an abstraction. Each thinking Spaniard follows a solitary path and whatever cohesion there is in the whole is due to the profound unity of the race which manifests itself in the several individuals. Hence that in Spain the sense of intellectual hierarchy is bound to be weak. We know that the intellectual gifts of Spain are mostly spontaneous, creative, and of the nature of genius, while she is weak in critical talent and in method. It follows that her thought is, in the deepest sense of the word, "popular." For the people are in every country the purest representative of the spontaneous qualities of the race. Conscious intellectual virtues are the specialty of the upper classes. If, therefore, Spain excels in subconscious gifts, she is best represented by her people. We shall have occasion to return to this point and incidentally to define more accurately what this expression *people* contains when applied to Spain. For the present it may suffice to put the fact on record and to draw from it a consequence bearing upon our present subject. A creative people feels instinctively strong in its genius. This feeling contributes to weaken its sense of intellectual hierarchy, while the inherent weakness of Spain's upper classes in the conscious qualities of talent, which are precisely the basis of their claim to occupy the higher ranks of the hierarchy, does but justify the attitude of the people towards them.

A further factor acting in the same direction is the synthetic attitude of the Spaniard. He beholds, and lets pass in him, the whole of life. This attitude creates a state of mind favourable to inactivity. For all intellectual work is apt to become local, partial, precise, in fact small and mean, when compared to the synthetic spectacle of the world. Hence the people feel instinctively a kind of quiet assurance, a self-confidence which thinks nothing of intellectual leaders.

Such are the reasons which explain the intellectual anarchy of Spain. And yet, circumstances might be imagined in which this anarchy would disappear and the whole social body of the country be brought together in a powerful and spontaneous unity. These circumstances must be sought in the light of the typical feature of the man of passion. We know that for the man of passion it is not thought, but passion which is the supreme aim. Spanish thought will therefore acquire a spontaneous unity when the soul of the people is seized by a sovereign passion. Such was the case when Spain, under the attacks of the Reformation, conceived the ambitious dream of purifying religion. Religion, which, as has been admirably said by Coventry Patmore, is in Spain a human passion, transfigured Spanish thought, making of it a whole, a unit. It was not a cohesion due to social pressure from the group, such as gives at least an external unity to thought in England; it was not a case of spontaneous intellectual co-operation, such as may be seen in the republic of letters and arts which governs the intellectual life of France; it was an inner unity which, while respecting the uncompromising individualism of all Spaniards, inspired their individual intuitions with the same spirit by making them drink from the same source.

VII

Passion in the Man of Action

THE CASE OF THE MAN OF ACTION IN A STATE OF PASSION RAISES problems which are the inverse of those observed in connexion with the man of passion in a state of action. We should therefore expect a certain symmetry between the features of passion in the Englishman and those of action in the Spaniard.

We have seen that the Englishman, bent on action, watches himself. The forces of nature which live in him are therefore carefully controlled by a power which resides in the will. Undoubtedly, this hold of the will is not always conscious. Used to being in harness, the Englishman often forgets the weight of it. The fact remains that the directing centre of his self-control is in his conscious will, and therefore it is there that the slightest commotion of the system is recorded and calls forth an energetic reaction to reassert the central authority which had been threatened. Two elements should be discriminated within this fundamental tendency: the first is that the passions are held and watched over; the second that they are held and watched with a view to action, namely, with positive aims. From these two observations a number of features of passion in the Englishman can be deduced.

And, to begin with, his lack of spontaneity. This feature corresponds by contrast to the spontaneity of the Spaniard in action. But such a contrast is evidence itself. Less evident is the subtle psychological symmetry which exists between the lack of spontaneity of the Englishman, whose passions are the slaves of action, and the lack of the instinct of spontaneous organization in the Spaniard, whose actions are the slaves of passion. Here, in my opinion, is the true symmetrical correspondence: the man of action, having enslaved his passions in order to reach positive aims, takes away from them all liberty to pursue their own aims as passions—which liberty is what we mean by spontaneity; the man of passion, whose actions can only be set in motion by the force of a passion, perforce individual, does not feel in him that spontaneous tendency to action which is the real inspiration underlying the instinct for spontaneous organization of the Englishman.

Thus, passion in the Englishman is normally withheld and constrained. It follows that the Englishman is normally calm, with a calm which corresponds also by a kind of symmetry to the indifference which we have commented upon when dealing with action in the Spaniard. For, just as under this Spanish indifference towards action, stores of active energy accumulate and manifest themselves now and then in sudden outbursts of exceptional activity, so, under the English calm, an accumulation of the explosives of passion takes place which a chance incident may at any moment set aflame. The English equivalents of the great heroes of action of Spanish history are not

English men of action, but great English men of passion. The Hernán Cortéses of England are its great poets—Shakespeare, Byron, Shelley—for, like the great crystalline peaks, witnesses of the oceans of fire which rage unknown under the Earth's cold plains, the great men of action of Spain rise in history to assert the high potential of energy hidden under the normal indifference of the race, and the great men of passion of England tower over the quiet levels of the English soul as a testimony to the profound passions hidden under the crust of her apparent calm.

The observation is important, for, led into error by the English calm—the famous British phlegm—the world has too often jumped to the conclusion that under this calm there was nothing but coldness. Far from being cold, the English soul lives rather at a higher temperature of passion than the average —if only as the effect of the pressure to which the constraint of self-control submits the passions of the Englishman. Properly observed, the English calm is by no means phlegmatic; on the contrary, it evinces an almost imperceptible vibration which shows that its immobility is due, not to the absence of forces, but to a continually renewed equilibrium between the contrary forces of a powerful passion and a usually more powerful self-control.

Self-control implies self-command, and self-command means a division between the subject and the object of the command. All these expressions are in fact inaccurate. We do not control ourselves. One part of our being controls another part. And though the expression might be understood in two ways by interchanging the roles of the commander and the commanded, what it actually means is the command of the passions by the conscious and enlightened will. Hence the man of action who is his own master does not give, cannot give, the impression of "integrality" which we have felt in the presence of the man of passion. Far from it, the very fact that his passion is controlled makes us feel that an important part of his personality is being concealed from our presence. The Englishman does not present himself entirely before us. Like the gear-wheel which he is, he commits himself only to the extent of the very small arc which is necessary to make the social machine turn round.

Other causes act in the same direction and particularly the profound disturbances produced in the life-stream by the English habit of self-control. We shall note here once more a case of symmetry between passion in the man of action and action in the man of passion. When dealing with the Spaniard in action we saw how the life-stream passed freely through the individual soul, which made itself hollow as it were to let it pass undisturbed as on a river-bed. In the Englishman, the life-stream is meddled with and disturbed by all kinds of dams and weirs which destroy its purity and its "integrality." The life-stream is divided and subdivided and localized and the state of soul becomes more sensitive to circumstances, less serene, under its apparent calm, than that of the man of passion. This is not an obvious feature of English psychology, yet it is a typical one which manifests itself in a curious lack of universal passions. The passions of the Englishman are all relative. In his life-stream the natural current is intimately mixed with social and artificial elements and this fact gives his psychology a singular complexity. So that, paradoxical as it may seem at first sight, this people of action which holds passion in distrust, represses it, and does not cultivate it, has reached, perhaps, the most complete, and certainly the most complex, development of passions amongst mankind.

Take for example the passion, so English, called *pride*, a word which no effort of ingenuity can translate accurately into either French or Spanish. It might seem at first sight that pride is a universal psychological species and that the Englishman who is proud is proud always and everywhere. The conclusion might be exact for the Spaniard. But, as concerns the Englishman, pride is not an absolute and constant characteristic of certain persons, so that it is possible to say that Smith is proud and Jones is not proud; in reality all the Smiths and all the Joneses of England are proud in certain circumstances and are not proud in other circumstances, which, of course, may not be the same for Smith and for Jones. For circumstances, that is to say the social world, act more deeply on English psychology than on other psychologies, precisely because, through the intermediate action of self-control, the group reaches the individual in his most intimate life and exerts its pressure there.

This conclusion, which forces itself on us when we consider the effects of self-control in itself, becomes even more imperative when we examine the consequences of the positive and utilitarian tendencies of self-control. The man of action does not bind himself to its constraint for nothing. He dons this harness in order to pull the chariot of utilitarian work. The life-stream is canalized in order to be utilized. Dams and weirs are there in order to direct its natural forces towards action and therefore to select them. From this moment the psychology of passion becomes, so to say, *polarized*. Any movement of the life-stream is considered no longer as a manifestation which carries with it its own justification, but as an element in a given mechanical problem determined by the aim in action which the subject has set before himself. Certain passions can be utilized and are therefore sources of power. Other passions cannot be utilized and must therefore be considered as forces of friction and waste, or, what is worse still, as antagonistic forces.

We may therefore expect to find in the life of English passion the influence of the group; and indeed, in the selection which the discipline of action imposes on the Englishman, it is easy to observe that the passions recognized as useful are those which it is possible to put at the service of the community, either as they are or after more or less deep transformations with that end in view. That is how the utilitarianism of self-control reinforces the tendency of self-control itself to deprive English passions of all universality. The group—in fact the nation, that is to say the British race—marks the frontier and colours the modality of the English passions which are considered as positive, that is to say, as useful. We shall have occasion to return to this point when dealing with religion, which might seem the very model of a universal passion, and yet *as a passion* is, in England, limited strictly to the frontiers of the race. The English language possesses an untranslatable word which expresses precisely this vital and irrational sense of the racial limitation of universal passions. The word *loyalty* does not correspond to the French *loyauté*, which implies a certain shade of intellectual honesty, respect for truth as recognized all round; no more does it correspond to the Spanish *lealtad*, which would rather mean fidelity of feeling towards other; *loyauté* and *lealtad* owe nothing to the group, of which they are entirely independent; both define relations which it is possible to establish between any two human beings. But *loyalty* is concerned with the relations between the individual and his group. Loyalty is a kind of internal discipline freely consented to, or rather previous to all consent, for it is instinctive. Through loyalty all the positive passions of the individual adapt themselves closely to the shape, and take on the colour, of the community, and therefore they lose their universality for the benefit of the group.

The other passions, the rebellious ones, the man of action, under pressure of the group, degrades instinctively to the rank of animal passions. It is possible to suspect that the true, profound origin of the puritan tendency lies in this degradation which the group inflicts on all individual passions which are not utilizable by the community. These passions happen to be those which result in purely individual sensations, generally accompanied with pleasure. Puritanism was once most severe with them. And it is curious to observe in this connexion that every time one of them has been reinstated into respectability, it has had first to pass through a kind of examination and prove before the group-jury that it was a good and useful passion for the community. The aesthetic passion, love of the Arts, is a striking example of this. It had to justify itself in the eyes of the guardians of the public good before the individual was able to enjoy without scruple the pleasure of listening to melodies unaccompanied by any moral teachings.

There are, however, a few passions difficult to justify from the point of view of the community. Having so admirably succeeded in disciplining the other passions to the service of the community, of the group, the Englishman is led to the conclusion that these rebellious ones are but the share of the animal which is in man. Strengthened in this view by that sense of matter which we have observed in him, he leaves to the flesh that which belongs to the flesh. These passions left to themselves tend, no doubt, to come nearer to earth, the more so from the fact that, being severely repressed, they live a life of obscurity and contempt and can only seek satisfaction in violence and repose in shame.

It is therefore in the domain of passion that the continuous fight between the individual and the community leads to the greatest havoc in a people of action. For such a people, as we have seen, evinces in an equal degree the sense of individual liberty and the sense of collective loyalty. The opinion is too general that, if the man of action makes self-control one of the most important categories of collective existence, it is because he under-estimates the force of passions. This opinion errs both on the side of observation and on that of reasoning. We do not watch closely that which we do not fear. "The price of liberty is eternal vigilance," a sentence which was born in England. The idea which it contains holds good in psychology. The man of action who wishes to be free—free, of course, from the hold of passions—must keep a continuous watch on his inner life. And in fact, the passions of the Englishman deserve to be closely watched.

The dissociation, discussed above, between passions that can be utilized by the group, and animal or rebellious passions, makes this vigilance easier and perhaps too perfect. Through the machinery of loyalty, the group settles itself solidly and surely in the individual. It follows that the animal passions feel that the master is at home. Following a psychological law, better known than understood, they sublimate themselves and tend to manifest themselves in the form of sentiment. Hence it is that this people, robust and masculine, whose reputation for coldness is as universal as it is mistaken, should be one of the most sentimental peoples on earth. Sentiment, in its turn, is held back by the law of self-control which governs all English psychology, held back but not abolished, for, after all, sentiment is "respectable" and within certain limits may even be useful for the community. But in so far as it is held back, it needs an outlet. It finds it in humour. It is to sentiment that English humour, even the dryest, owes its inimitable attraction.

But the group pushes its hold over individual life still farther. We have observed that it divides and subdivides the life-stream giving to all passions a relative and local modality. This effect is further complicated by the fact that the group vigilance finds access to the innermost folds of the English soul through the typically English phenomenon of self-consciousness. It is a kind of continuous presence of the observing ego on the observed ego; but, for the purpose of his observation, this observing ego adopts successively the eyes, the standards, the prejudices of all the countrymen and countrywomen which the observed ego respects and whose opinion he fears. Thus, all this ensemble of currents and under-currents which constitutes the life-stream subdivided by self-control doubles itself as it were with its own image seen in the social mirror and in this way the secret world of passion, which the active man strives to keep quiet, and even asleep, lives the more disturbed, the more sensitive to influences, sympathies, antipathies, and restraints. This agitation, always at work in the being under his apparent calm, does now and then come to the surface through the fissures of self-control. It influences, moreover, the whole of English life, which, despite its admirable discipline, is often troubled and always threatened by the intimate conflicts which it conceals.

VIII

Passion in the Man of Thought

IF THE ATTITUDE OF THE INTELLECTUAL MAY BE COMPARED TO vision, it follows that passion is inherently rebellious to such an attitude. For vision, as we have seen, implies the separation of the object from the subject, while passion is essentially an intimate union of life with the subject, the passage through the subject of the integral stream of life. The intellectual is dominated by a tendency to separate himself from the life-stream in order to place himself at the best distance for mental vision. We shall therefore observe in him a certain resistance to passion or perhaps, more exactly, a tendency to evade passion. We have seen the man of action strongly acting on the life-stream by means of his self-control and thereby mingling intimately with the life of passion at the moment when he is intent on controlling it. The intellectual, instead of coming nearer life, tends to get away from it by virtue, not of a decision of his conscious mind, but of a primary tendency which instinctively makes him draw apart from that which he wants to understand.

Hence two orders of consequences: on the one hand, those due to the fact that there is such a distance between the subject and his object; on the other, those which are due to the attitude of the intellectual, which is one of vision.

The distance, namely the instinctive separation between the active intellect and the life-stream, explains a certain coldness characteristic of the French type. Of the three peoples here studied, it is certainly the least inflammable. Perhaps one of the most entertaining and paradoxical facts of contemporary European life is the sight of hot and passionate English people reproaching in the calmest manner their French neighbours, sometimes irritable but always cold, for an imaginary tendency to passion. There never was a deeper error committed on the faith of superficial observation. It is true that the Frenchman does not give the impression of calm which the Englishman knows how to attain, not without effort, through the exercise of an admirable personal discipline. But the external calm of the Englishman ofter covers, as we have seen, keen intimate struggles, and it is surely strange to conclude from a victory that the enemy does not exist. Moreover, when these two peoples are compared, they are generally visualized in action; now we know that action is precisely the element of the Englishman, while the Frenchman is out of his element in it. It follows that the Frenchman in action lets himself go to a certain irritation caused by the resistances which the intellectual finds in irrational nature. In a state of pure passion, and when self-control is not solicited by an immediate action, English discipline is not altogether impervious to the robust vitality usually concealed beneath it. Now it is precisely in the state of pure passion that the coldness of the Frenchman can be observed, for in the

Frenchman the richest vitality is in the brain. The Frenchman is therefore more his own master in passion than in action, or, as we might say, paraphrasing a famous French verse, "he is more his own master than that of the Universe."

All this would not, however, justify the conclusion that self-control is a French feature. The word implies two characteristics, neither of which is to be found in the French *maîtrise de soi*. The first, more especially suggested by the prefix *self*, evinces an introspective tendency, a kind of meddling with the life-stream, which is both contrary to the principle of the distance between subject and nature mentioned above as typical of French psychology, and entirely unnecessary, since the attitude of the Frenchman towards the life-stream is wholly instinctive; the second, more especially represented in the word *control*, indicates an absolute hold over the passions, a repression or, at any rate, a most energetic damming of the life-stream. But things do not happen in this way to the intellectual. His attitude towards the forces of passion is more akin to the French meaning of the word *contrôle* than to the English meaning of *control*. I mean that the Frenchman supervises rather than represses. There is, however, a certain passivity, a certain neutrality in intellectual observation, and if, in actual practice, the Frenchman remains his own master, it is not so much because he makes a great effort thereto, as because the internal economy of his vital forces is established to the advantage of the intellect and to the detriment of passion.

The control of the passions takes place in him not in view of action, but in the name of the intellect. The Frenchman deeply feels the dignity of reason. He is as hierarchically ordered in his conscience as the world which he creates around him is ordered as a State. The Frenchman places on the summit of his own being the majesty of reason. It is out of respect for reason, out of a feeling of intellectual discipline that he supervises the life-stream in order that it should not threaten the foundations of so well organized a being. His attitude is one of precaution against eventual dangers which might arise after a certain moment, if a certain limit were to be overstepped. The situation does not require continuous self-control taut towards action, but mere foresight of possible exceptional cases—which does not prevent the most absolute liberty in normal life.

We find in the Frenchman, therefore, none of that constraint which we have observed in the English attitude towards passion. And this is the more true from the fact that the Frenchman brings to the life of passion that moderation, that sense of measure which are the manifestations of a character solidly built on reason. Reasonable he is even in pain, even in love, even in desperation. Like the compasses set on a double suspension which sailors use, he preserves the sense of the intellectual vertical with admirable determination even in the most terrific tempests.

No more do we find in him that crust which covers the hot passions of the Englishman by virtue of the external coldness generated by self-control. Passion in the Frenchman has free access to the surface and thus shows itself more frank, more spontaneous, and less capable of destroying by violence the equilibrium of thought. There is after all in French psychology a legitimizing of passion, a kind of instinctive and tacit recognition of the right to passion, which is wholly in harmony with the objective attitude of the intellectual. In the Frenchman, passion is not the enemy who is feared and watched, against whom the house is barricaded and defended, but the natural phenomenon which is foreseen, which has its laws and its rights, which plays a definite and necessary role in life, and which comes in its time and goes after having had its share and achieved what it had to do. This "matter-of-course" attitude towards passion is perhaps the typical feature of the life of passion in France.

It follows that, in so far as passion is concerned, the Frenchman is free from self-consciousness. For in the man of action self-consciousness, as we have seen, is due to the constant pressure of self-control stimulated by the requirements of the group. Now, neither self-control nor the action of the group is to be observed in the Frenchman. Licit for the individual, passions are licit for the group by virtue of that moral tolerance which we observed when discussing the Frenchman in action. Passions therefore emerge not only to the surface of individual life, but to the surface of social life as well, and are received with the same "matter-of-course" attitude by the group as by the individual. That curious foible which makes one people judge another by standards and ways of thinking of its own often causes this French attitude, whether social or individual, to be condemned as cynicism. Nothing, however, is farther from the truth than the view which would attribute to the Frenchman a cynical attitude in matters of passion. Faithful to his own type, his personality resides in his brain, and from this high observatory he looks down on passion. The liberty which he grants to it is almost that of a stranger, or at least that of a man who observes with detached curiosity the playful movements of the dogs which are in his keeping, knowing that he can always bring them back to order whenever he so desires. But in this confiding attitude it would be a mistake not to see a mastership as great as, and, in any case, a greater distance from passion than, that which the man of action can attain by means of self-control.

Though free from all self-consciousness, the intellectual evinces a feature, so to say, homologous, which might therefore go by the name of intellectual self-consciousness. I mean precisely this observant attitude of passion at work on which I have just dwelt. Though free, French passion is not spontaneous. True, it moves unfettered by self-control, but it lives under the eye of the introspection which observes it, analyses it, and judges it. Passion thus loses much of that unforeseeable volcanic character which it keeps intact in the true man of passion and even in the man of action under the crust of his self-control. Just as we have noticed in the Englishman the profound disturbances brought into passion under the individual and social pressure of self-control, so we can see in the Frenchman how passion becomes intimately mingled with intellectual elements developed by the continuous presence of an observant self. That is why the French are masters in the art of explaining states of mind minutely. For not only are they led towards this art by the natural superiority of expression and form which they owe to their intellectual structure, but the psychological matter which they observe is in itself richer in intellectual elements and therefore admits more easily of expression through verbal formulae.

It seems as if the intellectual attitude towards passion might have deeper consequences amounting almost to a kind of separation of the life-stream into two different currents, the one intellectual and the other bodily. We have duly noted in its place the intellectual tendency to neglect the irrational elements of life. Now the life-stream, irrational as a whole before all analysis, yields to reason two rational elements, or, at least, two elements the observation and explanation of which are rational: ideas and sensations. There is a third element, an irrational element this time, which manifests itself often in rich superstructures or, as the modern expression goes, in "sublimations." This complex phenomenon takes place more easily in the cases where the separation of conscious and subconscious functions is less clear. Now French psychology tends to define and to analyse experience through its apparatus for intellectual vision. A master in the abstract, given to precision, exacting in matters of definition and clearness, the Frenchman pitilessly attacks these superstructures which irrational life builds up in order to manifest itself to itself. The French mind detects in these superstructures that which comes from sensations and that which is borrowed from ideas. It separates these two elements, letting fall, perhaps, between them all that passion may contain of truly real, of ineffably real, and thus it tends to do away with what remains of the third irrational element of passion which an exacting analysis has already despoilt of the two rational elements which it contains.

Such a dissociation facilitates the calm and objective attitude which the intellectual is wont to take as regards passion. For, of the three elements of passion, the irrational element, the most ineffable and perhaps the most unstable, is also the most intimate and personal, the one which we live perhaps the most intensely. Ideas are abstract and universal; sensations are the affairs of matter, and, although lived and felt by the individual, they borrow from their physical nature a certain generality which makes them common experiences. The irrational element once destroyed or weakened by dissociation, the detachment and coldness of the intellectual can be easily explained.

Hence also the sobriety of the Frenchman. We have observed the role played in his *maîtrise* by his moderation and his sense of measure. These causes of ponderation come, so to say, from the outside of passion. Sobriety is a quality which flows from the characteristics of passion itself as it may be observed in the intellectual. For it is, as it were, a passion "dispassionated" by the intellect, reduced by the intellect to a sheaf of ideas and a gamut of sensations.

The intellectual, moreover, does not limit his effects on passion to a dissociation of the two elements which he discerns in it. He dwells also on each of these two elements separately. He enters the field of ideas in order to indulge in clever psychological analyses and determines the development of psychological situations along the laws of logic. We have seen how the intellect tends to destroy without pity the superstructures which irrational life builds in order to manifest itself; through a sort of curious inversion, this same intellect is wont to create for itself understructures of passion in order to satisfy the requirements of its psychological appetite. The Frenchman excels in the chemistry of the soul.

In a parallel way the intellectual acts also on sensations. We find here again the hedonistic tendency and the tendency to refinement which we had occasion to note down when dealing with the Frenchman in action. In spite of his pronounced taste for bodily pleasures, the Frenchman is by no means a slave of matter. Far from it. Here, as everywhere, he remains faithful to the law of his type and therefore resides in his brain. What characterizes his pleasures is precisely the intellectual character which they always evince, the mind being the agent of them, the body a passive instrument. Thus can be explained his tendency to refinement, that curious evolution through which the mind gradually trains the body and makes it more and more exacting, more and more capable of observing differences and of appreciating shades of pleasure. It also explains the forethought, one might almost say the premeditation, the study, the care, and perhaps the limitation of French hedonism. France is never more moderate, never surer of herself, never more balanced than in her pleasures. Orgies and disorderly pleasures are not in the tone of her life. In fact the taste for pleasure in the Frenchman is measured less by the quantity of wine he pours into his glass than by the time which he takes to choose his vintage.

All these premises naturally lead to the conclusion that the life of passion of the French people looks towards beauty. Beauty is attractive to the intellectual in that it is an abstract idea, the concrete manifestations of which are agreeable and pleasure-giving. Ideas and sensations both can feed on it, and even that light which irradiates from beauty is, though irrational, of a kind to appeal to this people eminently fond of clarity.

IX

Passion in the Man of Passion

THE MAN OF PASSION IN A STATE OF PASSION IS IN HIS ELEMENT. Tendency and state are harmonized. The life-stream finds in its passage no strange element, either individual or collective, of a nature to deflect, to divide, or to impoverish it. Its natural impulse flows in a channel ready to receive it.

Since passion is the natural law of the type, we shall see it manifest itself in complete spontaneity as a person who feels at home. But who says spontaneity does not necessarily say anarchy, and the ease of being at home does not necessarily imply an arbitrary conduct. Passion is suffering perhaps from a bad repu-

97

tation. Essentially passive, it has left its own name to the far from tender mercies of moralists and philosophers who, belonging to the active and intellectual types, have seldom understood it and often calumniated it. But passion is neither mad nor arbitrary. Like action and thought, it has its laws and disciplines. Being the supreme aim of the passionate type, it knows how to impose itself on him and how to oblige him to subordinate to it all other tendencies, whether they belong to the realm of action, to that of thought, or to that of passion itself.

The nature, so to say tacit, of these laws has perhaps contributed to their being forgotten. For while the psychology of the man of action develops mostly on the plane of the conscious will and that of the intellectual may easily be observed in the luminous atmosphere of the mind, the psychology of the man of passion is mostly subconscious, since it receives its first impulse and its most subtle reactions from the life-stream which reaches him straight from nature.

Save for this difference, there is a certain symmetry between the life of passion in the man of passion and the life of action in the man of action. We have seen that this last case is regulated by self-control, a psychological mechanism which ensures the discipline of the passions in order to safeguard a maximum efficiency. An analogous phenomenon may be observed in the man of passion, i.e. a mechanism for the protection of passion against all actions which might hinder its full manifestation. In the light of this observation we shall see more clearly the nature of the indifference to action which, under various names, such as laziness, passivity, or contemplation, has been recognized as one of the characteristics of the Spanish type. It allows us to give some precision to this psychological feature which is not, as we now see, a mere paralysis or negative attitude towards *all* action, but only a selective attitude, an instinctive filter which bars access towards the will to all solicitations to action from which passion may have anything to fear.

For, as we have seen, the man of passion is not absolutely inactive. From the fact that he does not feel *a priori* the urge to act, we are not justified in concluding that he avoids action systematically. It would be difficult, after all, to imagine a life rich in passion which would flow in total inactivity. Instinct, which protects passions against certain types of action, does not therefore go beyond determining an inhibition in the man of passion every time the action contemplated might trouble the spontaneous and integral character of passion. This explains the characteristics of the man of passion in action which were dealt with at the appropriate time. But we can now place these characteristics on a parallel with those of the man of action in the state of passion. We have seen that the instinct which protects passion in the man of passion corresponds to the self-control which, in the man of action, protects action against passion. And it follows that the effects of the former on individual and collective action must present a certain symmetry with the effects of self-control on the individual and collective life of passion in the man of action. Let us recall the mechanism of self-control in the people of action. We know that it tends to penetrate into the individual by pressure of the group, so that the passions of the man of action become localized and lose their universality in order to adapt themselves to the environment and to circumstances, to time and space. In a parallel fashion, or rather inversely, the instinct which protects passion in the man of passion subordinates individual action to the requirements of passion—spontaneity, integrality—and therefore exerts strong individual pressure on the environment and on circumstances, so that individual actions tend to become emancipated from the group and to reject the chains of solidarity. To the pressure inwards in the case of the man of action corresponds a pressure outwards in that of the man of passion. To the breaking up of passions in the man of action corresponds the breaking up of actions in the man of passion. And just as in the people of action it is sometimes possible under the surface of the individual soul, instead of personal passions, to detect mere movements of collective passions, so in the people of passion, under the surface of social life, we find, instead of collective actions, what really are vigorous impulses of individual action.

Often in the man of action, as a result of self-control, individual actions are purified of all anti-social passions and attain a higher solidarity. Inversely, the instinct which protects passion in the man of passion tends to raise a dam of inhibition before all actions whose strong collective nature might constitute a threat to the spontaneity and the integrality of the life of individual passion and thereby to defend the purity and the liberty of the human person threatened by the pressure of the group.

That is how we come to the paradoxical conclusion that the man of passion is at the same time more universal and more individual in his passions than the man of action. The paradox, however, is but apparent, since individual experience is the surest, if not the only, road towards universality.

There is a similar parallelism between the man of passion thinking and the intellectual in a state of passion. While the characteristics of passion in the intellectual are determined by the separation of the life-stream from the conscious subject, who resides in his brain, thought, in the man of passion, is, as we have seen, typified by a complete fusion between the subject and the object thought. The man of passion knows only that which he has assimilated, made his own. For him more than for any other human type, love is the first condition of knowledge.

Thus to the inherent coldness of the passion in the intellectual corresponds in strict symmetry the vital warmth which typifies Spanish thought. And this feature, which explains the synthetic character of Spanish thought, is also a guarantee which protects the spontaneity and the integrality of passion against the wearing influence of intellectual forces. We can see now why Spanish thought refuses to be caught into the complicated gear of technical work and to disperse itself in the numerous paths of specialization. Such fractionings of vitality are inherently inimical to the genius of the man of passion, since they tend to hinder in him the integral enjoyment of the life-stream.

We have observed how the intellectual tends to dissociate passions into ideas and sensations, that is to say, to "de-individualize" them; for the idea, which is universal, and the sensation, which is bodily, are the least personal elements in the vital complex which we call *passion*. Inversely, the man of passion tends to personalize his thought. We thus see as essential condition of the type the truly Spanish tendency to place man, better still, the ego, at the centre of all ideas. For at bottom, thought in the Spaniard is controlled by the life-stream or, to use an expression which Unamuno made famous, by the "sense of life."

Thus, whether as regards action or as regards thought, we observe how passion in the man of passion imposes its law of spontaneity and integrality. By mechanisms symmetrical to those which we observed in the man of action and in the intellectual, the man of passion defends the integrality of his life-stream against the pressure from the environment, from ethical rules, and from abstract doctrines. Moreover, the law of passion regulates also the life of passion itself. We know that this law demands respect for the spontaneity and the integrality of the life-stream. Now if one passion were to dominate over the others, the integrality of the human person would certainly suffer, since the other manifestations of its vitality would be impoverished. And that is why the man of passion finds a certain equilibrium precisely by granting free passage to all the waves of the life-stream which he feels within him. We find here, under a new aspect, that reserve, that spontaneity, that serenity of the Spanish type. They come, not from the constraint imposed more or less consciously by the will, as is the case with English self-control, nor from a philosophical coldness due to the intellectual distance of vision, as is the case with the Frenchman, but from the consistency of the life-stream itself, whole and indivisible, which does not allow itself to be divided by ephemeral and local influences. It is to this sense of the oneness of the whole that Spanish wisdom owes its substance. This wisdom is of course a gift of nature. Spanish wisdom is singularly independent of instruction—so necessary to the intellectual—and of education—so necessary to the man of action.

The respect for spontaneity, which is the second requirement of the life of passion, allows us to understand why the Spaniard seeks individual experience just as the Englishman seeks to insert himself within the framework of social cooperation. For just as social co-operation enables action to yield its maximum efficiency, individual experience enables passion to manifest itself with the greatest possible freedom and therefore to acquire the greatest possible wealth of vital elements. And we must therefore recognize in the sheaf of characteristics connected with the Spanish tendency to personal experience a symmetrical feature to that which we have observed in the Englishman under the name of instinct of cooperation. Individualism, humanism, amoralism are but the manifestations which, in the psychology of the men of passion, show the defensive instinct of passion at work opposing all social and intellectual forces the network of which might hinder the spontaneity of passion.

Collective life is therefore dominated in the people of passion by this main tendency of the individual psychology of the type. Man lives his life like a novel. The social framework, its laws, regulations, customs play in his life the role, not so much of organs which transmit the pressure of the group to the individual, as of forces which the individual utilizes, not with a view to collective efficiency, but under the inspiration of a human standard guided by the tendency towards individual experience. At every moment subjective vitality overflows the social cell within which it is supposed to confine itself. With the same spontaneity with which we have seen the men of action of England adapt themselves to the "laws of things," make of themselves things, so to say, in order the better to obey nature, we shall see the man of passion of Spain force things to follow the law of the person, personalize nature and oblige it to follow the life-stream which circulates in the individual blood.

The law of passion which controls and defines the type leads the individual Spaniard to place his personal experience in the situation of eminent finality occupied in England by the group and in France by intellectual order. The same psychological mechanism which, in the people of action, protects the group against all action contrary to solidarity, that is to say, contrary to the best yield of the collective machine, is at work in the people of passion to defend the individual against the invasion of gregarious passions. The most serious business—perhaps the only serious business—for the Spaniard is to "save his soul." This expression—somewhat technical since it belongs to the vocabulary of the Christian religion—is, in Spain, saturated with psychological elements which go farther than its purely orthodox meaning. To "save his soul" means to maintain the spontaneity and the integrality of the individual passion in face of the pressure of social activity, of generally accepted ideas, and, above all, of collective passions.

This is perhaps the key to Spanish egotism. All passions, individual or collective, must incarnate in the individual, must personalize themselves in him, in order to acquire a vital value. Now, it is natural that the process of assimilation of the passions should be the easier when it implies the absorption of a smaller number of elements external to the individual. This observation throws a new light on the tendency to invert the scale of social values which we noticed when dealing with the man of passion in action. We observed then, that, in the case of the man of passion, the self dominates the scale, for it provides the standard by which the places occupied by other social entities are determined, so that those which are most intimately linked with the individual are nearest the top of the scale: his family first, then his friends, and the State last. And even within the State, the town, the province, the region have often a hold on the individual in inverse proportion to their real or objective importance, but in direct proportion to the intimacy of the connexion which binds them to him. We are now in a position to penetrate farther into the psychological substratum of this tendency. We know now that things only become realities for the Spaniard when they live in him in the form of passion. And we understand that it should be the easier to vitalize and personalize what has been called here "social entities" when they contain more elements intimately connected with the subject.

Therefore, and without for a moment overstepping the hypothesis which explains the Spaniard as a man of passion, we may describe the rhythm of his life in passion as an oscillation between the ego and the whole. Egotism and integralism, all the passions and one passion. Intermediate stages between these two poles cannot serve as positions of equilibrium. Hence the weakness of this type in the workaday passions, civic, national, and so on, in a word, in all the small change of motives which allow people to go about in daily life. The man of passion is not interested in the usual and useful passions. We observed, in commenting on the psychology of the passions in the man of action, that the Englishman selects for cultivation those which are useful to the group. We know that, in the man of passion, what matters is not the yield in action for the service of the group, but the yield in passion for individual experience. We should not therefore be surprised if the Spaniard seeks above all the passions that are rich in vital experience, the most all-embracing, the most absolute.

It follows that the life of the man of passion takes place in a landscape, the background of which is universal; not only universal in space, but universal in time, that is to say, eternal. The most integral passion is the sense of life. When compared with this sense, the other passions are ephemeral, partial, and hardly worthy of the attention of a child. There is therefore in the Spaniard a tendency to consider everything *sub specie aeternitatis*. The popular language of Spain abounds in expressions of a striking synthetic nature which sum up in a few words taut with sense, not the idea but the passion for wholeness, which is the true substance of the soul of Spain. The Spaniard seeks universality without meaning to. It is precisely when he is most egotistical that he is most universal. For his egotism consists precisely in letting the life-stream pass in him in all its spontaneity and in its integrality. And the life-stream emanates from a Source which is the same for all.

Conclusion

THE DETAILED ANALYSIS OF THE NINE CASES OBTAINED BY combining the three tendencies—action, thought, and passion—with the three states—action, thought, and passion—confirms the existence of a considerable number of symmetrical and contrasting features which the mere inspection of the table of tendencies and states led us to anticipate. Let us look again at this table:

Prevailing tendencies which determine the active elements

Resultant states	ACTION	THOUGHT	PASSION
ACTION	I. 1. Action in the man of action	I. 2. Action in the man of thought	I. 3. Action in the man of passion
THOUGHT	II. 1. Thought in the man of action	II. 2. Thought in the man of thought	II. 3. Thought in the man of passion
PASSION	III. 1. Passion in the man of action	III. 2. Passion in the man of thought	III. 3. Passion in the man of passion

It is evident that the diagonal line which crosses this table from the left top square (I. 1) to the right bottom square (III. 3) is the axis of symmetry of the whole figure. From this fact two conclusions may be deduced: the first is the similitude of the three cases situated on the axis (squares I. 1, II. 2, III. 3); the second is the symmetry of the cases represented on the squares symmetrically placed on either side of the axis; such a symmetry applies respectively to three groups of two cases, namely I. 2 and II. 1, I. 3 and III. 1, II. 3 and III. 2.

1. *Similitude of the three cases placed on the axis*

These three cases present a common feature; in each of them the type is in its own element. They may be defined as follows:

I. 1. Action in the man of action.
II. 2. Thought in the man of thought.
III. 3. Passion in the man of passion.

In all of them the state and the tendency coincide. In all of them, therefore, we may observe how the type places itself in the state corresponding to its tendency with complete spontaneity.[1]

The Englishman goes to action, the Frenchman to thought, the Spaniard to passion, spontaneously. They are respectively states of satisfaction, states without conflict. The main tendency of the type acts without rival, without obstacles. By means of automatic psychological mechanisms, the main tendency secures the triumph of its own ends. We have noted the symmetry of these mechanisms in the appropriate place:

In the case I. 1 the man of action of England adapts himself to the "laws of things," becomes a thing himself in order the better to obey these laws, which are the laws of co-operation; self-control and self-consciousness defend the group against all individual actions antagonistic to solidarity.

In the case II. 2 the man of thought of France submits automatically to method (individual intellectual order) and to the republic of letters (collective intellectual order).

In the case III. 3 the man of passion of Spain forces things to follow the law of the person in order to bind them to flow in his own vital current, while he defends himself against the intrusion of gregarious passions by asserting his own personality against the group.

In the three cases we find the type at the service of its own tendency; they are, therefore, cases of absolute disinterestedness. All the other cases, namely, all those which are placed outside the axis, or, what comes to the same, all the cases in which the type is not on its own axis, reveal the existence of a natural force or tendency to come back towards the axis. Action for the Englishman, thought for the Frenchman, passion for the Spaniard are respectively the only forms of life which need no justification. Thus it may be explained why the

---

1. A distinction should be made between, on the one hand, the spontaneity wherewith the type lets himself go to its corresponding tendency, and, on the other hand, the way (spontaneous or otherwise) in which he exerts this tendency. The Englishman goes spontaneously *to* action, but is not spontaneous *in* action. Inversely, the Spaniard is spontaneous *in* action, but does not go *to* action spontaneously.

English should manifest themselves spontaneously in pure action (sports); the French in pure thought (all French culture, or, as might be said, intellectual sports); the Spaniard in pure passion (religion, love, Spanish life in general).

That the three types should be equally disinterested may seem paradoxical on account of the importance often granted to utilitarianism in English psychology. Yet, when properly understood, utilitarianism amounts to a tendency to exact fruits of action from thought and from passion, so that, once properly defined, utilitarianism does but confirm our view, since these fruits of action which it exacts are exacted in all disinterestedness.

The supreme law of each type, that is to say the satisfaction of its main tendency, is the basis of its subconscious ethics. Therefore, the English standard in life is ethical; the French standard is logical; the Spanish standard is personal. It is necessary to grasp this point in order to understand that hypocrisy, generally considered a typical British feature, is in reality a general feature. If hypocrisy is an artifice which allows us to bridge over the distance between standards and facts, the standards of the Englishman being ethical, his hypocrisy will be ethical; the standards of the Frenchman being intellectual, his hypocrisy will be intellectual; the standards of the Spaniard being vital and experimental, his hypocrisy will be that of passion. When weak, the Englishman feigns to behave; when unintelligent, the Frenchman feigns to understand; when cold, the Spaniard feigns to feel. The symmetry, however, is not complete, for standards, being collective, are weaker in France than in England and in Spain than in France. Thus Spanish, French, and English hypocrisies differ both in quality and in quantity.

2. Symmetry of the three groups of lateral cases

We know that in all these cases the type is outside its element, and therefore feels a force or tendency to come back to it. Such forces tending towards the axis are symmetrical and act in opposite directions for each of the two cases of each group. Thus the tendency towards the axis in the case I. 2 corresponds to the effort of the man of thought to avoid action in order to indulge in thought, while the tendency in the case II. 1 is the effort of the man of action to avoid thought in order to indulge in action.

Hence, a certain coercion upon spontaneity. For spontaneity is an impossible thing outside the axial cases.[2] No spontaneity is possible when the type, to satisfy his main tendency, is struggling against the state in which he is placed. These struggles are also symmetrical within each group, as can be seen by analysing each of them.

Finally, we shall observe when studying these lateral cases that the disinterestedness which we noted as a feature of the axial cases disappears and its place is taken by what might be described as a generalized utilitarianism. For in these cases the law of the type demands above all the satisfaction of the tendency, so that even when temporarily separated from his main tendency, being placed in a state outside it, the type seeks in this state a result in terms of his natural tendency. This observation allows us to generalize English utilitarianism, and to discover the corresponding features which might be described as French utilitarianism and Spanish utilitarianism. For, just as the Englishman seeks in thought and passion a "practical" result, that is, a result in terms of action; so the Frenchman seeks in action and in passion a result in intellectual experience, that is, in knowledge; and the Spaniard seeks in action and in thought a result in terms of passion, that is, in experience of life. Therefore, to English utilitarianism (utilitarianism of action) correspond French utilitarianism (utilitarianism of thought) and Spanish utilitarianism (utilitarianism of passion).

In each of these three groups will be discovered an obvious symmetry, due to the permutation of the tendency and of the state in each of the two cases which compose it. Thus in the

2. See, however, note on p. 108.

first group, composed of cases I. 2 and II. 1, the tendency of the first case (thought) becomes the state of the second; while the tendency of the second (action) is the state of the first. A similar observation applies, *mutatis mutandis*, to the two remaining groups of (I. 3, III. 1 and II. 3, III. 2). Let us now examine each of the three groups successively.

A. GROUP I. 2—II. 1

The first of these two cases is that of the man of thought in a state of action; the second that of a man of action in a state of thought.

The symmetry is evident, and manifests itself in many ways. Thus the way in which the intellectual abstracts and schematizes reality, in order to protect the integrality of his thought against the vagaries of action, is symmetrical with the way in which the man of action limits and curtails his thought through inhibition in order to defend the liberty of his action against the corroding influence of thought. We have already observed a similar symmetry between the diagrams which represent the two cases. The diagram of the intellectual in action is a series of straight lines tangent to the sinuous curve of reality, forming a broken line, the "elbows" of which represent the crises during which the intellectual rectifies his conduct in order to readjust it to reality. Similarly, the diagram of thought in the man of action is also a broken line, formed by a series of empirical opinions tangent to the most immediate reality, which the man of action rectifies when necessary by means of sudden changes of opinion. The very opposition which seems to exist between the tendency to prevision in the Frenchman in action, and the dislike of all intellectual prevision which is one of the typical characteristics of English thought, is but another form of this symmetry: *the Frenchman foresees because he mistrusts life; the Englishman refuses to foresee because he mistrusts thought.* Another case in point is that of tolerance. While the Frenchman is tolerant in morals and intolerant in politics, the Englishman is tolerant in politics and intolerant in morals.

Why? Because the essential, the immovable, the evident for the Frenchman is the idea, for the Englishman the act. Without agreement in ideas no intellectual community is possible; without agreement in customs there is no possible social community or co-operation. There is, finally, between these two cases a curious and subtle symmetry in what concerns collective life. On the one hand, English *thought*, although lacking in that internal and spontaneous order which distinguishes French thought, reaches a certain cohesion, thanks to the external pressure which it receives from the social environment in which it lives; on the other hand, French collective *action*, though lacking in that sense of spontaneous co-operation which is a typical feature of English collective life, reaches a certain cohesion, thanks to the intellectual order which, as a reasonable people, France creates and imposes upon herself.

B. GROUP I. 3–III. I

The first of these cases is that of the man of passion in action; the second that of the man of action in passion.

The parallel between these two cases reveals a certain number of interesting symmetrical features.

The precautions of the man of action to protect the purity of his acts against the influence of individual passion correspond to the precautions of the man of passion to protect the liberty of his passion against the pressure of social actions. The first explains the English lack of spontaneity in individual life; the second the Spanish lack of all instinctive and spontaneous organization in collective life. This symmetry deepens as we delve into each of the two characters. English calm, the crust which covers strong passions repressed by self-control, is a feature symmetrical with Spanish indifference, under which the energies of action accumulate. Just as the Englishman selects his passions, and only authorizes the manifestation of those which are useful to the group, the Spaniard selects his actions and only engages in those which enrich the experience of the individual. And just as, under the pressure of the group, the passions of the Englishman lose their universality to take on the impress and colour of the group, so, under the pressure of the person, the actions of the Spaniard lose their objectivity to take on the direction and tendency of the individual.

C. GROUP II. 3–III. 2

The first of these groups is that of the man of passion in thought; the second that of the intellectual in a state of passion.

The symmetry of these two cases is due to the fact that, while the Spaniard thinks by means of an intimate union of his person with the object thought, the Frenchman tends instinctively to place himself at a distance from the life-stream, the passage of which in his person constitutes passion. Hence a certain number of symmetrical features which may be observed respectively in Spanish thought and in French passion. We have seen that Spanish thought appears on the surface of the intellect still warm with the vital warmth of the intimate recesses of the soul in which it is formed, while French passion reaches the surface of life already cooled by the cold light of reason. Similarly, the integrality of Spanish thought, which appears all of a sudden and completely vitalized by passion, corresponds in strict symmetry to the dissociation of the elements of French passion which thought devitalizes. Spanish thought springs up spontaneously; French passion manifests itself in full consciousness and with method and measure; the Frenchman, moreover, revises and perfects his passion with a hedonistic artistry in contrast with the permanent "primitivism" of the Spanish mind, which, leaving aside all intellectual tradition, begins its work every time on the bottom rock of reality. The volcanic and ungovernable character of Spanish thought, so rebellious to all rules, will contrast with the moderation and the sense of measure which the Frenchman brings to his passion; and the calm with which the Frenchman contemplates his passions, sporting themselves under his eye, will be the symmetrical image of the fire with which the Spaniard maintains his opinions; finally, even that twist which Spanish passion gives to Spanish thought will appear to us as a feature symmetrical with those fantasies of passion which the Frenchman imagines he feels under the stimulus of an ever-ingenious and fertile brain.

Thus the table of the nine cases which has served us as the framework for the study of our three peoples reveals a whole system of symmetries and similitudes. Too frequently this rich field of observation has been darkened by erroneous opinions based on a mistaken idea of what a psychological parallel should be.

It is evident that a parallel between French thought and English thought, or between English action and Spanish action, can lead to nothing but precarious views and incomplete conclusions. The true symmetry must be found in homologous psychological situations such as those described above. Once this condition is borne in mind, the material observed appears spontaneously under a design of a beautiful natural symmetry. It is possible to observe then that features which seemed strange and peculiar in one people were but special cases of more general features manifest in all three. And in this way the three characters in question will appear, not as radically different, but rather as transpositions of the same melody in three different keys: the key of action; the key of thought; the key of passion.

PART TWO

Introduction

THE MAIN LINES OF THIS PARALLEL BETWEEN THE ENGLISH, French, and Spanish characters once established, it is possible to verify the conclusions thus reached *a priori* by direct observation of the individual and collective life of our three peoples. But before venturing on this ground it may be useful to forestall a certain number of objections and to clarify our own conclusions.

The first objection which might be made to the hypothesis here put forward, i.e. the assimilation of the Englishman to the man of action, the Frenchman to the man of thought, and the

Spaniard to the man of passion, is that it appears to be some-what too simple and systematic, and to exhaust the main psy-chological types of mankind with the first three peoples to which it is applied. It may therefore be necessary to say that our hypothesis does not claim to represent this group of three characters in an absolute and exact manner. It should be con-sidered as no more than what mathematicians might describe as "a first approximation." All human types contain simul-taneously the man of action, the man of thought, and the man of passion, or, if so preferred, all men are at the same time men of action, thought, and passion. The unity of the human race rests on this obvious fact. But it is no less obvious that in cer-tain men one or other of these tendencies predominates, and, though at this point we go beyond the obvious and venture into the hypothetical, we observe that the predominant ten-dency in the Englishman is action, in the Frenchman thought, and in the Spaniard passion.

But we may go one step farther. It is probable that, amongst all the national types in which the tendency to action pre-dominates, the Englishman is the one in which it predominates most. A similar observation, *mutatis mutandis*, might be applied to the Frenchman and to the Spaniard, so that our hypothesis might be formulated as follows: the Englishman, the French-man, and the Spaniard are respectively the national characters which come nearest to the pure type of man of action, man of thought, and man of passion.

It must, of course, be admitted that in every one of these characters the other two types are also at work, though less prominently, and moreover in different proportions. This fact, it will be seen, multiplies their psychological complexity. The secondary types interfere with the main type, producing a number of eddies and counter-currents which it is nearly im-possible to study in detail. Nevertheless, if a sufficient supe-riority of the main or predominant type is accepted, such eddies and counter-currents may be considered as "perturba-tions of the second order," which should not act as obstacles against reaching complete conclusions, though they may contribute to give such conclusions a somewhat tentative character.

A similar remark applies to the perturbations due to the mutual influence of some national characters on others. The progress in material and intellectual means of communication increases daily the areas of contact between peoples, and therefore the areas of their mutual influence. Due regard must therefore be given to the fact that the three characters here studied have to bear common influences, such as that of American mechanicism, as well as the influence of each on the other. These perturbations may lead in some cases to paradoxical situations which will have to be explained in their time. In all such cases national and extra-national factors may be discriminated by the criterion of spontaneity, national tendencies being innate, extra-national tendencies being acquired. In a great number of them it will be possible to observe an adaptation of the foreign element, which will have to nationalize itself more or less deeply before taking root. On the other hand, these mutual influences within our group are of themselves an excellent confirmation of our thesis. Thus, for instance, English influence on France, as on Spain, gives a distinctive quality to the recent orientation of these two countries towards action in all its forms: political (self-government), utilitarian (business), disinterested (sports). French influence over England, as over Spain, is mainly to be observed in the realm of ideas (literature, style), of refinement (fashions), and of moral tolerance. Finally, Spanish influence over England and France is particularly at work in the areas of life pertaining to the passions, and we may notice that it is not without a certain passivity on the part of the influencing country (Spanish themes in art, prestige of Spanish ways of living, and the picturesque).

Once these qualifications are borne in mind, our hypothesis remains to be confirmed by comparing the conclusions to which it leads with the direct observation of reality. At first sight the best method for such a comparison would appear to be a parallel study of the different aspects of life in each of the three peoples so as to verify whether the Englishman really excels in those aspects of life in which action prevails, the

Frenchman in those in which thought prevails, and the Spaniard in those in which passion prevails. But such a method would be based on an obvious error. We are about to observe manifestations of human character, and shall therefore be in the presence of vital movements which will not be acts, ideas, or states of passion pure and simple, but complex systems in which the soul, the intellect, and the will always co-operate, though in different proportions.

Let us attempt to analyse one of these psychological units, which are, so to speak, the raw-material of our observations. It may be in its origin a "state of soul" unconscious at first, and then felt with a growing intensity, which will eventually call the attention of the intellect; at this point the state of soul begins to enrich itself with thought, and little by little it takes consciousness of itself and, therefore, is cast into form; finally, passion, strengthened by thought, gives a definite direction to the conscious state which thus tends to appear on the surface of external reality. The will then takes possession of the tendency and converts it into a fact.

There is no doubt that other processes might be imagined. The initial moment might equally well be a thinking or an active attitude; moreover, the evolution may take, and it is even safe to say that it generally does take, more complicated forms, less linear than the one outlined above. But the fact remains that, in each psychological unit, three phases or aspects may be discriminated: conception in the soul; formation in the intellect; execution in the will. It would be childish to take such a classification literally and to specialize these three faculties in an absolute way. In each of the three aspects of our psychological activity the three faculties are intimately blended. Life is one, and all that happens partakes of its indivisibility. The analysis here sketched has no other object than to bring a certain precision, in so far as this is possible, to the structure of the phenomenon which we are to study. This allows us to anticipate that the facts of life will not present so perfect a symmetry as that which might be expected if our main hypothesis were applied with an uncompromising rigidity. Life does not present facts which it is possible to ascribe exclusively to action or to thought or to passion.

Moreover, on the one hand, the facts that we are to observe appear in the form of a synthesis of the three elements, action, thought, and passion; while the beings which are the object of our observation present themselves in their turn as composed, though in *typically* different proportions, of the three corresponding tendencies of character towards action, towards thought, and towards passion. If, therefore, our hypothesis is correct our observation will suggest two laws:

(*a*) There will be in each of the three peoples a certain proclivity to specialize in those manifestations of individual or collective life in which the predominating tendency is in harmony with the type. However complicated and indivisible, these manifestations will evince the predominance of one or other of the three psychological elements: politics, social life, historical development, we shall find woven mostly with materials of action; culture, ideas, criticism will be principally connected with the tendency to thought; in literature and the arts we shall see a transition between thought and passion; while passion itself will almost entirely govern love, patriotism, and religion.

(*b*) Within each fact observed there will be a kind of selection of the element in harmony with the predominant tendency of the type, or, in other words, each type will excel in the particular aspect within the psychological fact (conception, formation, or execution) which is most deeply in harmony with its main tendency. It is therefore to be expected that the Spaniard will excel in conception, the Frenchman in formation, and the Englishman in execution.

I

The Structure of the Community

A. THE NATION

THE SOCIAL STRUCTURES OF ENGLAND, FRANCE, AND SPAIN CLOSELY
correspond to the general lines of the parallel here sketched
between their three national characters. Generally speaking, the
social structure is aristocratic-organic in England, bourgeois-
mechanical in France, and popular-anarchical [1] in Spain.

1. This word should be understood in its theoretical sense. It has
nothing to do with anarchism. It merely means a tendency to evade and
to do without collective fetters.

I

The English structure is the direct outcome of the genius of the race for spontaneous organization. No law, no force imposes on the people the carefully poised hierarchy on which all social life rests. The hierarchy is so naturally accepted that the Englishman is hardly aware of its existence, and to this day believes himself to be living in the land of equality. Now, equality is a category completely outside the purview of English psychology. It is a category of the thinking mind, the consequence of a measure. It is therefore, as we shall see, a characteristic of French life. But English life ignores it altogether. It is true that all Englishmen are supposed to be equal before the law,[2] but then, the law in England is always administered in equity by judges whose discretionary powers are considerable, and moreover the law in a country like England is but a small part of the nation's life. The true category of English life is not equality but liberty. For liberty is the absence of political constraint, and we know that political constraint is unnecessary in a people gifted with a genius for spontaneous organization which puts its citizens automatically at the disposal of the community.

In this atmosphere of liberty the English nation organizes itself and naturally adopts a hierarchical structure. Empirical, this structure must of course rest on continuity and tradition. We thus find by direct observation the characteristics which we were led to attribute to the English people when analysing the case of a people of action in action. English society is not homogeneous, but naturally divided into classes and sub-classes, each of which plays a distinct part in the work of the whole.

The norm, the model of this society, is the aristocrat. This appreciation of the aristocrat may be foolish or enlightened, deep or superficial, frank or shamefaced, conscious or subcon-

2. With some exceptions. Peers cannot vote. Non-peers cannot enter the House of Lords. Catholics have (or had until quite recent times) certain limitations to their rights. Younger brothers can inherit but a small part of the paternal estate. And so on.

scious, but it is wellnigh universal in England. For the aristocrat incarnates the perfect man of action and the perfect leader.
He is a representative individual, for he has power, but he is
also a representative community type, for he has tradition and
he embodies leadership. He thus combines in his personality
the sense of action and the group sense, which are the two
dominant forces in the English character.

This granted, the rest follows. From the pure type, the 100
per cent aristocrat, your dukes whose names and mansions all
Englishmen know and love to hear about, more and more diluted types of English aristocracy occupy lower and lower
reaches of English life and live according to standards which
resemble more and more faintly the standards of the exalted
summits. Thus the social structure of England may be assimilated to a pyramid solidly built on a wide basis of willing and
debonair lower classes, which support a whole system of upper
classes gradually tapering as they approach the apex. The apex
is the King.

No pressure, no coercion is needed to maintain the balance
of this structure standing so securely on its wide basis. A
moderate amount of observation of English life will suffice to
yield abundant examples of the inner sense of equilibrium
which immediately reacts in the social body on the slightest
provocation from a disturbing factor. Thus the British press,
the freest press in the world, is also the safest for a statesman-
like government; for, though it cannot of course be relied upon
when the purely political, i.e. party, interests of the government
are concerned, it is sure to behave with instinctive wisdom
when the interests at stake are those of the nation as a whole or
even those of its social structure. A typical case in point is the
attitude of the British press towards the royal family. A word
of criticism in this connexion is unprintable. For the King is
the apex of the pyramid.

This case is, after all, but another illustration of that gift for
spontaneous organization which we have considered as the
typical feature of the English people in action. But then this
gift determines practically every manifestation of English col-

lective life. In the political sphere it accounts, as we shall see hereafter, for the fact known as self-government, a spontaneous growth of political institutions rather than a local freedom granted from or by a central authority. Similarly, in every nook and corner of English collective life, cases will be found of spontaneous organization which amount to manifestations of self-government in spheres other than the political one. Charity is an obvious example. The care of the sick and infirm, which, in other countries, is organized by the State, is left in England to the initiative and responsibility of the nation at large, and the nation's answer to this call fully justifies the method chosen. An ever-growing number of private institutions take upon themselves the numerous tasks which a modern nation has to fulfil: education, the protection of children, of animals, of the landscape, of the theatre, Shakespeare's memory, the language, Washington's manor, and what not. The co-operative urge acts as a coalescing element with wonderful facility, thus producing associations based on the most unexpected and at first sight unpromising motives—a common admiration for Browning, for instance. All these institutions live and thrive. All find, not merely the necessary funds—which after all is not so surprising in a rich nation—but the necessary vital warmth, the necessary number of devoted enthusiasts ready to give up to their obscure tasks a generous slice of their life. Ultimately, this mystery has to be solved in that individual *sanctum sanctorum* in which the claims of the self and those of the community are weighed and balanced. The observation of English life amply shows that, in the immense majority of such cases of weighing and balancing, the claims of the community win.

2

The social structure of France is more rigidly framed than its English counterpart. In it, custom is an element of lesser importance and law, or more exactly, *droit*, a more potent force. The framework of society has been and is constantly thought out, deduced from general principles. These general principles themselves are the object of continuous study and discussion.

Now and then a deep change alters their very essence and the crystal of social structure passes from one rigid shape to another shape no less rigid.

The category of French social life is equality. In the French mind, equality is a postulate of social science which asserts the equilibrium of rights between any two citizens. This word *citizen* represents an abstraction. It is somewhat in the nature of a diagram of man, the *homo politicus*, that which in each man can be equalized to the similar part in any other man. Equality is thus a geometrical plane made of human points. It is beautifully level.

As a contrast to the living pyramid which liberty erects in England, there rises upon this plane of equal citizens a purely official pyramid—the hierarchy of the State. This hierarchy does not foster in France any of the feelings which genuinely arise in a true British breast out of the subtle and complicated differences of status which the English aristocratic structure implies. Napoleon's efforts to revive a French aristocracy by means of the Légion d'Honneur have ended in a pure mechanism for the distribution of seniority badges to officials and others.

Such an evolution was to be anticipated. A rationalistic people, the French tend to reduce facts to ideas and ideas to numbers. Equality is but the political and social manifestation of this tendency. The Code Napoléon is its legal monument. The inheritance laws of the French nation have pulverized the country into an aggregate of small owners. The typically French tendencies to foresight, limitation, moderation, thrift, and the like have transformed these small owners into *petits rentiers*. The *petit rentier* is the norm and model of French social life. His *aurea mediocritas* is the goal of most Frenchmen. His well-fed, secure, unambitious, jolly, bon-vivant, expert-in-wine sort of type is the genuine representative of the nation as a whole.

The French, though perhaps less varied in type, less individualized than the English, are, notwithstanding, more individualistic in their requirements. Their enjoyment must be their own. Less intimately attached to the community than the English, they do not possess that wonderful capacity for vicarious enjoyment which distinguishes the true Englishman. When the Duke of Devonshire's daughter is married, all true Englishmen feel happy. When the Duke of Richmond rides with his hounds, all true Englishmen blow their horn. But the Frenchman holds to his own poet: *Mon verre n'est pas grand, mais je bois dans mon verre,*[3] and, unless he drinks himself, he does not smack his lips.

A more exacting individual, less given to delegate his enjoyment or his power, the Frenchman lives nevertheless in a relatively ordered community, thanks to the existence of a well planned-out system of State action. The multifarious activities which are met in England by the free and spontaneous growth of private initiative, must in France rely on the help and leadership of the State. The State takes upon itself many extra-political duties with significant spontaneity on its part and a no less significant acquiescence on the part of the nation. Thus, not only does it take charge of the hospitals and all that in France goes under the general name of *Bienfaisance*, but it also assumes the official leadership of the scientific and artistic life of the country. The universities, free bodies in England, are in France part of the State bureaucracy. The State owns and administers the Galleries and governs more or less rigidly the four most important theatres in Paris—one of which, the Comédie Française, has for its statute a decree signed by Napoleon in Moscow. The quarrels between actors and managers, the staging of certain plays give rise to heated parliamentary debates. A ballet-dancer's *faux pas* may bring about the fall of the Cabinet.

We see, therefore, how the French, lacking in spontaneous organization, reach nevertheless a considerable degree of order through the mechanization of their collective life. The movements of their collective life are not so natural and free as is the case in England, for they cannot be left to the spontaneous

3. My glass is not large, but it is my own.

play of the social instinct, but must be pre-arranged, laid down beforehand by some foreseeing mind well trained to imagine moves on the chess-board of possibilities. The relations between people are therefore apt to be more rigidly defined than in England—especially in the case of the relations between the citizens and the particular piece of the State machinery with which they have to deal. Hence the fertile and entertaining branch of French literature devoted to the vagaries of the Rond-de-Cuir. But, though paid for at this price, the order which prevails in the collective life of the French nation is the more impressive from the fact that it rests on an assumption of equality intellectually established and recognized by all—an assumption which would have sufficed to ruin the collective life of any people less endowed with the constructive gift of reason.

3

Neither the aristocratic-organic nor the bourgeois-mechanical structure of the community is possible in Spain. This much can be said *a priori*, since the one implies a spontaneous tendency to group-life and the other a spontaneous tendency to intellectual order. Observation confirms that Spain is lacking in all hierarchical sense—whether in the natural and instinctive form which this sense takes in England, or in the outward and political form which it assumes in France.

We shall find in Spain a strong *sense* which, for lack of a better word, we describe as *sense of equality*. But the *sense* of equality which permeates all collective life in Spain is as different from the *idea* of equality on which French order rests as is this intellectual order of France from the anarchy which constitutes the normal latent tendency of the Spanish nation.

French equality, being an idea, is aired and asserted whenever necessary—sometimes even unnecessarily, if there happens to be in the air the suspicion of a challenge. Spanish equality, being a living sense, is unconsciously assumed and regulates all human relations in the country without the parties concerned being aware of the fact.

Such is the main condition of the environment in which the social structure of Spain is built. It is easy to see that such a condition cannot foster the development of a hierarchy after the English type which implies the spontaneous recognition and acceptation of inequalities. Nor does it afford a better basis for the erection of a State hierarchy after the French pattern, since the sense of equality is subconscious and does not level the people down to a flat plane of citizens. All the efforts of political propagandists to make the Spaniard feel like a citizen have failed. He feels like a man, "nothing less than a whole man" is the striking expression of Miguel de Unamuno. Nothing less than a whole man in every conceivable situation.

It follows that the social structure of Spain is bound to be lax, like that of a body the several members of which are stronger than the force of cohesion which keeps them together. This—incidentally—explains the paradox, so often observed, that the value of Spain as a whole should be less than the sum-total of the values of individual Spaniards might lead the world to expect, as well as that Spaniards should often be powerful forces in foreign countries, where they benefit by the atmosphere of solidarity which enables their ability to reap its due success. No one who knows Spain can have failed to be struck by the impressive amount of individual effort lost in activities at cross purposes or, even worse, *in vacuo*. A typical case in point is that of the intellectual "minority." Spain seems unable to provide an adequate framework for its intellectuals. Most of them fail to find within the country the necessary mass which will absorb their effort by offering them the resistance indispensable to the balance of their work. The result is that they tend to lose their balance and to develop along lines of extremely individualized thought less and less useful to the community and to themselves.

We know that the force of a superior passion can group Spaniards together. Spanish collective life counts thus on two forces which give it a certain amount of external, superimposed cohesion, such as the shell gives the tortoise: one is the Army, the other, the Church. The influence of these two forces on

Spanish collective life has often been attributed to plausible though superficial reasons, such as "the ignorance of the masses" and what not. Measured by that most misleading of standards, the number of illiterate people, the Spanish nation may be inferior to most Western countries. But if a more subtle criterion is applied—one, for instance, which would rightly exclude from amongst the educated the readers of some Western newspapers of enormous circulation—the people of Spain can hardly be deemed inferior to those of other countries much better organized politically. The influence of the Army and of the Church in Spain may be better explained in the light of the general views put forward in this essay: these institutions are the two best organized communities in a country in which most collective life is lax, and therefore weak—and, moreover, they owe their better organization to the fact that they possess a collective life of their own based on passions which appeal strongly to the Spanish soul: honour, the fundamental passion in the Army; and religion, the fundamental passion in the Church. While the rest of the nation lacks cohesion, the Army and the Church hold together. Hence their power.

But their sway over the country is a fact, and no more than a fact. The people does not acquiesce in it, does not recognize it, and, taken as a whole, neither approves nor disapproves it. The people takes things as they come, lives and lets live, but will have no hierarchy. In fact, the people does not know, or rather does not feel what a hierarchy is. As in England the aristocrat, and in France the bourgeois, in Spain the people is the norm of the nation. Just as every Englishman consciously or unconsciously fashions himself on the aristocratic model, and every Frenchman, of whatever station, is, in his heart of hearts, a *petit* bourgeois, the Spaniard, no matter his class, is a man of the people. A typical proof of this fact is to be found in the subconscious tendencies which govern the style of dress in each of the three nations: the English style of dress is dictated by its leisured aristocracy; the French is governed by a preoccupation for "correctness" which is deeply bourgeois. Dress in Spain is under the leadership of the people, and, while the

English mill-girl strives to follow, though at a considerable distance, the fashions laid down by duchesses, the Spanish duchess, when she wants to look smart, dresses like a mill-girl on Easter Sunday.

B. THE FAMILY

Left at this point, the parallel between the social structures of England, France, and Spain would give an incomplete picture of our three peoples. The individual and the community are not the only types of human unit which are to be considered in this connexion. The comparison of the family in the three countries concerned is also indispensable.

I

As was to be expected, we find the English family much weakened by the all-powerful influence of the national group. The dominant feature in this respect is the public school, for the public school substitutes itself for the family as the character-moulding agency. Now, the public school is a powerful element of standardization. In it the English boy is carefully moulded to type. The little Toms, Dicks, and Harrys of England are transformed into the one and only type: the British gentleman. It is a well-known fact that the battle of Waterloo was won on the playing fields of Eton, but all the Waterloos, military and civil, which have gone to the growth of the British Empire were also won on the same playing fields. The public school boy is undoubtedly one of the greatest assets of the British nation. But the measure of his success as a type is precisely the measure of the victory of the national group over the family group. What the public school begins, the university completes. Public school and university standardize the men, leaving but few characteristics, but few outstanding features to mark the family line. Every family is as every other family. They have, no doubt, the virtues which characterize all English human units—stability, continuity, co-operation. They are all solidly built on a hardworking *paterfamilias*, whose life is safely insured and whose income is devoted to the welfare of the little community for which he feels himself responsible. But the foreign observer, used to a somewhat warmer, more spontaneous, and less official, if less well organized, family life, is apt to feel that the English family owes more to the English nation than the English nation to the English family. Whatever is strong and stable in this family is, one feels, of exactly the same nature as what is strong and stable in the English Civil Service or in English banking. The father, in one word, is *the governor*. As for the family in its wider sense, it is in England little more than a loosely built association of friends, or, better still, of acquaintances, divided, rather than united, by their common interests.

2

The dominant feature in the French family is perhaps the *mariage de raison*. There is no need to go to extremes and to describe French family life through the romantic, naturalistic exaggerations of M. Brieux. Yet M. Brieux's view, though exaggerated, is not altogether unreal. A marriage in France is a carefully discussed business, in which the feelings of the future partners being taken for granted, the positive side of the contemplated concern is attentively examined in consultation with the family solicitor. The *situation* is the main preoccupation of both sides. The typical French tendencies connected with foresight, planning, scheming, marshalling one's forces contribute to enlarge the idea of the family so as to include in it all collaterals, each in its place in the family army. This tendency works alongside of the tendency towards intellectual order—*droit, règlement*—and thus it is that the French family acquires an almost official dignity and rigidity. Hence that proclivity towards official stiffness to be noticed in French family gatherings, particularly in funerals. A French funeral is probably the most rigidly regulated ceremony of the present time.

There is no doubt that, within the framework of the State, the framework of the family is one of the strongest elements, if not the strongest, in the social structure of France. The family, in France, may be considered as the field in which social and individual tendencies come to terms and compensate each other. It does not, as in England, yield before the pressure of the national group. Yet, through it, the individual perceives the pressure of the group and, thanks to it, a sufficient standard of collective behaviour is maintained in the nation.

This useful function is made easier by the fact that the family has in France a character of its own. Though usually founded on calculating reason (perhaps because it is so), it is remarkably stable. Reason, moreover, in a reasonable people, seems a particularly favourable ground for the fostering of feelings which, though free from passion and sentiment, are singularly tough and resilient. The atmosphere of a French home is cordial in its order and calm. The high level of intellectual culture which prevails in it contributes to give a great variety of characteristic features to each home. Family traditions are rich and complex to a degree sufficient to stamp the individual with a family seal, yet not to hinder the development of his original personality.

3

While the family is, in England, but one of the many forms which the spirit of co-operation takes in the people of action, and, in France, a kind of State writ small, in Spain the family is but the first collective sphere which the individual meets in his expansion as he travels outwards from his egocentric self. It is therefore the strongest of the group units in Spanish life. This conclusion, to which we were led when analysing the man of passion in action, is confirmed by direct observation. In Spain a bad citizen, a mediocre Civil Servant, even a doubtful friend may often be, in fact generally is, an excellent husband and father. While in England the nation is stronger than the family, and in France the family is the meeting ground or line of equilibrium between collective and individual tendencies, in Spain the family is stronger than the wider forms of the community.

We know that this is due to the fact that the family falls

more directly within the vital experience of the individualistic Spaniard. The Spanish family is therefore rich in emotion and life. And its strength does not lie in the formal traditions and rigid organization which are so characteristic of the French family. Far from it. Family life is in Spain singularly free from formalistic laws, as may be observed often in the matter of style and language. In fact the strength of the Spanish family life lies in its strong feeling of *consanguinidad*, "community of blood," a vital feeling which brings home to each member of the family the natural unity of the whole.

Hence its solidarity. But we are not, of course, to expect in the Spanish family a kind of solidarity like that which is fostered in all English group forms of life by the English genius for spontaneous organization. The solidarity of the Spanish family is not directed towards action. It is a solidarity of feeling, perhaps even only of being, and if it manifests itself in action, it does so independently of the merits of the action considered and, in particular, independently of the claims of the community at large.

By virtue of this solidarity, the family in Spain is often a self-sustained unit, or nearly so. In other countries, and notably in England, the family sheds its surplus individuals right and left—the community, moreover, absorbs the loose individuals in national activities, but this is by the way. In Spain the family keeps them by it and utilizes them to the advantage of the whole. Thus to the spinster, a *social* type in England, there corresponds in Spain the maiden aunt, a *family* type, without whose devotion and help large families would be impossible.

Though often the rival of the claims of the community, the family is, in Spain, one of the strongest assets of collective life. No other tendencies could curb the extreme individualistic tendencies of the Spaniard and force him to rise above his egoistic outlook. Indeed, without the family, the Spaniard would drop from egotism to egoism.

II

Leadership

NOTHING COULD BE MORE TYPICAL OF THE SUBJECT UNDER discussion, or better confirm the main line of thought which underlies these pages, than the fact that the idea expressed in English as *leaders* should be expressed in French as *les élites*, and in Spanish as *las minorías*. *Leaders* suggests a people led, willingly, spontaneously led. *Les élites* suggests a mere selection of the best, a setting aside of quality. *Las minorías* is but the bare statistical recognition of the fact that a certain type of man, endowed with a certain number of powers, is in a minority. Here again, language faithfully represents facts.

I

The people of action is always on the move—on the move as a people, knowing that it has a collective existence and that it goes forward. It wants, therefore, to be led. The people of action trains its leaders for this high task. It develops in them the qualities which are indispensable in the man of action: resolution, self-confidence, self-discipline, authority, knowledge of the laws of things, knowledge of men. It carefully avoids weakening their will power by developing in them any taste for intellectual sport, which not only deflects our vitality from the channels of action but, by making us wonder, makes us hesitate. The would-be leader must beware of the light of reason as of the fire of passion. He must concentrate on sense and will.

This exacting education is carried out in two kinds of establishments: the public schools and the universities. It would be absurd to deny that there are considerable differences between the several types of public school and of university which cater for the education of English youth. It is a far cry from Eton and Harrow to the Manchester Grammar School. Similarly, between the University of Oxford and that of Glasgow the differences in spirit and atmosphere are so deep as to make all generalization impossible. Yet we know by now that the social structure of England is solidly built on the principle of classes, each of which endeavours consciously or unconsciously to follow the fashions and to imitate the ways of the class above. To all intents and purposes, therefore, and even though it may be necessary to qualify our conclusions in order to allow for an evolution in English education, the type of education which has made England what she is must be found in the types of public school and university which are looked up to by all Englishmen as models of the kind. There are two such public schools: Eton and Harrow; and two such universities: Oxford and Cambridge.

The most important items in the curricula of these schools are undoubtedly the sundry types of sport which they cultivate. Their heroes and representative men are the captains of their cricket, football, and rowing teams. Their true competitions are those in which these teams are pitted against each other. Here, in his early youth, through the play of his muscles and not by any brain work, the Englishman cultivates the sense of fair play, the spirit of co-operation, the self-denial for the sake of the community to which he belongs, the capacity for fighting with grit and determination, yet with detachment and good humour—in a word, all the virtues-in-action which are those of his race.

Here, also, he receives on his yet tender soul the impress of the group. One by one, all the elements of the psychology of the people of action in action will appear and play their role in the life of the public school and university student. The force of *tradition* in these public schools and universities of England could hardly be exaggerated. Ways of living and dressing, relations between masters and boys and between boys themselves, festivals, religious services, every step in life is regulated by precedent, and, as in the portraits scene in Victor Hugo's *Hernani*, an impressive gallery of old Eton or Harrow boys of world-wide fame, hanging from the walls of history, watch in eloquent silence every one of the boys in every one of their actions.

This long historical ancestry of the school, its undisturbed development over so long a lapse of time, the close personal ties which attach it to the history of the country itself give a strong *aristocratic* atmosphere to English public schools and universities. For after all, what is aristocracy but a tradition preserved in comfort and conscious of itself? This very sense of aristocracy predisposes the mind of the schoolboy to accept the *hierarchical* sense which is, as we know, one of the most typical features of English collective life. But the whole organization of the public school is strongly *hierarchical*, as shown even in the curious system known as "fagging," a practice unthinkable in French or Spanish schools, whereby the younger boys serve the older ones and humbly obey their orders.

The *empirical* spirit of the race manifests itself in the unpopularity of the intellectual boy, the "brainy" fellow, as well as in the tendency to shun intellectual work and cultivate sports.

Self-control develops rapidly in this closely watched environment so strongly dominated by group-influences, and *self-consciousness* follows self-control. Though apparently free and easy, at any rate in what concerns the material liberty of the boys—moving about, coming and going, working or playing—the public school, and, perhaps in a lesser degree, the university, keeps a close watch over their actions. It is no official, no State watch; but the mere action of a vigorous collective being controlling all its members. The boy or student is free to do what he likes, but he is fully aware of the things which his school or university does not want him to do.

In the immense majority of cases, this education is completed by tuition in classical languages, history, and English. Here again we meet the wisdom of the race, instinctively choosing the best possible preparation for its leaders. A general study of the roots of European culture, to be found in the classical languages and literatures; history, i.e. facts about human nature; English, i.e. information about English character. The man of action is now ready. He knows all he needs to know. He does not know enough to doubt and moon at inaccessible truths.

Sometimes—this is particularly the case with many a political leader—the student reads law. (Let us underline in passing that word: *read*. It is a delightful revelation of the empirical character of English tuition.) Law, however, that is, English law, is an absolutely safe occupation for a future man of action. The possession—either on his desk or in his brain—of a bulky repertory of precedents can hardly be said to hamper his resolution through an excessive development of intellectual activity. The fact may be recalled here that, to be called to the Bar, a would-be barrister must eat a certain number of dinners at the Inns of Court on the registers of which his name has been written down. In this quaint custom we may see a valuable symbol: manners and environment are as compulsory as knowledge in the formation of the man of law.

2

The French word *élites* is the nearest approach to the English *leaders*. But we may observe that while *leaders* implies leading, and therefore movement, *élites* conveys more than an idea of position: it is static. All it suggests is that the persons it designates are the selected few, and therefore occupy the highest ranks in the hierarchy of the established order.

The French system differs from the English in two points—both of which were to be expected: it is directed towards the cultivation of the intellect, not of the will; and it is organized by the State.

The English public school is wholly independent of the State. It is a private enterprise, for indeed, in the phrase *public school*, the word *public* means in actual fact *private*, i.e. not official. Similarly, the two great universities are congeries of colleges founded and endowed by private individuals or institutions alien to the State, and the State has but little say in their internal organization, nor does it appoint its professorial staff.[1]

Not so in France. The whole apparatus whereby the *élites* are selected and educated is State-manufactured and State-handled. The secondary schools, or *lycées*, dotted all over the country are built on a uniform pattern and, so to say, on an interchangeable system. Their staff is organized on a national basis as part of the Civil Service, so that teachers pass from one *lycée* to another as a major or a colonel changes garrison. These teachers, moreover, teach whatever subject they happen to specialize in, but do not otherwise interfere with the life of the boys. If day-boys, as the immense majority of *lycée* students are, they come to the *lycée* for their lectures and then go home. If boarders, they lodge within the walls of the *lycée*, subjected to a quasi-military discipline. There may be some football played in the quadrangle, perhaps, now and then, a game in the open, on Thursdays or Sundays, but that is a matter for the boys. Their teachers have no concern with sports.

1. With a few exceptions, for a rule without exceptions would be unthinkable in England—far more so than elsewhere.

French secondary education is therefore specialized in the development of the brain. As an intellectual education, it is excellent. It does not limit itself to providing information. It does aim at the exercise of intellectual powers both for themselves and with a view to the creation of an *élite* as an indispensable part of the order which underlies the State. The education of the will and character is no special concern of the school. This does not mean that character and will are left uncultivated in France, but that, in this sphere, the school abstains in favour of the family—a fact which shows both that the family has a stronger formative importance than in England, and that character and will are not thought to be the concern of the nation to the same extent as they are in a community so strongly self-conscious as the English.

French secondary education is, therefore, one of the manifestations of that official order and uniformity which stand in France in lieu of the genius for co-operation characteristic of England. By means of an extensive system of scholarships, this educational apparatus automatically selects the more intelligent types of students, enabling them, whatever their financial limitations, to rise to the higher ranks of education, and therefore to the higher ranks of the established order. Here again we must observe the contrast with the English system. Though scholarships are not lacking in England, the system is not sufficiently uniform and, above all, the costly public schools provide too safe a filter for a great, or even a moderate, influx of fresh blood to invade the upper ranks of society. England believes too much in other than intellectual gifts to allow such a revolution to transform her body politic. But, in France, the aim of education is to develop the intellect of the educated, and, as we know, the true basis of French hierarchy is intellectual distinction. Hence no obstacles prevent the State from organizing the picking of the best brains of the people on a uniform and automatic basis in order to utilize them to the best advantage. A true intellectual measure, this system is radical in its theory and profoundly conservative in its effects.

From this uniform ground of secondary teaching the future

élites pass on to an admirable system of higher education. As befits an intellectual nation, this system is carefully specialized, in striking contrast with the somewhat general character of English university education. A considerable number of the young *élites* are absorbed by what is known in France as *les Grandes Écoles*. The École Polytechnique, the École Normale Supérieure, the several technical schools make a powerful appeal to French youth. They stand for a highly specialized education of the mind. Technical schools, yes, but profoundly theoretical and ambitiously universal in the scope of their teachings and in their outlook, they prepare first-rate leaders for industrial and State services and provide a continuous flow of scientific workers for the nation. The universities in their turn are also organized on the basis of specialized work. Though they aim at the formation of all-round intellects, they demand from each of their students a thorough knowledge of a particular subject. They are exacting in point of intellectual discipline but also in point of originality. And above all they develop in their students the love of knowledge, culture, and ideas.

Thus it is that we often find in France types of men whose intellectual refinement far exceeds, not only their physical appearance, but even their refinement in other than the intellectual sides of nature; while it sometimes happens in England that men of great physical and social distinction go about quite at their ease, with a mind so incurious and undeveloped that it is unable to realize its own shortcomings.

3

When passing from the English idea of *leaders* to the French idea of *élites* we lost the notion of movement but retained that of hierarchy. In passing now from the French *élites* to the Spanish *minorías*, the notion of hierarchy itself goes by the board. The *minorías* are merely a small number of people who happen to have reached a higher mental development than the rest. That is all.

This observation will save us from the error which we might

otherwise commit if, following a hasty and superficial parallel, we expected Spain to prepare her *minorities* by a carefully organized education of the passions. Such an argument would of course miss the main point. While England organizes herself spontaneously and France submits herself to the framework of her intellectual order, Spain's individuals are refractory to all national or State hold over them. The non-committal expression *minorías* is a timely reminder of this tendency.

We are here in the presence of one of those cases where it is indispensable to bear in mind that all manifestations of life contain action, passion, and thought. There is no doubt that, in so far as it manifests itself, the educational tendency of Spain, in full confirmation of our main hypothesis, is directed towards the education of an all-round man, and particularly of his passions. Spain's great humanists of the past—such as Luis Vives —or of recent times—such as Don Francisco Giner—may be quoted as excellent examples in this connexion. But the primal tendency cannot manifest itself in actual collective life without the co-operation of tendencies of thought and action, which are notoriously weak in the Spanish character. Hence it is that the intellectual minority of the country is reared under conditions amounting to the absence of any system whatsoever.

Secondary education is given in State *Institutos* and in a number of private establishments, many of which are owned, staffed, or controlled by the Church. Their level and value depend entirely on the persons in charge. Some of the best and no doubt some of the worst secondary schools are to be found in Spain. As for the spirit and orientation of this education, it also depends on the persons in charge. The weakness of the Spanish State, an obvious consequence of the individualistic character of the people, does not permit its *Institutos* to be governed by a uniform spirit such as that which makes all French *lycées* copies of the same pattern. It goes without saying that this applies with still greater force to private schools. The Church, of course, has its own standards and tendencies. But on the whole it cannot be said that Spanish education specializes in either character or intellect. Wherever it is conscious and conscientious [2] it is humanistic and general, and aims at the formation of all-round men for the sake of the men themselves.

Over the anarchy of secondary education rises the anarchy of the universities. All State-owned, enjoying a modicum of autonomy, they are but just beginning to revive from the long period of atony they have suffered since the days when Alcalá led the world in Biblical studies and edited the wonderful Polyglot Bible, and Salamanca ranked with Paris and Oxford as one of the three leading universities of Christendom. But, though there is a general revival, this revival is worth what the particular men behind it make it, and considerable differences may be observed not only between the several universities of the country but even between the several faculties of each university.

As if further to complicate the conditions under which the intellectual minority of Spain is reared, the Spanish family is a most unreliable organ for choosing studies for their young. Sometimes for lack of means, sometimes for other reasons of a greater or lesser importance, it often happens that Spanish students are bound to devote themselves to studies for which they feel but little inclination, to the neglect of others for which perhaps they were born. Add to this the typical Spanish tendency against specialization and it will be understood why Spain should be the land of missed vocations. When a Spaniard speaks convincingly of medicine, the chances are that he is an artist; if he shows a more than usual knowledge of painting, he may be a colonel; should he appear to be a specialist in strategy, he is sure to be a cathedral dean. Men of letters come from all professions.

A minority so chaotically raised could hardly be expected to be homogeneous and compact. The atmosphere of intellectual culture is somewhat thin and rarefied in Spain. Each individual seeks ideas and sensations by his own unaided effort, both be-

2. As in the institutions of all kinds created by the JUNTA DE AMPLIA-CIÓN DE ESTUDIOS.

cause his own character as a man of passion requires him to do so and because the environment itself provides but scanty food prepared, so to say, for wholesale consumption. Exceptional men in Spain rise therefore from sea level, not from the high lands of a social culture already established. They bring to their position all the peculiarities, singularities, and angularities of their isolated growth.

Thus the merely statistical expression—*minorías*—is a find of the language, for, while English leaders are a team and French *élites* are a class, the Spanish *minorías* are a number of loose units without any connexion or solidarity—save perhaps a vague fellow-feeling of isolation.

III

Political Structure

AT FIRST SIGHT, THE POLITICAL STRUCTURE OF THE THREE PEOPLES of western Europe is the same. They are three democracies organized under a parliamentary system. In reality, the political structures of England, France, and Spain differ as much as the differences in the three national characters lead us to expect. We may at the outset point out that, in England, political institutions are the outcome of an empirical evolution; in France, they result from a constitution carefully planned out and discussed beforehand; while, in Spain, they are at present in a plastic state under the masterful hand of a dictator.

This general observation could not fit better than it does the general scheme which underlies these pages. A more detailed analysis will but confirm our first impression.

I

We find England organized under an unwritten constitution which rests on tradition, convenience, and rule of thumb practice. Under this constitution the king reigns but does not govern. The wisdom of such a formula no one can deny. Its success in England, and in other countries not unlike England in their political organization, has given it such powerful roots in political thought that it is difficult to realize how utterly allogical it is. Such an idea could only germinate in the allogical consciousness of the Englishman. As if further to emphasize his contempt for logic in political matters, the Englishman has carefully preserved in his official language all the externals of kingly power. In his royal messages to Parliament—which are written by his Ministers—the King of England speaks of "My Army," "My Navy," "My Ministers." The House of Commons answers in the most humble terms, knowing itself all the time the mistress of the cash.

The parliamentary system itself is another typical English invention. It consists in a subordination of the executive to an assembly which discusses off-hand and verbally what the executive has carefully studied in long days or months of specialized work. This absurdity works. It works even admirably, but why? Because the Englishman does not care for ideas as such, and wants things done. Now it is obvious that, in a country, the agent that gets things done is the Government, and when the Opposition has "put up a show" and feels its brains fagged out, it ends by letting the Government work. We may even add that, were it not for this intellectual indifference of the average Englishman, the existence of a strong parliamentary system would be impossible. The party system rests on the assumption that there will be no more than two parties in the country. Its success cannot, therefore, be depended upon save in countries trained by cricket and football. And, in fact, as we have pointed out, English politics do not differ fundamentally from English sports; both are ruled by an unfailing, though vague and unformulated, feeling of fair play (the Speaker, the Umpire).

The present moment of English politics may be taken as an illustration. Of the intellectual indifference of the Conservative Party it is hardly necessary to speak. As for the Labour Party, its very name is characteristic. In every other country the corresponding party is styled *Socialist*. In England, despite the efforts of the most dangerous of its enemies to brand it with a label suggesting intellectual activity (thus destroying its chances with the electorate), the Labour Party is not a political, but a Trade Union party. It has no system of ideas generally accepted by its members, and its electorate is most suspicious of its small but brilliant intellectual General Staff, very few of whose members are ever elected to Parliament. As for the Liberal Party, it has not recovered yet from the devastating effects of the flood of ideas which fell on it from the hills of Wales.

The Cabinet is another picturesque product of this empirical and traditional people. Neither it as a whole nor any of its numerous members is what he seems. The Cabinet is, in practice, a Committee of party leaders freely chosen by the party chief. In theory, and in tradition, it is a Committee of the Privy Council, yet it numbers amongst its ordinary members the President of the Privy Council and the Presidents of several specialized committees of the Privy Council, such as the Board of Trade, the Board of Agriculture, the Board of Education, of all of which the Prime Minister is an ordinary member. This Prime Minister himself, who is the undisputed Chief of the Cabinet, does not appear in practice until the reign of George I, and then only owing to the fact that the King knew no English and could not preside over Cabinet meetings. This wholly fortuitous accident of history is the origin of the corner-stone of the party system, i.e. the collective responsibility of the Ministers of the Cabinet, which became an accepted tradition when Ministers were put under one political Chief, the Prime Minister. But the Prime Minister, though a part of English politics since George I, did not become a recognized and official personage until 1905. Till then he had access to the Cabinet over which he presided, not as its *de facto* Chief, but as the First Lord of the Treasury, a title which, of course, must be understood as meaning that he has nothing whatever to do with Treasury affairs.

The Treasury is one of the numerous English Departments of State which are "put in commission," i.e. which are managed by a Committee instead of by an individual. But here again, this is a purely theoretical complication, for of the seven Lords of the Treasury who are supposed to decide this and refuse that, and who, therefore, are referred to as "My Lords" on all Treasury papers, the First Lord is the Prime Minister and nothing else, while the Junior Lords are the Whips and officials of the party, dealing only with party machinery, and with what is modestly described in English as *patronage*. The true Minister of Finance is the Chancellor of the Exchequer, one of the old Crown dignitaries whom modern cabinets have inherited from the Middle Ages, preserving their picturesque manner and the complexity of their functions. Other dignitaries of this traditional and decorative kind are the Lord Chancellor, the Lord President of the Council, the Lord Privy Seal, and the Chancellor of the Duchy of Lancaster.

This cumbrous, heterogeneous, and picturesque body, a mixture of old dignitaries, Presidents of Boards, Secretaries of State, whose rights, duties, and organizations are so fluid that an eminent statesman was able to revolutionize it without stepping outside the constitution, is a typical growth of empirical England. From the English Cabinet all other constitutional cabinets have been copied—but as wax trees are copied from a living tree.

The true force behind the Cabinet is the Civil Service. It is difficult to do justice to so admirable an institution. Two of its eminent qualities must be commented upon, for they aptly illustrate the point of view here maintained. The first is its public spirit. No bureaucracy in the world can vie with the English Civil Service in its devotion to the interests of the country. The second is its efficiency. Now, this is in a way a natural consequence of the first, but it owes much also to that instinct for co-operation, that objectivity, that absence of self-seeking, of vanity, and of personal passion which are typical of the whole race. A race whose main tendency is to get things done is sure to have a good Civil Service.

A similar remark would apply to local government. In most continental countries, certainly in France, the organizing principle emanates from the central government and is distributed through bureaucratic channels to the provinces and departments all over the country. In England, local government is a spontaneous local growth, due to the same public virtues which can be observed in central and national institutions. It is but the genius of spontaneous organization, which we have seen at work in charity and other general and social activities, applied to the sphere of public local affairs. It follows that local government is in England singularly free from central fetters; varied and adapted to the characteristics of the different regions in which it grows; traditional; directly under the control of the members of the local community and usually in the hands of public-spirited citizens. Its vigour is its own and not a strength received from the centre of the nation. Both its motive power and the critical control which it needs for its right working are at hand on the spot where it has to work. Its relations with the central authorities are mostly of co-operation and co-ordination rather than of subordination. In short, local government is in England a true manifestation of genuine public life.

The basis of the political life of a country is, of course, its people. Now, there is no doubt that the people of England are a good-humoured, easily led nation. The deep-rooted hierarchical sense which is typical of it predisposes it to believe what it hears from its leaders. Its own sense of action makes it patient and trustful with the man at the helm. Its gregarious tendency is ever ready to make allowances whenever an appeal to national union is made, without looking too closely into the reasons which prompt such an appeal. The people of England, moreover, come to politics with a strong sense of the national scope which politics must have. No doubt, in the heat and passion of political argument they may accuse each other of thinking more of their own class than of the country, but, in comparison with the peoples of other countries, the English are truly patriotic in their political activities, and a national argument is sure to go very deep with them.

2

The political evolution of France is in typical contrast with that of England. In England, the constitution evolves slowly and empirically with wonderful continuity. In France, the political mould of the country is broken now and then and a new cast made in a new mould. France is the specialist in constitutions amongst nations. We recognize here the French tendency to plan everything beforehand, to define and limit areas of thought and action, to lay down *le droit*, to foresee all possible things. The parallel between the political evolution of the two peoples will recall to mind what has been said about the diagrams of action when the agents are respectively the man of action and the man of thought. In the first case the diagram is a continuous line winding along in order to keep as close as possible to realities; in the second, a series of straight lines tangent to the winding profile of realities, the direction of which is constantly rectified, now and then by sharp angles. The first diagram represents the evolution of the unwritten and elastic English constitution, always changing, yet always the same; the second might do for a diagram of the constitutional history of France, in which written constitutions follow each other through sharp turns or revolutions in the political life of the country.

French political life is at present ruled by the constitution of 1875. It is all in black and white, perfectly planned out beforehand and unchangeable. When the National Government, which took office in 1926, wished to give exceptional solemnity to the laws which it proposed to have voted for the restoration of the franc, it had to give assurances that there would be no attempt to use the constituent machinery with a view to revising the constitution. Needless to say, the French constitution is clear, precise, logical, and complete. It sets up a parliamentary system based on certain rules and regulations, according to which either of the two Houses of Parliament can eject a government from power. This logical wonder does not work.

It does not work because, leaving aside other less worthy motives which may act here and there, the French nation is above all interested in ideas. The deputies believe in what they think. As a matter of fact, thinking is the only way of believing in France. Thus, a debate in the French Chamber is a real debate: none of that sense of sport which pervades an English parliamentary debate—when the opposing teams face each other in perfect good humour, follow the ball of argument as it passes to and fro from the Government team to the Opposition team, acknowledge the good stroke by whatever side secured, and bow to the wigged umpire, and know all the time how the thing will end, for "He is a jolly good fellow, and so say all of us." None of that good humour of a cricket-playing race. In France, a debate is a battle, and arguments are loaded. Every pair of eyes looks like the two barrels of a double-barrelled machine-gun turning at high speed, throwing ideas at the enemy with the utmost alacrity. Arguments, innuendoes, accusations, insults are hurled through the air like projectiles. The President does his best to keep outside the area of fire lest some missile hit his neutral figure and thus impair his dignity, while ruining his neutrality. No one ever knows how the battle will end, and when, in the small hours of the morning, the beaten army sounds its retreat, the *huissiers* go about from bench to bench wakening up the dead and wounded asleep in the trenches.

In these conditions it is difficult to obtain a sufficient amount of agreement for stable government, the more so as the beautiful party system of England, that chariot smoothly running on two wheels, cannot be realized in France, since it is too much to expect that an assembly of five hundred minds should hold no more than two opinions. Let us remember that, in the English assembly, opinions are not the leading forces at all—

the leading force is the conviction that things must get done. Now, in the French Chamber and Senate the desirability of getting things done must wait on the all-important questions of how they are to be done, who is to do them, and in the name of which principles; and it is easy to see that while roads to action are bound to converge, roads to thought radiate in all the directions of the mind.

The place which efficiency occupies in England is taken in France by intellectual honesty. In England the man who, instead of coming round and joining the others in the work in hand, sticks to his opinion is branded as pigheaded. The average Englishman finds it wellnigh impossible to believe that any one but a pig could be so fond of an opinion at all. But, in France, a man who gives up his opinion in order to get on with the business is looked upon with suspicion, for an opinion is the most cherished possession of the Frenchman.[1]

Thus, the working of the French Parliament differs profoundly from that of its English model, both politically and technically. Politically, the French Parliament is divided into groups representing a considerable number of shades of opinion. Cabinets and majorities are put together by a careful blending of such groups, very much as a doctor concocts a prescription by mixing carefully balanced doses of several drugs. Technically, the work of the French Parliament is carried out in commissions which specialize in the several branches of the executive in order to scrutinize its work. Debates in both Houses are fed by the technical work done on the details of government business in these commissions. There is no doubt a considerable amount of passion in such debates. It would be absurd to present the French Parliament as a purely platonic academy, debating in beautiful calm on the intellectual problems raised by the exercise of the art of government; but the passion of French politics is born of the clash of ideas. Nothing, not even personal ambition, which, like copper in gold, is an

1. A popular Paris newspaper brandishes this title, *L'Intransigeant*. Such a title would be unthinkable in an English newspaper.

indispensable alloy in the politician, nothing raises the fire of passion in a Frenchman like intellectual opposition. Passion in French political life, therefore, is like the heat which develops in machinery in motion. It would be wrong to mistake it for the motive power of events. It is a concomitant phenomenon—in fact, a waste. The motive power is not in the heart but in the brain.

A similar observation applies to the French Civil Service. Its motive power is in the brain, not in the heart. Its intellectual efficiency is, therefore, higher than its efficiency as the servant of the public. It does not so much serve as administer. Language again points out this fact, since the French expression for civil service is *L'Administration*. There is more than meets the eye in this verbal difference. The expression *Civil Service* reminds us that in England the State is but a machinery at the service of the nation. In *L'Administration* we find an assumption of the State as central authority. Thus we meet again the now familiar opposition between the English genius for spontaneous co-operation (which evolves a State as a service) and the French intellectual order (which imposes a centralized discipline from on high through an Administration).

The Administration is the strongest force working for uniformity and centralization in France. It possesses a marvellous capacity for absorbing public functions which in other countries, such as England, remain outside the State. We have seen that such is the case with secondary teachers and university professors. Magistrates and judges are another example of the kind. But the most impressive proof of its unifying power is the admirable organization of its local government. Gone is the autonomy of English local institutions. By a bold intellectual operation the Préfet and his Sous-Préfets are made to represent the whole executive in their local capitals. Each Préfet is surrounded with the necessary number of specialists to enable him to follow up all administrative business with due competence and efficiency. Thus the neatly constructed intellectual order of the centre is reproduced in all its details in every one of the Departments of France: hill or valley, north or south, Teutonic,

Basque, Breton, Flemish—all live and work according to the instructions evolved under the abstract skies of the Île-de-France.

But what of the people? The people are too intelligent really to believe in liberty; too calculating to compromise on the subject of equality; too busy with their own affairs to care to take over those of the community, and too mistrustful to allow the community, i.e. the State, to take too much care of their own. Their formula is that the State must do its job so that they can do theirs. They are interested in politics generally from an intellectual standpoint. More often than not political battles are fought round the principle of freedom of thought, by which Free-thinkers understand that all should be allowed to think as Free-thinkers; or round the principle of freedom of teaching, by which Catholics understand that all should be free to be taught by Catholic schools. The electorate, compared with an English electorate, is perhaps more preoccupied with local, or even personal, interests, than national issues. Yet, in so far as it brings to politics a deeper concern with ideas, it often strikes a universal note. Occasionally a first-rate political scandal or "cause" rends the country into two factions, earnestly possessed of the idea that truth is with them, and then the capacity of the French nation to serve an idea is brilliantly, if perhaps tragically, brought to light.

3

At first sight the political evolution of Spain is not unlike that of France. In both countries sudden changes are brought about by dramatic moves, and new constitutions are laid down for the guidance of the country during a more or less protracted period of internal peace. A closer scrutiny, however, reveals considerable differences. French political revolutions are the outcome of evolutions in the mind of the nation. This is evident in the case of the Great Revolution, which was merely the refashioning of the country-as-a-fact in order to adapt it to the country-as-a-theory described and prescribed by the Encyclopaedists. The leaders of French revolutions are intellectuals, priests of Goddess Reason or of Goddess Glory, that other moving spirit of the French Olympus, of which more will be said anon. Spanish revolutions are not made in the name of a school of thought. They are crises in a drama. The political life of the country is like a novel or drama, in which the moving forces are not principles but all-round personalities. No doubt in France principles do incarnate in persons. No doubt in Spain characters on the political stage are moved by principles more or less obscurely held. But the point is that, as a general rule, in France, principles drive the persons and give them their greatness, while in Spain the characters on the political stage owe their prestige to their own personality, and their own personality it is which gives strength and driving power to the principle or cause which they happen to have espoused.

This is what was to be expected. We know, on the one hand, that the Spanish genius is individualistic to such an extent that the Spaniard enters wholly wherever he enters; therefore Spanish political leaders make of politics a sphere not merely of action as in England, or of ideas, as in France, but of action, thought, and passion rolled into one. On the other hand, we have seen that the Spaniard tends to judge things and people with the standards of a theatre-goer. He is in the stalls. Contrary to what is often thought by superficial observers—even Spanish observers—he is not indifferent in matters of politics; he is most interested, only he follows political events not as a member of a concern (which is the English way), nor as a member of an intellectual sect (which is the French way), but as the reader of a novel in instalments, or as a man at the play. His criterion is dramatic. He is held by the vicissitudes of the continual fighting for power and for the spoils of power between a certain number of people who, less wise than he is, have left their quiet seats in the pit and gone on the stage.

That is the fundamental fact in the situation. It explains more than one puzzling feature of Spanish political life. First the fluidity of political opinion. In the politicians themselves, this particular feature might be lightly dismissed with a cynical smile. Yet the smile would be unfair, for why judge political persons more unfavourably than the mass of their countrymen? Now, it is a fact that the political opinions of the immense majority of Spaniards are fluid and wayward. The reason would appear to be that, their political allegiance being more personal than objective, they feel disposed to allow it to evolve along with the evolution of their hero's character.

In a similar manner we may explain the relative facility wherewith political situations are won and lost in Spain. A capital political failure in most other countries means political death. Not so in Spain; for a great and forceful villain is as important a character as a great hero, and the spectator instinctively accepts the right of such prominent men to be on the stage. The criterion of English politics is ethical and economic. Sir Charles Dilke and Parnell were hounded out of politics for being involved in social scandals. Other political leaders failed because they mismanaged the affairs of the country, or had to raise the rate of income-tax. France, as a whole nation, does not dismiss her leaders. She splits into sects, and leaders come and go as their sects are or are not in power. Spanish political life is, we know, a drama. Therefore, just as once an actor always an actor, once a political man always a political man. A *pro-hombre* (a typical Spanish expression meaning a protagonist in the theatre of life) may be off the stage for the time being, but no one dreams of denying that he is a person in the play.

Such is the most natural explanation of the political phenomenon known in Spanish as *Caciquismo*. The political district is "organized" in England by the local branch of the party. It is a cell of a living body covering the whole country, with its secretaries, its committees, its discussions, and what not. In France the political life of small districts takes the form of a permanent warfare between the two schools of thought, the Clerical and the Anti-Clerical—usually centred round the priest and the schoolmaster. In Spain local political life is entirely in the hands of the local dictator or *Cacique*. *Caciquismo* has often been denounced in Spain as the source of all political evils, and a galaxy of remedies have been suggested in order to extirpate it. It is doubtful whether such remedies would have proved effective, and, if so, whether their application would have been desirable, for *Caciquismo* is so natural a form of Spanish public life, so consonant with the national character, that its extirpation might prove to be a loss rather than a gain. Local government by the most energetic and able man will in all probability be for ever the basis of Spanish political life, and Spanish statesmen may have to concentrate on the ways to ensure that the *Cacique* is a man worthy of his responsibilities.

The above remarks would suffice to establish a thorough-going distinction between French and Spanish political life. But they give rise to further observations, which carry this distinction still farther. There is no doubt a constitution-drafting mania in Spain. This is one of the cases of the influence of France over her southern neighbour. Others will have to be pointed out. As poor in conscious as rich in subconscious gifts, Spanish genius has often sought to imitate French talent in matters of organization as in many other matters. The number of constitutions enacted during the nineteenth century in Spain is only inferior (if it is inferior) to that which the fertile brain of France has contrived in the same period; but, in France, they are applied.

In Spain they never ventured out of the paper on which they were written. It is only an intellectual people, that knows by instinct how to live according to plan, which can make a written constitution live, if with difficulty. The others must choose: either they evolve an empirical, unwritten, elastic constitution, which is not the dress but the skin over their body politic, or else they must resign themselves to live an unconstitutional life. England has taken the first course, Spain the second.

This was to be expected for more than one reason. In the first place, the political evolution of Spain, like the line of action in the man of passion, is best represented as a series of lines of quiescence followed by fits of activity. Spain lacks, therefore, the continuity of political life which enabled England to evolve her constitution. In the second place, a constitution is a set of rules contrived in order to limit the power of the rulers. The rulers tend to overstep them. The ruled must, therefore, be the guardians of their constitution. Now, we know that the average Spaniard is not made that way. He watches the conflict of powers on the stage. For him the constitution is one of the elements in the play. Is it strange then that, if and when one of the protagonists finds it to be an obstacle, it should be turned or even brushed aside by an energetic hand?

We are now in a position to realize how deeply Spanish revolutions differ from French. A French crisis marks the moment when an intellectual evolution reaches its logical conclusion on the plane of facts. A Spanish revolution is generaly a *pronunciamiento* or an *alzamiento*, words which both suggest an outstanding person who *pronounces* a new order of things, or who *rises* in order to impose it. A Spanish revolution is a dramatic event, an act of power. Its leader is nearly always a commander of men, often an army chief.

All these characteristics work in Spain against the establishment of a democratic system of government on a strong and durable basis, though not, be it understood, against democratic life. We saw the English man-in-the-street go to politics with an eye to action; the French citizen voting in accordance with his ideas. The Spaniard is too much of a realist to attach much importance to his vote, and too much of an individualist to multiply its importance by co-operation with other voters. Moreover, in virtue of his tendency to invert social values, classifying them in an egocentric order, the Spaniard often gives his vote for reasons entirely foreign to objective politics— to oblige a private friend, for instance.

Similar psychological obstacles stand in the way of a good organization of bureaucracy. The personality of the Spaniard leads him too often to adopt an attitude of ownership rather than of service in connexion with his functions. This is particularly the main defect of the *cuerpos*, or organizations of the several branches of State functionaries, which apportion the duties of the State amongst themselves with a jealous watch upon their bureaucratic territory which suggests rather the fear of invasion felt by tribes occupying land than eagerness to serve the nation to the best of their ability. Here again, we may recognize features which we were led to expect in the people of passion in action.

IV

====

Historical Development

A. IMPERIAL HISTORY

CHARACTER AND DESTINY, FOR PEOPLES AS FOR INDIVIDUALS, ARE
the two forces which shape history. The history of a people,
therefore, is not exclusively the outcome of its character. The
length of Cleopatra's nose, a matter of pure destiny, had a considerable influence on the history of Mark Antony, and therefore on that of the Roman Empire.

I

Destiny rather than character explains why the imperial
development of European nations should have begun with

Spain. The several peninsular kingdoms were unified by a series of monarchs both before and after Ferdinand and Isabel, thanks to the vigour of the religious passion then prevailing in the country. The fall of Granada symbolizes the union of all Spaniards under one faith. Now that a sufficient time has elapsed for that religious passion to have subsided considerably, it is possible to wonder whether Spain would not have been happier and ultimately stronger if she had allowed a greater variety of faiths and races to live and thrive on her soil. The impulse gathered up to beat down the gates of Granada carried Spain on to a religious adventure which lasted three centuries—through glory to ruin. But "ifs" in history are but vain conceits, and the fact remains that Spain enters European history as a people of passion.

The next, indeed contemporaneous, event which Spanish history registers is even more important for our purpose. Christopher Columbus discovers America. Here again Spain manifests herself as a people of passion, with all the features which we have analysed in the type. The discovery, exploration, and colonization of the new world is the greatest epic of the white race. It has not yet found a Homer worthy of its greatness; it has found many a carping critic. For three centuries Spain has been the enemy of a large part of the world, a part which was precisely the most industrious and the most skilled in the use of information. The ideas of the world on the subject of the American epic are inadequate. The history of the subject must be written afresh—without omitting any of the mistakes made, yet bringing out the whole enterprise in its true colossal proportions.

It will then be realized that the first navigators and explorers were men of astounding courage, daring, imagination, and even, in many cases, wisdom. These men acted as individual adventurers. Sooner or later, of course, either before or after their expeditions, they endeavoured to secure a royal charter giving them some sort of official status. But the initial impulse and consecutive efforts were theirs alone.

We find in these men the typical Spanish feature which we

have described as the co-existence of contradictory tendencies. Taken as a whole, the exploration and colonization of America by the Spaniards is perhaps the most inhuman, but also the most human, of its kind. Spaniards were, no doubt, the men who committed the abuses and ill-treatments so often exposed since; but Spaniards also those who laid down the standards of humanity by which the inhuman acts of their countrymen were condemned. And while the former, the brutal and unscrupulous colonizers, found imitators, and do to this day, the latter were far in advance of their time, and even of ours.

Spanish colonization, as a system, was established on the principle of the equality of races, itself a consequence of the religious basis of all Spanish law. This accounts for the absence of the colour bar in the Spanish colonial empire, which led to the fact that Spanish America should now be the crucible in which a new race is being prepared out of the white, red, and black elements which history has blended on its territory. A second consequence of the religious inspiration which animated the Spanish nation at that time is that the colonizing State considered itself in duty bound to educate and convert the native population. The main orientation of the Spanish Empire is, therefore, not economic nor political, but spiritual. This assertion is eloquently proved by comparing the dates on which the educational establishments of the two American continents were founded. It will be seen that the oldest are all of Spanish foundation, and that the creative effort of Spain in this field is wellnigh incredible.

There is nothing in the remaining history of the Spanish Empire which our reading of the Spanish character cannot explain satisfactorily. Economically the Spaniards had to pay for being the first in the field. They made mistakes, they monopolized the trade of their colonies. The idea, though absurd, has returned in recent times, somewhat rejuvenated as an ideal for the British Empire, which shows that errors die hard. Politically the Spanish Empire was, like Spain, governed very badly or very well, or indifferently, according to the Viceroys who were sent over. The *Leyes de Indias*, or Laws for Overseas, are considered today excellent in doctrine and shrewd in procedure, but it was the man on the spot that mattered.

Ultimately the disruption of the Spanish Empire came about —leaving aside such foreign factors as English and American help—through the action of internal psychological causes with which we are now familiar. The overseas Spaniard was as individualistic as his European brother. The centrifugal force, so typical of the man of passion in action, revealed itself rather unexpectedly on the first opportunity. The history of the emancipation of Spanish America is another chapter of Spanish history which must be revised. Practically every one of the movements which compose it was born as an outburst of loyalty to the Spanish crown persecuted by Napoleon. It was through a natural evolution, determined by the dispersive tendencies inherent in Spanish psychology, that such movements ultimately led to the wars of emancipation. These dispersive tendencies did not cease acting when the colonies cut themselves loose from the motherland. Under their influence, the old Spanish Empire was disrupted into an ever-growing number of nations, and, in contrast to the United States which the English race created in the north, the Spanish race formed in the south the dis-united States.

The Spanish Empire, however, as a positive and original force did not die with the wars of emancipation, for it was dead already. It was killed on the day when the Armada was abandoned by its Great Admiral, the Lord, i.e. the Catholic God. When Santa Cruz, who had organized the Armada and was to command it, died shortly before the date of its departure, Philip II appointed as his successor the Duke of Medina Sidonia, who humbly requested His Majesty to relieve him from the post, for, he said, he knew nothing of sea strategy, and, moreover, was a bad sailor. But the King answered that the fleet would be led by the Lord himself. The Lord led it to defeat. The great Catholic force sent to put down heresy in England was beaten by an English admiral who was himself a Catholic. Henceforward, the Spanish nation, though unaware of it perhaps, was a nation without ideal. *Don Quixote* was written a few years after that fateful date by a man who had fought at Lepanto, under the Spanish flag, a victorious battle against the Turks.

The people of Spain went into quiescence for several centuries.

2

We expect to see the imperial evolution of France as a systematic effort to establish a beautiful intellectual order in the world. Order, we know, is the intellectual category of action, and an inherent requirement of French psychology. We know that in their collective life the French people establish order by means of a State and an official hierarchy, and that, therefore, contrary to what happens in England, the State in France occupies a prominent and central position.

It is only natural then that, through a generalization or a universalization, which is itself in keeping with the intellectual turn of the French character, the history of French foreign policy should evince a tendency to organize the world as a kind of solar system, having Paris for its centre and sun. In so doing the French nation is led by no mean or selfish motives. The impulse which drove her in her age-long fight against the House of Austria was, at bottom, but the manifestation of this primary need of her genius—order, and therefore an intelligent and peaceful grouping of nations round Paris.

There is a considerable difference between this tendency to order which dominates French foreign policy and the tendency to unity which inspires Spanish imperial wars. Spain fights for a spiritual principle. She believes herself the soldier of God. France's policy, even that of the monarchy of the "Roy très chrestien," was always lay, and indifferent in matters of religion. The first Christian monarch to strike an alliance with the Turks was Francis I. Henry IV thought that Paris was well worth a mass, and acted upon it.

To this difference in inspiration corresponds a difference in aims and methods. Spain's aim is one only monarch:

Un monarca, un imperio y una espada.

Her method is uncompromising whenever matters of religion are at stake. When Philip II, having tried ruthlessness in the Low Countries with Alba, decides to try conciliation, his instructions to Recassens, Alba's successor, are to compromise in everything but in matters affecting the purity of the faith, for, says the King, "I would rather lose the Provinces." The aim of the King of France has much less to do with the other world, and his conscience is far more political. So long as the supremacy of France was undisturbed in the world—as that of the State of France—the French nation would have let other nations do their sweet will in a world which would add to the blessings of peace those of French polity and civilization. Such an aim, in which—at any rate in the eyes of France—the French nation gave more than it took, admitted of a certain amount of elasticity, compromise, and diplomatic give and take. Spain, the soldier of God, could not compromise, for it was not her own she would give away. France, the protagonist of order, could compromise, for, though at bottom interested, her own interests were not directly involved in her policy. French diplomacy soon superseded Spanish diplomacy, for it was freer in its methods and less ambitious in its aims.

This policy was served by two forces of considerable importance. The first was the military genius of the French race. When dealing with French individual psychology we have noted how the military tendency is but the natural outcome of the combination of two groups of tendencies—the group connected with foresight and distrust, and the group which comprises intellectual contemplation, appetite, subjective speed, and "go." The military tendency in an intellectual race naturally leads to the sense of glory. Glory, moreover, is but national vanity, and we know that vanity is a typical French feature. The French people are the most sensitive to military glory in itself, independently of the positive results which it may bring them. They see it as a pure spectacle, while the English, when they think of it at all, only view it as one of the several expressions of their power and of their capacity for action.

This French tendency to military glory explains why the

French idea of order should so often have taken the form of a military empire. The military empire dreamed by Louis XII and Francis I, prepared by Henry IV, and realized by Louis XIV, prepared again by the French Revolution, and achieved by Napoleon; again attempted by Napoleon III, the French military empire was not a business of this world—race and commerce, like the British Empire—nor a business of the other world—theocracy, like the Spanish Empire—but an intellectual creation, or, in the words which Victor Hugo applies to Charlemagne's empire, "un beau spectacle à ravir la pensée." There is a vast universality in it all. We begin to perceive it in Henry IV's dream of a great confederation of nations—a dream which was several centuries in advance of its time, yet which inspired Henry IV's workaday policy. It reappears in the generous international principles proclaimed and advocated by the first revolutionists of the great Revolution; and to this date it inspires and elevates whatever may seem too naïvely national in the French belief in the intellectual supremacy of France, which is the second formidable force at the service of their imperial expansion.

Belief in their intellectual supremacy. But it really goes farther than that. It is a desire to irradiate the light of their spirit over the whole world: *le rayonnement de la France*. The name "Ville lumière" given to Paris has become silly for French people, because Paris has become self-conscious about it, but there is no doubt that it must have caused her deep pleasure the first time she heard it, for that is precisely what she loves to think herself. And today when the world has grown too big, and wars too technical and too scientifically barbaric for a military empire to be possible and pleasing to the French mind, this lofty ideal of being a torch-bearer of the world remains in the heart of France as the most refined form of her imperialism. The French Empire is intellectual.

3

Just as the Spanish Empire is inspired by religious passion, and the French Empire is guided by an intellectual vision, the

English Empire results from a growth-impulse which manifests itself in its effects, which is vital and always potentially active, but which maintains throughout the secret of its whence and whither, always ready to turn natural obstacles by following the curve of compromise. Here, no dominant passion, no intellectual vision; therefore, no intransigent conditions, no pre-established plans; a force which proceeds forward, and knows nothing but other forces on its road. And towards these forces it offers the simple and straightforward attitude which is known in mathematics as *the composition of forces*; if the growth-impulse of the empire is stronger than the obstacle, it overruns it; if not so strong, it turns it.

The growth of the British Empire is thus empirical, continuous, and limited to the sphere of action.

Empirical. So empirical that the growth-impulse manifests itself sometimes with greater clearness in this or that individual Englishman than in the nation or State. Drake, Raleigh, Clive, Cecil Rhodes are typical cases. But though these men feel the growth-impulse, they cannot be said to have had before them a clear vision, a plan of some total future arrangement. They are as the buds on a vigorous and powerful tree, as the limbs of a healthy and youthful body.

The empirical character of this development is one of the greatest assets of the empire, for it allows it to adapt its forms to all sorts of climates and conditions: from the imperial pomp and luxury of the Indian Viceregal Court to the republican simplicity of the Australian Commonwealth, all forms of government, all types of colonization can be found under the world-wide mantle of His Majesty the King. In this encyclopaedia of colonizing forms nothing is lacking—not even a failure. The British Empire shows the scar left by the secession of the American colony with the pride of an old veteran who has washed away a defeat in the blood of numerous victories, for this defeat is an indispensable element in the history of the British Empire. It vouches for the empirical character of all its successes.

This continuity of growth is the imperial form of the continuity of British politics in general. The body politic is ever active, because it is ever alive, and being the body of a people of action, life and action are for it synonymous. We must point out the intimate connexion which exists between this continuity observed in English political life and the spirit of co-operation which we know to be one of the strongest virtues of English life in general and of English political life in particular. Nowhere is it possible to observe the team-work of English politics in more beautiful harmony than in the foreign and imperial policy of Great Britain. The art of collaboration in opposition could not be carried farther. Conservatives add to the empire; Liberals denounce them for doing so, and, their consciences thus laid at rest, consolidate the new acquisitions by applications of Liberal cement in the form of self-government and such-like soothing fomentations.

The orientation of the English colonial system towards action manifests itself in its eminently economic character. The main preoccupation of all empire-builders is to make the colony a paying proposition. This aim is often pursued with a true regard for the interests of the governed—particularly in our day; at other times, the interests of the governed pass to the second plan, and the more general view, the economic interests of the whole, plays a preponderant role; but in every case the main inspiration is one of economic development. That sense of matter and of the material, which we had occasion to observe in the English character, shows itself at work here, drawing English empire-builders towards things rather than people, and even when dealing with people, towards their material rather than their intellectual or spiritual welfare.

The neutrality of the English towards native religions, and their respect for local forms of belief and worship, is but the quality-defect derived from this economic orientation of their overseas activities. At bottom there is much indifference in their neutrality, and their impartiality is the natural outcome of the distance—a distance upwards—at which they feel themselves from their "subjects."

Our parallel is thus fully justified by a survey of the colonial ways of our three nations. The colonizing ways of Spain, when Spain had definite colonial ways of her own, were inspired in a spiritual tendency and based on an equalitarian sense rooted in religion. French colonization is led by the idea of intellectual order, which it seeks to generalize and extend to the "Frances overseas"; it also rests on equality, but on an equality which is an idea based on intellectual preconceptions. The British Empire is conceived rather as an ambitious commercial concern, in which each territory plays a definite role according to climate and geographical position, and the race which occupies it fulfils certain functions according to blood and development. No idea, no feeling of equality is there to complicate matters which are of themselves complicated enough. The leading race throughout is that of the mother country.

This, again, was to be expected, in view of the all-important consequences of the feeling of group-limitation which we have observed in English psychology. We know that fair play and the genius for spontaneous organization have, for their frontiers, the frontiers of the race in which they manifest themselves. Any weakening, crumbling down, breach or opening in the race wall would be fatal to these racial virtues. The race, no doubt, is aware of it, and guards against the danger at all costs. The pressure of the group thus well defended acts at its best in each of its individuals. If it prevents them from winning-over the hearts of other peoples in whose midst they live as strangers, it enables them, sometimes in trying circumstances, worthily to bear the white man's burden.

It is well worth notice that the historical evolution of the Spanish, French, and English empires may be fairly represented by the respective diagrams which we have attributed to the action of each of the three corresponding psychological types. Thus the diagram of action in the man of passion, described as a long horizontal line of inaction, cut now and then by a sudden peak of exceptional effort, faithfully represents the history of Spain; the diagram of action in the intellectual, which we find to be a series of straight lines tangent to the winding line of reality, and connected by successive sharp curves or elbows, aptly represents French history with its several attempts at empire-building: Louis XIV, Napoleon, Napoleon III, the third Republic; while the diagram of action in the man of action, a winding curve closely adapted to life's own sinuosities, is an apt image of English evolution, taking at every moment the direction most favourable to England's interests compatible with the drift of events.

B. HOME HISTORY

It seems hardly necessary to point out that the development of the home history of the three nations coincides in its general lines with that of their international history, and therefore fits in equally well with our psychological premises. The leading group in each case is Castille, in Spain; the Île-de-France, in France; England, in the United Kingdom.

I

Castille seeks not so much to centralize and organize as to unify the Peninsula, and to unify it not so much politically or economically as spiritually. The typical move, taken in utter disregard of political or economic consequences, is the forced conversion of the Jews and Moors, and the subsequent expulsion of the recalcitrants. No racial prejudice; nothing but the all-absorbing concern in the religious welfare of the nation. A pure example of a religious passion, acting at home with the same intransigence and disinterested zeal wherewith it buried itself and its own power in the Netherlands.

Later, the disruptive tendencies of the nation show themselves at work in the Peninsula. Just as in America, the English United States of the north face the Spanish disunited States of the south, so in Europe to the English United Kingdom corresponds the Spanish disunited Peninsula. Portugal breaks away from the other Spains, turns her back to the Peninsula, and looks wistfully across the ocean to the spot in the horizon on which the sun of her empire once set. A party of Catalonian dreaming youths sets its heart on a separate nationhood, never more Spanish than when indignantly refusing to be so. Every region, as it awakens to political life, feels the lure of centrifugal forces in her Iberian heart. The twentieth century will witness again in the Peninsula the struggle between a Castille, not always intelligently, but always wisely, bent on unity, and the other disruptive forces which the Iberian soul carries within it.

2

The evolution of French home history is a triumph of State organization. Placed in the most frequented thoroughfare of Europe, not particularly favoured from the point of view of racial unity, the kingdom of France constitutes itself from Paris as its head on a strongly centralized pattern. Among the forces which explain this miracle should be mentioned as particularly significant: the law, the sword, and the road. The law, defined by the *légistes* and providing a basis of *droit* for the monarch; the military activity of the monarchs, well served by first-rate commanders; and, finally, a system of communications admirably planned and executed. All these forces are eminently intellectual. The centralizing tendency of French communications is perhaps the most striking feature of the system. It was so with the old roads; it remains so with the advent of railways. While open competition in an active commercial community determines English railway construction, French railways are carefully planned beforehand by an intellectual statesman, Monsieur de Freycinet, and this plan is in the form of a star with Paris for its centre. Clearness, foresight, State order, centralization are the typical French features which preside over the home history of France.

3

In British home history the leading factor is the English people. English monarchs do not always see the way, and often waste their lives and the nation's money in useless French wars. The English people feel that their interests lie first at home, where everything is still to be done in order to make a well-disciplined team out of the several elements which have developed in the island. They begin by making England strong through self-government;[1] they absorb Wales; they absorb Scotland; but such operations are typically carried out with a minimum interference with local ways, such as language and religion. It will be seen that this process takes place in strict harmony with the main tendencies—empiricism, utilitarianism, spontaneous organization—with which we are now familiar in the people of action.

Yet in the gradual process of federation England fails for a long time in Ireland. This failure, and its subsequent transformation into a success, are not without a deep psychological interest. England fails in Ireland because Ireland is beyond the barriers of the national group. The fellow-feeling of co-nationality is extended to the Scot and to the Welshman, and therefore co-operation can be set up in the great island with relative ease. In passing to Ireland this feeling is "refracted." The Irishman at bottom is a stranger. In these conditions, as we know, the typical virtues of the Englishman in action are warped, not merely, be it understood, through his own fault, assuming that fault there is, but through the fact that there exists a cleavage, a flaw, a frontier, so that the Englishman does not find in the Irishman a sufficient reflection of his own self for spontaneous co-operation to take place.

For the Irishman is a man of passion like the Spaniard. He is, therefore, strongly individualistic, poor in collective virtues, apt to feel patriotism rather as a passion to burn in his isolated soul than as fuel to be usefully consumed in the national factory. The history of Anglo-Irish relations is thus outwardly an unequal fight between a nation endowed with a strong sense of unity and team-work, and a dispersive and individualized people, weak as a nation. Ireland was hopelessly divided by her own weakness as a community, as well as by the pressure of her foe.

1. They eliminated the foreign influence involved in the Roman organization of the Church.

But, beneath the surface, this struggle determined an evolution of great spiritual significance. In her trials Ireland's character evolved towards the character of England. The people of passion, under the historical pressure of the struggle, gradually learnt the virtues of the people of action. When this anglification of Ireland was sufficiently advanced, Ireland was welded into one nation with a strong *spontaneous* discipline. It was not in the pro-English Irishman that the incarnation of such a process was to be found, but, on the contrary, in the Sinn Feiner, the Irishman who represented the group-dominated, group-moulded, and group-disciplined individual. It was the Sinn Feiner who was the most deeply anglified Irishman. The Mayor of Cork dying for Ireland marks the dramatic moment when England, though blind to the fact, has conquered Ireland at last, since she is at last fighting against Irishmen who are like Englishman. The fight is no longer necessary.

V

The Language

A COMPARISON OF LANGUAGES WITHIN THE FRAMEWORK OF A parallel study of national character cannot be based on mere philological grounds. Indeed it may be said that philology, if narrowly understood, is more apt to hinder than to help the psychologist, for very much the same reasons which tend to give most medical men a materialistic philosophy.

Philology is too often understood as the mere study of the body of languages. But languages are something more than hosts of words aligned in grammatical order. It is perhaps unscientific to exact from science a kind of insight without which poets—at any rate—feel that knowledge is not worth its name. The botanist who cannot tell us why the cypress is so intensely lyrical and why the willow lets itself go down the vale of life, the zoologist who cannot explain why the magpie is a thief and the parrot a talkative old woman, why the dog is loyal and servile and the cat mystical and proud will no doubt smile in sympathy with the philologist. But we can return the smile when we are told that the Spanish and the French languages belong to the same family. Perhaps they do, as dead languages, but certainly not as the living languages which we know them to be.

Languages are the most direct expression of national character. They are the first impress of the mind of man on the outer world. The words he coins in order to describe objects and emotions closely correspond to his idea of them; the system he contrives in order to use such words is a direct image of his way of thinking. A grammar is a philosophy.

In the case of most modern languages, however, an important qualification is necessary. An historical accident, emigration, immigration, conquest, may have driven out the native language, replacing it by another one alien to the genius of the people. In most cases the genius of the people is itself altered by such an historical accident, implying, as it does, racial and social changes. In all these cases, the language thus transplanted evolves more or less rapidly towards a new type. It is as if the national character shaped the philological mass into a new form in order to adapt it to its own requirements. The innate tendencies of the aboriginal people will, in such cases, appear in a continuous struggle against the invading language and its natural forms and laws.

Now, it is evident that, from the point of view of national psychology, what matters is not the philological inheritance from a language now dead, but the features of the new language which are the direct outcome of the national character which has brought it into existence. Thus, what is significant in the "Latin" languages is not that they are alike in grammar and vocabulary—an accident of history—but that the Latin, from which they all come, has evolved so differently under the several national characters which it had to express.

Let us listen to our co-Europeans with this idea in mind. We shall be surprised to find how revealing their words—merely as words—become to us as expressions of character. The German word, a voluminous encyclopaedia of the idea which it embodies; the Italian word, a relish which the speaker tastes and enjoys; the English word, a snapshot of the act; the French word, a diagram of the object; the Spanish word, the object itself four-square before our eyes.

I

There is deep satisfaction in the thought that English—the language of the man of action—is a monosyllabic language. For the man of action, as we know, lives in the present, and the present is an instant with room for no more than one syllable. Words of more than one syllable are sometimes called in English "dictionary" words, that is, words for the intellectual, for the bookworm, for the crank, almost for the un-English. They are marvellous, those English monosyllables, particularly, of course, those which represent acts. Their fidelity to the act which they represent is so perfect that one is tempted to think English words are the right and proper names which those acts were meant to have, and all other words but pitiable failures. How could one improve on *splash*, *smash*, *ooze*, *shriek*, *slush*, *glide*, *squeak*, *coo*? Who could find anything better than *hum*, or *buzz*, or *howl*, or *whir*? Who could think of anything more sloppy than *slop*? Is not the word *sweet* a kiss in itself, and what could suggest a more peremptory obstacle than *stop*?

Such persistence in success cannot be explained away as a mere whim of nature. It is in fact one of the ways in which there is shown at work that infallible sense of matter which we have observed as one of the features of the English character. But in the monosyllabic tendency of the language, other English features co-operate, as for instance, the utilitarian sense which disregards all considerations but results, quick and efficient service. Utilitarian and empirical, the Englishman sees no difficulty in cutting down *perambulator* to *pram*, *omnibus* to *bus*, *bicycle* to *bike*. He is helped here by his indifference to mere matters of form. The English language has an exceptional capacity for swallowing and digesting foreign words without taking the trouble to cook them. From *desesperado* he makes *desperado*. Brunette may suggest a delightful coquettish vision to a Frenchman, yet in English it means no more than a certain hue of human skin, and may be applied to a sergeant-major. *Nurse*, in its origin so bountifully feminine, was first dried up in order to pass from nursery to hospital, and then changed sex and became *male nurse*.

Such linguistic adventures are only possible with a language endowed with the flexibility of the English language. The differences between masculine and feminine, between noun, verb, and adjective do not affect the shape of the English word. Let us observe in passing the correspondence between this feature of the English language and a well-known feature of the English character, i.e. its empirical tendency, its refusal to bind itself beforehand and to cross the bridge before coming to it. Verbal forms prejudge the use to be made of the words which are caught in them. The Englishman keeps his words in an interchangeable state, so that he can put one and the same verbal tool to any use he likes at the time it is to be used. His words are equally apt to turn right or left, up or down, as time and tide require.

The final adjustment of each word to its function is in English a matter mostly of intonation. The vital element is, therefore, particularly strong. But the inflexions of voice and manner which enable the speaker to express himself concretely, though manifesting themselves through the individual, are social in character, and should be considered as part of the language on an equal footing with its vocabulary and syntax. Thus the vital element of the English language is not, strictly speaking, personal, but social. It might, in a way, be considered as the linguistic manifestation of the genius for spontaneous organization of the Englishman, since it is a social force acting, if and when necessary, in order to "organize" the language at the moment when such organization is needed. The evolution of the language still points that way. Three verbal auxiliaries, *would*, *should*, and *had*, are in everyday speech reduced to one only form, 'd. The important, nay, the essential differences between the three respective meanings are conveyed by tone and context, i.e. by the "language community." It will be seen that in the English language, as in English life, the individual is but little; the community gives him his value.

This becomes particularly clear if due significance is given to the fact that, in English, the tonic accent of the sentence is more important than the tonic accent of the word. Not that English words are entirely without a tonic accent—English words at any rate in which there is room for it, since we cannot expect it in monosyllabics—but, when a word has more than one syllable, its tonic accent is energetic, usually placed at the beginning, or towards the beginning of the word, and clearly marked. (Let us note, in passing, that the tonic accent becomes singularly vacillating in very long words such as *laboratory*; a feature to be related to the dislike of the English mind to enter on a long argument with any degree of precision.) The tonic accent is the predominant factor in the personality of the word. The English word is therefore far from lacking in personality. Yet, as we have observed, the tonic accent of the sentence predominates over the tonic accent of the words which compose it, and, in this again, the national language is a faithful image of the national character, which tends, not so much to merge individuals in the community, as to group them harmoniously in it and give them a social stress over and above the personal stress.

The tendency to action explains, no doubt, the admirable aptitude of the English language to turn anything into a verb. Other languages have to disguise words with verb terminations before than can use them as verbs. Thus in French from *graisse*, *graisser*; in Spanish from *hierro*, *herrar*. The Englishman takes *grease*, *iron* as substantives and turns them into verbs by a mere twist of his will, by filling up the inert noun with a momentum of action. No mental operation is involved. Now, verbs are word representations of acts and the above observation should be interpreted in the light of this fact. It amounts to this: languages in which words must take a preordained form in order to become verbs correspond to peoples who must think their actions and see them as categories; while the English language, with its direct turning into verbs of any word which happens to be passing, suggests the purely empirical people for whom thought and action go generally together.

This parallel between a feature of the language and a feature of the character is confirmed by its own exception. There is a whole category of English words which cannot be turned into verbs without a previous transformation which casts them into a standard mould, such for instance: *system*, *systematize*. They will be found to be words which belong to the intellectual field, as opposed to words of action; and we may point out in passing that, while in English action-words are turned into verbs with the utmost ease and even grace, the transformation of thought-words into verbs is usually cumbrous and elaborate in contrast with the ease which distinguishes such a verbal operation in the intellectual language—French.

The direct manner of the man of action, superbly illustrated by the direct way in which his language gets hold of any odd word and turns it into a verb, just as it is, in its native form and vigour, seems to go with a kind of impatience, the impatience of the man of action, as manifested in the summary way in which the language gets rid of verbal endings whenever possible. Thus the Englishman chops down *beginnen* into *begin*, and *commencer* into *commence*.

Similar tendencies explain why English verbs should have been simplified by evolution to a degree unknown in other languages, for this evolution aimed at establishing the present as the key-tense of the English conjugation. We know that the present is the tense of the man of action, and therefore we are not surprised to find that it is on the present that the English verb is built. The fact that all English verbal forms are simply the present tense accompanied by auxiliaries, which might be styled verbal adjectives, clearly suggests an empirical mind. We are here in the presence of a case similar to that mentioned above in connexion with action-words. Other languages *think* the future, the present, the subjunctive, and the indicative as intellectual categories, and therefore grant them definite forms, the abstract character of which is shown by the fact that they are the same for all verbs. But in English, the present form stands out clearly and is accompanied by a verbal adjective such as *shall* or *should*, which shows that the past and the future are felt as modified aspects of the present, of the here and now which is the immediate reality, one might almost say the only reality, of the empirical Englishman. This fact is aptly illustrated in the particular verbal form attached to certain kinds of future, such as in the phrase *when he comes*. The event described in such a phrase is obviously in the future, but the verbal form is the present pure and simple. When providing for a future condition, the Englishman therefore imagines it in the present. A brilliant proof of empiricism provided by the language.

Further examples may be found by observing the peculiar character of English vowels. "Vowels," I have said, in order to humour for a while a general delusion on the subject. The English language is supposed to have many vowels. I believe they have even been counted and estimated at twenty-six. This is mere science. The fact is that there is only one English vowel or, if preferred, only one vowel-mass, a vowel-cloud, a vowel-sea, a vowel-nebula. It is universal and protean. It is now broad and dark, now sharp and pointed, now deep and musical, now dry and short, now stiff and opaque, but it is always vague and always ambiguous and shifting, so that it hardly ever ends as it begins, and it seems always to be turning up from somewhere, appearing for a time, then withdrawing somewhere else, dragging along with it bits of uncomfortable consonants. The English vowel-nebula is the true representative of the English empirical mind, always fluid and in process of becoming, only in actual use at the fleeting moment of the present which action fills, and even then, always ready to compromise.

That there is such a thing as an English grammar is a debatable point. The fact is that a grammar, being something like a pre-established regulation of the language, could hardly appeal to a people which frets at the mere idea of rules. Whatever rules may be said to exist in English are so rusty and exception-eaten as to amount to very little indeed. The strongest force of cohesion in language, as in every other form of English life, is social leadership. Fashion, as dictated by "our betters," is the living grammar which all Englishmen willingly follow. There are in England two centres of such leadership in matters of language: society and the university. They mix but do not blend.

Hence a few curious consequences. On the university side, the uncouth, pedantic form which many words drag into plain English from the classical dictionaries, whence they came: *formulae*, *aesthetic*, *archaeology*, *genii*, *rhythm*; on the social side, the chaotic pronunciation (or spelling—it comes to the same) of the language, a chaos due to a galaxy of causes, some of which are even sound and reasonable, but the mass of which doubtless must be the accumulated effect of centuries of capricious affectations. The empirical and vague characteristics of the national genius allow a considerable elasticity in matters of pronunciation. "Should you say 'aheether' or 'eether'?" a Yorkshireman was asked, and he answered: "You can say oother." What is called *King's English*, which leaves beyond its somewhat official borders stretches of untold philological wealth, itself comprises an impressive variety of accent, from middle-class Glasgow to scholarly Balliol, from Mayfair to Salisbury Plain, from Liverpool Docks to the Stock Exchange. The strongest moulding influence over this plastic matter is undoubtedly society. But society has no rules, no particular erudition, not even a definite standard of taste, and under its guidance the language evolves in perfect empirical freedom, happy in its ever-ready adaptability to events, the despair of all men who believe in logic.

2

French is a "Latin" language. What has Latin become after having served several centuries as the vehicle of French thought?

Let us look at a few words. *Anima* has become *âme*; *cathedra*, *chaire* and *chaise*; *calidum*, *chaud*; *aqua*, *eau*; *famem*, *faim*; *accapare*, *achever*; *benedicere*, *bénir*; *Augustus*, *août*. The Latin word is in all cases, not merely simplified, not merely shortened, but flattened out. It is obvious that we are here in the presence of a linguistic evolution wholly different from that which simplified English words. The English language handles the words very much like the peasant who chops off leaves and twigs from the stalk which he wants to use as a stick. In the French case we observe a simplification carried out under laws which, while respecting a certain framework within the word, schematize it and reduce it to its essential elements. It is a process similar to that of abstraction. The words of the French language are like geometrical projections of the Latin words. In passing from Latin into French, words seem to lose their volume and colour and to become flat, black-and-white diagrams of their Latin forms.

Such is, in particular, the effect of the loss of the tonic accent. In French the Latin tonic accent disappears and all but the so-called mute syllables bear exactly the same stress. No doubt the Latin tonic accent plays an important role in the new word (French) as it did in the old word (Latin), but, while in the Latin word it was, so to say, the centre of gravity of a body having volume and mass, it is, in the French word, the mere centre of a geometric figure, the point round which the projection of the Latin word on to the plane of the French language has taken place. This fact must be considered as the linguistic manifestation of that intellectual and abstract outlook which makes the French mind disregard the vagaries of life in order to bring some intellectual order into its vision. We find here the same analogy between linguistic features and collective life which we had occasion to observe when commenting on the English language. English words we saw—like English citizens—free and individual, yet always ready to serve in sentences spontaneously regulated by the laws of a phrase-accent, eminently social in their unwritten infallibility. We see now, not merely French words, but even French syllables, put all on the same plane, as we saw French citizens in the State, all vital differences abstracted, on a footing of perfect equality. Let us note in passing that this important feature of French speech is also in harmony with the tendency to clearness so typical of the French character. Clearness demands an equal, well-cut enunciation of every part of each word. It is as if that "separating-power," which we discussed in connexion with intellectual vision, were at work here to separate each syllable and make it stand out in its place as a clearly drawn line of the word-diagram.

French is a most carefully pronounced language. Every letter receives its value and remains in its place. French does not tolerate the capricious inversions of letters, the traditional singularities, the social affectations, the elastic latitude which make English spelling and pronunciation the grammarian's despair and the delight of the exception-hunter. French pronunciation is accurate and precise, and it follows its own rules with such perfect docility that it might even be erected into a deductive science as exact as French *droit*.

One of the most potent amongst the factors which contribute to render French pronunciation so clear and precise is the clearness and precision of French vowels. In English the one vowel-nebula is perpetually mobile, and, save in short-vowel words such as *snap*, is always compound, not merely a diphthong, but a sound floating within a range of three or more simple vowels. French vowels, on the contrary, are always simple, and diphthongs do not exist. Let us observe this fact and give it its true importance. Old French had diphthongs; it inherited them from its Latin mother. But French genius is opposed to the ambiguity which diphthongs imply. *C'est ça ou c'est pas ça.* Diphthongs try to be both. The evolution of the French language has resolved them into one or other of their components, or, more often still, into a third sound which is, phonetically speaking, their logical conclusion (thus *au* into *o*).

French owes some of its clearness also to the harmonious proportions bewteen vowels and consonants, which is one of its typical features. The vowel gives spirit to the language; the consonant weight and matter. Some languages, such as German, are overburdened with consonants; others, even if more evenly composed, mix their vowels and consonants in irregular groups, owing to an excessive frequency of diphthongs. The absence of diphthongs and a happy balance between consonants and vowels give the French language, in which each syllable stands by itself, an equal measure of breath and sound. The typical French word is composed of vowels and consonants in almost perfect alternate succession.

This feature contributes also to that black-and-white impression which the French language is apt to produce. We have observed it in connexion with the shortening up of words as they pass from Latin into French, becoming, so to say, their own diagrams. We find it again as the result of the French tendency to reduce the coloured vowels (*a*, *i*, *o*, *u*) to the colourless and non-committal *e*. *E* is the key-vowel of the French language, and substitutes itself for nearly every other value in the immense majority of French words as compared with their Latin origins. This is particularly the case with the mute *e* ending, so frequent as to be almost the normal one in French. It is to be found in words evolved from origins so different in form as *vaccam—vache*, *carmen—charme*, *asparagum—asperge*, *arborem—arbre*, *amat—aime*. But it applies also to the transformation of such different forms as *cellarium—cellier*, *christianum —chrétien*, *clarum—clair*, *hospitalem—hôtel*, *amare—aimer*, and even to the evolution towards *e* revealed by the transformation of Latin *o* into French *e*, such as in *bovem—bœuf*.

To be sure, complete sets of phonetic laws have been carefully drafted to preside over such evolutions. But what interests us here is not the how, but the why. The how is phonetics; the why, psychology. The fact that the French language should have guided its phonetic evolution towards the predominance of the vowel *e* over all other vowels seems to us of the utmost psychological importance, for it comes to confirm all we hold about the geometrical, abstract, black-and-white character of the French representation of life.

It reminds us also of the French sense of moderation and

measure, for *e* is the middle vowel, equally distant from the full-blown vowels *a*, *o*, *u* (oo) and from the unrestrained *i* (ee). While French was still in the making, the south influenced the evolution of the language towards fuller vowels than did the north. Such words as *laborem*, *horrorem*, *furorem*, *amorem* evolve towards forms in *our* in the south, in *eur* in the north. In some cases the south triumphs (*amour*); some other words such as *labour*, *labeur* evolve simultaneously towards two forms, but in the immense majority of cases the north prevails (*horreur*, *fureur*, *supérieur*). And it is worth noticing that the *ou* form is closely linked up with a shade of fullness, excess, lack of measure, exaggeration. The *Dious*, in *Cyrano de Bergerac*, when the cadets of Gascogne enter the stage swearing abundantly in the name of Dious, instead of the northern *Dieu*, is a typical example. But may we not find another in the fact that *amorem*, a passion whose very nature is inimical to the sense of moderation, should have been guided by this same psychological force towards the full and frank *amour*? Now the significance of such evolution goes deeper than mere phonetics. While the *eu* form suggests measure and moderation, the form *ou* expresses fullness and over-abundance. *Little* in French is expressed by *peu*; *much* by two full vowel-sounds: *beaucoup*. Thus the fact that the tendency of vowel-sounds to evolve towards one of the varieties of *e* should be the dominant tendency in French vowel evolution must be considered as one of the many manifestations of the group of features connected with the sense of measure inherent in the French character.

It will be seen that in thus depriving its vowels of their mass and colour, the French language reflects the tendency towards abstraction of the French mind. But we have also noted that French pronunciation is neat and precise. We may, therefore, say of the language, what we have observed of the mind of France, that it is both abstract and precise. An identical conclusion would be reached by a study of French style. An English humorist—and nothing inspires English humour like the observation of the French—once said that French was the language in which it was most difficult to speak the truth. Now this is a most unfair statement if taken without qualification, for, on the contrary, its very clearness and precision make the French language one in which statements must crystallize with neat edges and planes, which accurately limit their meaning. But the English humorist was probably more used to *sense* truth than to think it, and therefore was apt to feel that, in thus cutting cubes and pyramids out of the mass of reality, the French language failed to render its living spirit. In short, what worries the English in the French language is that it falls naturally into an abstract style. Abstract and precise, it sins therefore twice over against English tastes, which are concrete and vague.

Such inner necessities of the language determine its grammatical structure. The French language has, if anything, stiffened the grammatical framework which it received from Latin; each piece in this framework is clearly labelled and fulfils its definite function, each piece has therefore its definite shape. Nor is this arrangement of its grammatical system merely theoretical. In actual use French is perhaps the most rigid language of Europe. "Cela n'est pas français" is a sentence often passed in French and always without hesitation.

Characteristically enough, one of the features which contribute to give the French language its rigidity is its dislike of inversions. The English can say *home he went*; the Spaniards more freely, *a casa se fué*. The French must say *il s'en alla chez lui*. They are tied to logical order, prisoners of it. This feature is a manifestation of that French tendency to leave nothing to chance, to foresee everything, and to ensure clearness by all possible means. Thus in order to ask *What is it?* the French language might be content with *Qu'est-ce?* but the sound of these three words is a simple monosyllable, and the Frenchman, fearing obscurity, lengthens it to *Qu'est-ce que c'est?* and even to *Qu'est-ce que c'est que ça?* The negative form, *ne . . . pas, ne . . . point*, must undoubtedly be ascribed to the same tendency. A short word, such as *ne*, based on but one vowel, and that obscure, is a wholly inadequate instrument for conveying the important idea of negation in a language so bent on clearness. This explanation would seem to be confirmed by the fact that the two words which have remained as auxiliary negatives, *pas* and *point*, should both begin with the same strong letter *p*, while the other words such as *mie* or *mot*, equally well placed from the historical point of view to play the same role, but weaker as sounds, have been lost.

Logic and clearness are therefore the main laws of French grammar. As an illustration in point, let us compare the English and French forms of an hypothetical future. The Englishman, we saw, places himself in the future, turns that future into a present, and says *when he comes;* the Frenchman remains firmly on his logical ground, and his way of saying it is *lorsqu'il viendra.*

Thus we see that the life and evolution of the French language are governed by intellectual laws and not by social and empirical laws, as is the case with the English language. The French Academy is not, of course, the legislator, but it is the codifier of such laws. And it is precisely because it codifies and does not legislate that it is respected. For the French Academy governs in a sphere in which order is spontaneous, since it is the expression of an intellectual tendency inherent in the race.

3

It is a fact of experience that of the three languages here considered Spanish is the most tiring for the speaker. French is spoken mostly with the teeth and lips; English between the teeth and palate; Spanish between the palate and throat. Of the three languages Spanish is the one which draws most on the inner man. You may drawl English; you may pronounce French trippingly on the tongue; you must speak Spanish fully and frankly and fill up with your own life's breath the ample volume of its words. It is therefore a language fit for the people which is itself fully whenever it is at all. Its words are not like English monosyllables, snapshots of acts; nor like clear French polysyllables, black-and-white diagrams of their Latin originals.

They are the objects themselves four-square, with all their volume, colour, and mass.

Nothing could better illustrate the force of the psychological tendencies which acted on the Latin inheritance common to French and Spanish than the difference between the words evolved by the two languages from one and the same Latin root. Thus: *âme—alma, chaire—cátedra, chaud—caldo, eau— agua, faim—hambre, achever—acabar, bénir—bendecir, août— agosto*. In each case the schematization which typifies the verbal evolution of French is absent in Spanish, the evolution of which is limited to changing the Latin ending *um* into a more luminous *o*, and, in the case of verbs, to the dropping of the weak vowel ending. The dominant vowels of the language are thus *o* and *a*—the fullest and the most sonorous. Their pronunciation, moreover, is straightforward and simple. Spanish is, perhaps, the European language in which the number of types of vowels is smallest. This feature suggests again mass, colour, and volume rather than nuance as with the most delicately tinted French vowel, or rather than vagueness and fluidity as is the case with the English vowel-cloud.

Such an impression is, if anything, enhanced by the laws of the tonic accent in Spanish. In English we know the most important tonic accent is that of the sentence, not that of the word. Moreover, so far as words themselves are concerned, most of them are monosyllabic signs of action, while polysyllabic words are generally stressed at the beginning, thus: *carpenter, midshipman, deputy*. This tendency comes out even more clearly in the case of compound words, such as *windowsill*. It explains alliteration, the true English form of rhyming. It suggests the dominance and the energy of action. French spreads the accent evenly over the whole word; it corresponds to a language in which, for the sake of clearness, all is put on the same level and neatly brought out. French, in fact, is a language in two dimensions. It is no longer nature but art. Spanish is a contrast to English in that the word-accent is stronger than the accent of the sentence, so that it is somewhat "stonier" when heard, more like an undisciplined company of individuals. Moreover, within each word the Spanish language tends to stress the penultimate syllable, but with quite different effects from those produced in English in similar cases. *Widow*, *casa* seem at first sight to follow an identical tonic law. Both are disyllabic words stressed on the first syllable. But there are three differences. Firstly, *widow* wavers between *wid-ow* and *wi-dow* while *casa* sounds clearly *ca-sa*. Secondly, the vowel *ow* is vague and poor, apt to be blurred, while the *a* of *sa* demands and obtains its full measure of breath; and thirdly, the actual stress is stronger in English than in Spanish. It will be seen that in the aggregate these three differences tend all to increase the force and the weight of the accent in the English word, which is thus forcibly pulled back on to its first syllable; while the Spanish word is almost evenly split by its accent into two equal parts. This evenness of the Spanish accent is evident in the immense majority of its trisyllabic words, most of which are stressed in the middle syllable—*sombrero*. This, with few exceptions, is a universal law of the language. Most Spanish words are accented on their centre of gravity. Thus the mechanical laws of the language confirm the psychological laws of the race. The very words are individualistic and self-centred.

This individual energy concentrated in each separate word tends sometimes to become excessive and unruly. Hence the sense of "throwing" which is so characteristic of Spanish when unguardedly spoken, as if words were flung, rather than drawled as in English, or deliberately doled out as in French. Such is perhaps the psychological explanation of the Spanish proclivity towards diphthongs or triphthongs. The French language, we know, resolves its diphthongs into clear vowels, preferring even an hiatus to a diphthong. Words such as *li-ai-son*, with its three syllables, are typically French in this respect. The Spanish language, on the contrary, finds a diphthong more congenial than an hiatus. Thus, from the Latin *regina*, stressed in its middle syllable, through *re-i-na* in three syllables with an hiatus, Spanish has evolved *rei-na*. The tendency is not merely to be found in the past as one of the agencies whereby Latin becomes Castillian, but is still active in our time, and contributes as much as any other to the evolution of the present-day language. Thus the *ado* endings are normally pronounced *ao* (*delgado—delgao*). It will be seen that in all these cases the diphthong tendency forcibly expresses the sense of "throwing" born of cumulative energy. This fact becomes particularly clear when extreme cases are considered, such as the popular tendency to concentrate several vowels in a triphthong; for instance, from *cuidado*, *cuidao*, and then *cudiao*.

Such whip-like effects suggest energy, and in this feature the Spanish language would appear to resemble the English, which is also, as we know, an energetic language. But a closer consideration will show that, while the energy of the English language is contained within the word, carried with it, one might even say *utilized* by it, the energy of Spanish words is let off, thrown off. It is energy for its own sake. Let us note the static character of this feature. Though there may be an apparent paradox in attributing a static character to an outburst of energy, the fact remains that energy is not dynamic unless it is used, since only then does it become a *force*. English is the dynamic language *par excellence*. Energy *qua* energy is static. Spanish is static. When forcible it is so for the sake of being forcible; when calm for the sake of calm.

Hence, its tendency to sobriety. Let us observe it first in the words themselves. Spanish words, compared with English monosyllables and with French verbal diagrams, are fuller and bulkier, yet they produce an impression of sobriety, because, though they are full enough to carry the bulk of the object, they are no fuller than necessary, they do not overflow, they do not "wave" or flap with superfluous texture. This can easily be felt in a comparison with Italian words; it will be seen that, on the whole, Spanish is more shorn than Italian: *dottore—doctor, omettere—omitir, infelice—infeliz, ambizione—ambicion, universale—universal*. In all these cases the sense of throwing and the somewhat brusque simplicity of the Spanish language is in contrast with the softer cadence which Italian derives from its final *e*, not mute as in French, but constituting a kind of coda to the song of the word.

It cannot be denied that Spanish has a grammar; whether this grammar is generally respected is another question altogether. Here is a clear case of conflict between the foreign genius and the genius of the native people in whose mental soil the invading language was transplanted. The Spanish people received a grammar from the Romans. They have been fighting against it ever since, and this struggle is one of the main elements in the evolution of the Spanish language. Under the various aspects of this struggle between the language and its grammar—i.e. between Spanish and Latin—may be observed the efforts of the Spanish character to force the alien language to adapt itself to its new country and people. Inversions, short-cuts, all sorts of breaks and seams are opened on the smooth soil of the grammar by the volcanic spontaneity of the people who speak it. Rules become elastic or are dropped. There is a feeling of freedom and breadth in sharp contrast with the rigidity of the terse French speech and style; it is more unaccountable, more unruly than the empirical way of English, which, even though not bound down by rules, follows its own instinctive laws. And withal there is in this spontaneous language a deep-lying wisdom born of the synthetic tendency of the people who speak it. No better example could be given than the Spanish version of that hypothetical future which has served us already in comparing English and French. *When he comes* says the Englishman, forcing the future to become the present, since from the present he will not budge. *Quand il viendra* says the Frenchman, seeing the future abstractly in the future to which it belongs *de droit*. *Cuando venga* says the Spaniard, with a subjunctive, which puts the event not in a future theoretically *de droit*, therefore certain, but in an all-round and vital future, with all the uncertainty which attaches to events which we do not hold yet. Thus in his subjunctive the Spaniard manages to satisfy his synthetic principle, holding at one and the same time the thing and its opposite.

Such an attitude of rebellion against grammar may perhaps

explain why grammatical questions appeal to Spaniards, though they do not seem to appeal to other peoples more grammatically minded. It is like the attraction which theological questions have for the sceptic. A grammatical discussion in England is unthinkable because there is no grammar, and grammar is theory anyhow; it is rare in France, because grammar is well known and universally respected, in fact taken for granted; but, in Spain, grammatical rules and their exceptions, and above all the evolution of both exceptions and rules, are so intertwined that the subject is always alive. Hence the peculiar position occupied by the Spanish Academy. Why an Academy in Spain? Of course in imitation of the French; but while in England the cohesive authority over the language comes from social leadership, and in France from that government or assembly of the republic of letters called L'Académie Française, in Spain the real leader of evolution is the people—the people of all classes of course, but the people, in that it knows neither organization nor hierarchy. The Academy decrees this or that, and as was to be expected, often gets far away from realities. For a long time the Spanish Academy insisted on defining the pronunciation of v as equivalent to that of the French or English v, ignoring the fact that the Spanish people refuses to pronounce it otherwise than as Spanish b. Thus in the matter of academies as in that of grammar the parallel leads to the same conclusion. In England, none; in France, grammar and Academy in harmony with the national genius, and therefore respected; in Spain, grammar and Academy both alien to the national genius and both neglected.

VI

Art and Letters

IN THE BEGINNING OF ART THERE IS PASSION. THE FIRST INSTANT of art is a touch felt within—whether from beyond or merely from outside does not matter for our present purpose. This touch starts the soul vibrating. From the moment when it takes place in the passive soul of the artist till the production of the work of art and its further absorption by the artistic life of the community, there exists a long and complex gamut of phases in each of which new elements—intellectual, volitional, and, finally, extra-individual—come to complicate and enrich the initial stage.

In ordinary language, opinions on the art of this or that nation are based on the observation of the main facts connected with its artistic life; they include the quality of the inspiration of its artists, together with the average level of beauty of its household furniture and the aesthetic value of its folk-lore. Even if sufficient for everyday consumption, opinions thus formed would be more misleading than illuminating for our purpose.

I

Now, if it be true that the first instant of art belongs to passion, we must expect to find Spain the richest of our three nations in the raw material of art. And this is, in fact, what experience shows. Of the three countries, Spain is the only one in which an aesthetic attitude is natural, spontaneous, innate, and general. The river of life flows in the Spanish people, carrying with it like rich gold sands these "instants" of aesthetic sensibility, which shine here and there in the multitude. Hence the exceptional wealth of popular art. The strongly popular character of Spanish art is a byword with students of literature and music. It becomes evident in such combinations of these two arts as the popular song. It may be observed that the popular song confirms all we know already about the spontaneity and the individualism of the Spanish character, for, like Spanish popular music in general, it is not choral but the song of the lone man. One of its most beautiful genres is even known as "Solitudes" (*Soleares*).

That art is, in Spain, a spontaneous and universal attitude is evident to the most unobservant. In differing degrees, according to local climate, occupation, and economic conditions, it is one of the most potent manifestations of popular life, influencing directly the house, the dress and personal attire, the language, habits of living, of travel, ceremonies, religion. The obvious objection is that life is not always artistic, still less beautiful, in Spain. But this, though well founded as a statement, is unfounded as an objection, for an artistic, or rather an aesthetic attitude does not necessarily mean an artistic achievement. Far from it. Precisely because art in Spain is always, as chemists say, *in its native state*, it is often unripe for consumption. Like the fruits of nature, the fruits of art require a maturing process which must take place under the light of the intellect.

The success of Spanish art is in inverse ratio to its distance from nature, and in this observation must be found the key to numerous characteristics of Spanish artistic life. Thus its "untranslatable character," the strong local flavour which typifies it. Spanish art, whatever its manifestations, is, above all, Spanish; one might even say that it is more Spanish than art. For in it nature has the strongest say from the fact that Spanish nature is in itself aesthetic. Thus we touch again that vital and integral character which we recognized before in all forms of Spanish life, and particularly in those closely connected with passion. There are some forms of Spanish art which are hardly more than spontaneous movements of life without any training or conscious attempt at form. A typical example is dancing. Spanish dancing is untranslatable. It must be performed by a Spanish dancer or else result in failure.[1]

One other feature of Spanish art which follows from its close dependence on nature is that it is at the same time strongly individualistic yet strongly national. Let us observe Spanish painting, for instance, though our remarks would equally apply to any other art. How little in common there is between Ribera, Velazquez, El Greco, Goya, Picasso, Zuloaga, and yet how forceful the impression of their country in them all. The paradox is more apparent than real, for the strong individualism of Spanish art is but the unavoidable consequence of its volcanic character. It is, we have said, more nature than art, and therefore, precisely because all these Spaniards are so strongly

---

1. As an illustration, the gallant attempt made by a company of excellent Swedish ballet-dancers to interpret Albeniz's music—a scene which, performed by a group of Spanish women, would have been full of vigour and natural ardour became, in the more conscious northerners, a show of wilful brutality.

themselves and therefore so different as men, they are so
strongly Spanish, and therefore so equally Spanish-like.

A digression may perhaps be permitted here in order to point
out that we are in the presence of one of those symmetrical
features, the recurrence of which gives strength and balance
to our triangular structure. Spanish artists, though wholly individualistic, manifest spontaneously the community of Spain.
This fact is in strict symmetry with the genius for spontaneous
co-operation of the Englishman, which makes English men of
action (the type symmetrical with Spanish artists), though acting independently, manifest spontaneously in action the unity
of England.

A third consequence of the spontaneity of Spanish art is the
all-important role which improvisation plays in it. We know
that, in its essence, art in Spain is more a gift of nature than a
conquest of man. It is genius rather than talent. The Spanish
artist is therefore apt to let nature produce in him free from
all critical fetters.

The contrast between the strength of its creative genius and
the weakness of its critical talent is the key-note of Spanish
artistic development. It may be observed equally in plastic arts,
music, or literature. It explains the disparity of the various
artists who happen to be producing at the same period, with
hardly any other feature in common than the fortuitous fact of
their being coevals. It explains also the inequality of the production of each artist.

Colour is the predominant category of Spanish art. Colour
is the spontaneous gift of nature to the artist, that which leaps
to the eye. Drawing, composition, arrangement, purpose are
more complex and later elements. Colour is the first impact of
nature on our senses. It is therefore in colour that Spanish art
manifests itself in its strength. This may seem at first sight
somewhat paradoxical. Spanish classic painters do not revel in
colour as do Italians, and particularly some of their Venetian
masters. But we are not dealing here with the respective intensi-
ties of colour in this or that painter. What concerns us is more
the respective value of the several elements of art in each artist.

Now it is evident that the general rule of Spanish painting is that it is predominantly painting and not coloured drawing. That is no doubt what El Greco had in mind when, in conversation with Pacheco, he said that Michael Angelo was "a good man but he could not paint." He could not, that is, paint direct, catch colour, and put it neat on canvas. What he did was to draw superbly and then to colour his drawing with a masterly hand. That is not the Spanish way. The impression of a great Spanish picture is not that of a coloured drawing, but of a flaming picture vibrating with living colour. Drawing in it is the mere result of colour, coming after it, as a consequence of it. For neither drawing nor composition is a first impression; they are complex observations which imply mental interference with the first impact of nature on the artist's soul.

This predominance of colour has its spiritual significance. It suggests that the Spanish artist perceives aesthetic objects bathed in that divine atmosphere for which the surface of things does not exist. Hence that feeling of rawness which Spanish pictures give—an impression of more than mere nakedness, as if things and people had been skinned and were showing their inner bodies to the world. More nature than art.

If Ribera or El Greco are compared to Raphael, the contrast will become impressive. Italian painting is an exquisite production of art. When clothing with its formal perception the deep insight and intellectual excellence of Leonardo, the result is a marvel; but even when its perfect form holds nothing but the smiling inanity of a Raphael, it is still a joy. An inane Spanish painter is an impossibility, for if his soul does not give itself to the canvas his art will not be sufficient to conceal the fact or to compensate for it. Ribera, El Greco are creators, transmitters of life, of their own life; Raphael is an exquisite designer who remains outside his work.

This and other features common to all Spanish art may perhaps be best observed in literature. George Borrow was, I believe, the first to remark that the Spanish language was superior to its literature. True, but is not that another way of saying "more nature than art"? In literary work the language stands at the "nature" end of the scale; it is, in fact, one of the raw-materials, or, if preferred, it is the work of art in which the conscious or artistic element is at its minimum. There is no doubt that, of the three languages, Spanish is the richest in spontaneous aesthetic effects. The pith, the energy, the picturesque quality, the sonority, the colour, the relief of Spanish short expressions, sayings, proverbs, popular songs are unrivalled.

In true harmony with all we know by now about Spanish social structure and history, the language is controlled and led by the people. So is literature. For even when literature is considered as an intellectual art in the hands of the learned, it is easy to observe that it is led by what is "people" in them. This amounts to saying that the creative element in Spanish literature predominates over the critical and conscious—a fact which, of course, determines the evolution of Spanish literature, since we know that it determines the evolution of all Spanish arts.[2]

No country has ever worked with greater disregard for rules in literature; yet in no country have men of letters believed in rules with greater faith; while the critical intellect of Spain asserts the rules of the literary game, its creative spirit breaks through them, and this opposition appears even in one and the same person. A score of names might be quoted, but all may be represented by Cervantes himself. *Don Quixote* contains in one and the same work the masterpiece of freedom from rules and the precepts which Cervantes respected in theory, and which in practice he fortunately forgot.

Cervantes may serve also as an example of another feature of Spanish literature and art in general—its concentration on man. This is, as we know, consonant with our views on the Spanish character in general. Landscape, for instance, plays an insignificant role in Spanish art. There is hardly a scene of nature in the whole of Spanish painting, and as to literature, we have to wait till the nineteenth century to read an outstanding

2. For further particulars on this point, see my *The Genius of Spain* (Oxford University Press, 1923).

description of nature in a Spanish book. Animals are also rare, save for references to one or two famous horses. Cervantes has written an immortal dialogue between two dogs, and he has, of course, made Rocinante and Rucio climb the steep heights to Parnassus with their respective masters, Don Quixote and Sancho. But that is about all, and even that is not genuine literature about animals, for neither the two dogs of the dialogue, nor the two quadrupeds in *Don Quixote* are presented from a really objective point of view. Their treatment is seen almost entirely from the point of view of man.

Man, in fact, is the centre and almost sole object of Spanish art. Man complete and precise. He fills the galleries of Spanish art with its unforgettable faces, created with so much intensity that one seems to remember them as one does friends. This sense of man concrete and precise, standing well individualized out of all the social or collective mass, is perhaps the strongest cumulative impression which Spanish art leaves behind. It comes from two sources: the subjects first, and then also the artist. With Spanish artists there is little or no handed-down tradition. Every man is wholly himself. So in the subject of Spanish art, what we see is not the type—a king, a general, a monk, a beggar—but a definite and well-defined man whose immortal soul is before us, though he happens to be wearing the clothes of this or that social rank. And it is so with authors. We never see merely a romanticist or a classicist, or a symbolist or a parnassist, but So-and-so, a man who has lived and learned by himself, and whose experience and knowledge begin and end with his own. Hence the heterogeneous character of Spanish art, as compared with French art. French art is a polished surface. Spanish art is a cross-section in human nature, cutting through every layer from the polished surface to the deepest formations. With Voltaire, with Anatole France, we are always in the same level of evolved and final excellence; with Quevedo, with Unamuno, we perceive the finished thought together with the elementary lucubrations. Every Spanish artist or man of letters begins afresh, from the bed-rock upwards, and as he gives himself without stint and without artifice, one finds in his work a blend of all the "qualities" from the primitive and naïve to the polished and sophisticated.

2

If passion is the first instant in the creative process, the second or form-giving phrase is controlled by the intellect; in its narrower and more concrete sense, the word *art* means precisely the form-giving power of the intellect moved by aesthetic emotion. France is therefore the country which excels in *Art*. She is, we know, poorer in the raw materials of art than Spain. Her people cannot compare with the Spanish in those spontaneous manifestations of aesthetic life which we have observed in Spain. The stress in France comes a little later in the creative process; it is a moment in which conscious effort and constructive thought have a wider share. Compare French with Spanish dancing; French feminine elegance with Spanish feminine movement and grace. French excellence will be found to reside in a greater intellectual control over the aesthetic emotion, even if the emotion itself is found to be less vigorous at its root. Hence the typical French distinction in all manual arts which require a close intellectual co-operation. If we want to seek in France the equivalent of those popular manifestations of aesthetic life which are so abundant in Spain in a primitive and unconscious vigour, we must turn to the almost universal ability of French men and women to arrange materials for life's uses with refinement and taste. In such artistic productions, the person is less present than in their Spanish equivalents. He is no longer himself the raw material of his art, both the channel and the flow of his emotion, but the artificer who, from the outside, works on the material and gives it shape.

Hence that sense of objectivity which we find as the keynote of all French art, in contrast with the subjective value of Spanish aesthetic manifestations. Even when the Spanish anonymous poet tells a ballad or drops a proverb in an impressive way, there seems to sound in his words a note of hidden lyricism. Objective as the truth may be as a truth, it is deeply subjective as an experience, and we feel it in the way it is said. Inversely, even in her most personal and lyrical moments, the French muse manages to keep a universal, an almost abstract outlook.

> Lleva el que deja, y vive el que ha vivido,[3]

says Machado in an immortal line, and this philosophical theory of general and abstract import is, nevertheless, inseparable from the poet who sings it, in a recognizable voice matured by experience. But when Baudelaire, in one of his most purely lyrical songs, draws the picture of the ideal land of love, he defines for all time the ideal features of the French mind in lines of cold and perfect beauty:

> Là tout n'est qu'ordre et beauté,
> Luxe, calme et volupté.[4]

Nor is this the only way in which French art manifests the intellectual nature of French character. Thus, in contrast with Spanish art, we find in France a better balance between the critical and creative elements. This can be observed in all the arts. French artists are conscious, they know where they are going, they know what they want. Racine, writing to a friend: "I have finished my tragedy; nothing remains but to write it," is a signal example of the French attitude towards creative work. It is all planned beforehand. Method, foresight, all the qualities we know to be those of the intellectual, shine with special brilliancy in French art.

This importance of the critical element at work in the individual contributes to keep up the high standard of formal excellence in French artistic work. The critical mind it is which puts into shape the shapeless lava thrown up by the imagination, after having purified it of all the worthless material which usually comes up with it. France is the teacher of the world in matters of form and of composition.

3. He takes with him who leaves behind; and he lives who has lived.
4. There everything is order and beauty,
   Radiance, calm and abundance.

Collectively, the vigour of the critical sense acts as a power-ful stimulus to the continuous study of artistic methods and technique. In the community as in the individual the assiduous presence of the intellect leads to consciousness. France works always under her own attentive eye, and each epoch knows, while working, that it is fulfilling a specific mission in the history of French art. "We are the knights of the Middle Ages," sings a chorus of ironclad men in a somewhat naïve musical comedy. A French literary and artistic generation al-ways feels happier when it is working under a banner and knows what it is doing.

Hence, those "isms" which appear periodically in the fields of literary and artistic criticism in France: symbolism, parnas-sism, romanticism, classicism are the names of generations, ban-ners, labels which the critical intellect affixes to this or that period of French literary and artistic life. They usually have but little meaning outside France, and if non-French critics were not, as they usually are, bamboozled by their brilliant French colleagues into believing that things must happen in the world as they happen in France, these "isms" would have remained what they really are, mere accidents of French life, perfectly clear and plausible in a country which evolves ac-cording to plan but inapplicable elsewhere. The least exclu-sively French of them—romanticism itself—when applied out-side of France leads to such utter absurdities as classifying Victor Hugo and Lamartine with Wordsworth, Byron, Schil-ler, Espronceda, and Leopardi—a strange cauldron of eagles.

In point of fact these "isms" of French artistic life must be considered in the same light as similar manifestations in other spheres of French history; for instance, the constitutions in French political life. They began like new political eras, with a manifesto and a fight. Victor Hugo's manifesto is a kind of declaration of the rights of man, and Théophile Gautier's famous red waistcoat is—if an Irish bull can be permitted in these matters—a kind of tri-colour.

This is of course another sign of the French tendency to plan out future work. Theory precedes practice; manifestoes precede poems and plays. Schools, "isms," and literary generations bring intellectual order into the anarchical field of aesthetic creation. So much for artists. But what about their works? A similar effort towards intellectual order leads to their classification in "genres." The garden of the Muses, as seen by a true French critic, resembles a botanical garden in which every work bears a label with its genus and species clearly set out. And it goes without saying that all these literary genres are rigorously defined by rules to which future artists must conform their creations if they do not want them to be branded as anti-natural monsters.

There is more than meets the eye in this invasion of literary lands by scientific preoccupations. A mind given to thought and thinking is predominantly interested in knowledge. France can no longer keep that wholly disinterested aesthetic attitude, spontaneous in the Spaniard. No sooner is he moved by an aesthetic emotion than the Frenchman instinctively and unconsciously deflects it towards intellectual aims, i.e. towards aims of knowledge. Hence the frequent use of a scientific vocabulary in literary spheres: *le document*; *un livre très documenté*; *qui révèle une observation pénétrante*; *recherches*. French literature would seem a branch of science, so keenly interested is it in truth rather than in beauty. Naturalism, *verism* (the very word is a revelation) are the manifestations of this scientific invasion of art. Impressionism itself, the nineteenth-century revolution in painting, is little more than the application of scientific methods to the technique of the painter, and a French artist can put forward as his greatest claim to glory that he painted a haystack under all possible laboratory—I mean natural—conditions of light and shade.

By dint of intellectual pressure the French artist tends therefore to lay special stress on clearness, order, and composition. Hence a tendency to simplify, almost to schematize, to abstract irrational elements. French art in fine gives the same black-and-white impression which the French mind and language leave in us. Just as Spanish painting is based on colour, French painting is based on drawing. France, along with northern

Italy, is the country in which black-and-white art reaches its highest excellence. But this observation, born in the sphere of the plastic arts, applies equally well to the other arts. French music, French literature are mostly line and composition.

More art than nature, more intellect than passion, more line than colour, French art is always on a high level of distinction and excellence, but shows no giants. Giants, in fact, are an insult to that sense of measure which we know to be a French psychological category. It is true that Victor Hugo, Rabelais, and Balzac may be mentioned as three living arguments against our case. But are they so very formidable as arguments? Balzac is impressive mostly as a man with an immense capacity for work and production. He is big rather than great. Moreover, in dealing with great French artists it must be borne in mind that they are *ex hypothesi* intellectuals with a greater proportion of passion in them than is usual in their country's type. This observation may suffice to explain many an apparent exception. Rabelais seems to have no sense of measure, but has it to such an extent that he can play with size without ever losing his proportions. And, moreover, when he sins against measure, he does it knowingly, and after having sized the leap. As for Victor Hugo, he is not wholly himself. Victor Hugo is not a self-contained artist; he is possessed of the idea that he is a genius, and that he must bellow genius-like and show big. In his way he also sins against measure wilfully and to show what he can do. But out of measure he is like a fish out of water—as a Frenchman is bound to be.

No, the strength of French arts and letters is not in its peaks, but in its general level. The truly specifically great French men are not geniuses but supreme talents: Voltaire, Racine, Anatole France. Like France herself, her art is even, cultivated, fine, and never overwhelmingly great. And this is one of the reasons why French culture is universal. It is the only culture which covers the whole world; for, being black-and-white, it does not lose so much in passing from country to country and from continent to continent as other cultures more varied and coloured, richer in irrational and untranslatable elements. The same qualities and shortcomings which make French culture universal make it less apt to receive and understand other cultures. Of course, the small minority, the well-read and well-trained critic can understand anything. France possesses today perhaps the best exponents in the world of other than French cultures. But her cultivated mind is, as a whole, less open to other cultures than are the cultivated people of most other countries, for, again, it is a mind given to rationalize, simplify, and project everything on the two-dimensional plane of the intellect, so losing many of the vital elements in which the essence of non-French culture often resides.

3

Considered in its first instant, the purely aesthetic sensation, which is the seed of art, is in itself its own justification for the man of passion. Evolved and worked out into a "work of art" by means of the form-giving intellect, it is also its own justification for the intellectual. Art, however, whether raw or finished, does not justify itself in the eye of the man of action. And this fact, which lies firmly rooted in the unexplained, the unargued, the unexpressed, and even the unconscious, is the crucial element in the artistic life of the English people.

The seed is lacking. England, therefore, provides as poor an atmosphere for the life of her great artists as does Spain for the life of her great men of action. The people do not feel art. We find thus, by a curious effect of symmetry, small groups of devoted men trying to preach the gospel of art to the English people as similar groups of devoted men try to preach to the Spanish people the gospel of collective action. No one who knows the two countries can fail to notice the strange likeness of the two movements, the striking family air between the two types of men. The preachers of virtue in Spain and the preachers of beauty in England have, amongst other common characteristics, that of being self-conscious about it.

For self-consciousness in art is, of course, inevitable in England. The process is here in its final stage. Unconscious in

Spain, conscious in France, art was bound to be self-conscious in England. For in Spain art is volcanic and springs up in the individual from cosmic forces; in France it is the result of an intellect trained to make the most of natural promptings; while in England it has to rely on the stimulus of social forces, traditions, and requirements.

The bulk of English art is, therefore, more subservient to the community than is the case in France or Spain. Its mood is less purely aesthetic, more blended with considerations of time and space, more anecdotical. The work of art in England must *tell a story*; art, in the terms of a famous business man, a protector of music, must "deliver the goods." The artist must hand over something tangible, substantial. The public are, of course, reasonable. They are quite willing to accept as substantial the soap bubbles made by a little boy, provided he is fair-headed and clean, and shows every sign of belonging to a good family, but there must be a story.

Let us recognize here that sense of matter and of the material which we have noted in due course as typical of the people of action. Not in vain is the story called the "matter" of the book. Nor will it do to argue that the story may be all in the succession of moods in a soul in pilgrimage, as in *Hamlet*. When H. B. Irving gave a scandalously abridged version of *Hamlet* at the Savoy, an utterly unintelligible version for any man understanding Shakespeare, he put forward that his aim had been to make the *story* of *Hamlet* stand out clearly. He meant the outward material events.

But, apart from the sense of matter and the material, this feature of English artistic life will recall to mind English utilitarianism. We know by now what to understand by such a word. We mean by it that tendency which expects fruits of action from every expense of energy. The story is the form which action takes in art. And, moreover, by insisting that art must have a story, the Englishman makes it carry an ethical load; it must mean something. It is all very well for the artist to say that his art is meant to convey an emotion. The true Englishman asks what is the good of an emotion, i.e. are your emotions fit to move the wheels of the social mill? If so, show it. If not, keep them to your unholy self.

Hence, the frequency of English works of art with an ethical meaning, or at least with an ethical intention, and the popularity, even amongst the educated, of such things as Watts's "Hope"—pictures in which the externals of art have been filled up with that most nobly utilitarian of notions, a lesson.

But the ethical is only one of the forms of the utilitarianism of action. The other is the social. Social influences act deeply on English art. The sense of social distinction is the predominant impression which remains in the mind after a mental review of the great English painters: Gainsborough, Reynolds, Romney, Constable, Landseer. A favourite criterion with English critics is whether the author is or is not a gentleman.[5]

Finally, it may be noted that the influence of a rich society is to be observed in the presentation of English works of art. Frames of pictures, stones and metals in sculpture, paper and binding in books reach a more exacting level in England than in France or Spain. We are, of course, at the other end of the artistic process. As we have been led to foresee, experience shows that while Spain is strongest in the initial phase, conception; and France in the middle phase, formation; England is strongest in the final phase, execution. As an example let us note the fine level reached in England by certain ancillary branches of literature, such as printing.

Of all the arts that which best tolerates the addition of unaesthetic matter is literature, and that is probably why literature is by far the best and most successful of English arts. Literature is in England eminently social. The novel is a direct reflexion of the life of the people, woven with all the complicated threads which cross and re-cross in so evolved a society. Along with the novel, England produces in abundance other kinds of works which would be incomprehensible, nay,

5. Not, to be fair, a purely social criterion in their minds, yet *mostly* social, and at any rate social in its origin.

which would not exist, were it not for the intensity of the social life which feeds them. To this kind belong books such as Boswell's *Johnson*, or Pepys's *Diary*, as well as the impressive mass of biographical works which is an English specialty, and, last but not least, the flow of memoirs and reminiscences which endeavour to give some kind of literary dignity to drawing-room gossip.

We may observe that, by definition, an artist is a man of passion. An English artist, therefore, is a man in whom there is a permanent conflict between passion and action tendencies. Hence the evolution of English literature should be determined by the play between the aesthetic and the ethical tendencies. Inasmuch as ethical tendencies are the disturbing factor in art (whether they be positive as in Wordsworth, or negative as in Oscar Wilde), the best English artists are to be found amongst those who sacrifice least to them. A survey of English literature will show how the two sets of tendencies intertwine, so that now the one, now the other predominates. With Wordsworth the ethical social tendency reaches its zenith. Wordsworth becomes the most representative English poet, the poet best appreciated in England and least abroad, the poet of goodness, purpose, and utility.

But in a greater or lesser degree that which he stands for manifests itself also in all but one or two of the great names of English literature, even in those who at first sight might appear least Wordsworthian. Shelley himself, the Shelley at least of the great poems, has a strong didactic and ethical propensity which prevents him from reaching poetical serenity. Hence the superiority of his shorter and more truly poetical works, such as the "Ode to the West Wind" or "Adonais," over his long poems, such as "Prometheus Unbound," which carry too great an ethical load really to soar as pure works of art.

This conflict between action and passion tendencies, always alive in English artistic circles, explains the permanent controversy between the "art for art" and the "art for improvement" schools. The scrap between Ruskin and Whistler is a typical example of this controversy—a scrap to which we owe that monument of "arty" self-consciousness, "The Gentle Art of Making Enemies." It is a controversy in which both sides manage to be in the wrong. It has produced that other tragic monument of self-conscious artistry—Oscar Wilde. The truth is that, though ethical tendencies should be absent from the mood in which the work of art is conceived, they should not be absent from the artist who enters into that mood. Far from it. Granted that the state of soul is wholly aesthetic, the richer that soul in intellectual and moral value, the greater the work of art.

Now we know that the English people tends to organize itself along the lines of a natural hierarchy led by an aristocracy. In direct contrast with the case of the Spanish people, literature in general and poetry in particular are in England the almost exclusive appanage of the upper classes. In these classes social and moral experience is particularly rich. Hence it is that English literature, though loaded with moral tendencies—and as such defective—is rich in moral substance—and as such valuable.

Hence also that when England produces a genius of passion, able in his poetic mood to stand aloof from all moral pre-occupations, his creations should reach such heights of excellence, for they are cast in the crucible of pure beauty, while made of the rich moral metal of the people of action.

Such seems to be the true explanation of this apparent paradox, that the usually inartistic, unpoetic people of England should have produced the greatest poets in Europe. Her poets are by definition men of passion, able—Shakespeare always, Keats nearly always, and the others often—to conceive their poems in a mood of serene contemplation—but, as men born of the people of action, endowed with a rich substratum of moral values. And it is obvious that such a combination is the ideal one for the creation of great art.

VII

Love—Patriotism—Religion

LOVE IN ITS NARROWER SENSE, RELIGION, AND PATRIOTISM ARE
ultimately three manifestations of Love in its wider sense. They
differ as to the object on which this Love exerts itself. The first
seeks for its object another human being of the opposite sex;
the second, the Divine Being; the third, the Country. The
object, therefore, is individual in love, universal in religion,
and national or racial in patriotism.

A. LOVE

I

Love has its roots in sex but its foliage and flowers are in the pure light of spirit. It is truly human in its complex impurity. It refuses to be dragged to earth by the cynic, or subtilized into the thin air of platonic heights by the idealist. Considered thus as an absolute, all-round, all-absorbing passion, it will be found to fit in with the most typical features of Spanish psychology.

And in actual fact, love is in Spain the vigorous human passion which we expect it to be. It is absolute, complete, exacting, and exhausting. It demands the complete surrender of the lover and possession without reservation. But to say that it demands is to misinterpret it, for it obtains without asking. Love is in Spain as spontaneous, as uncalculating, as volcanic as Spanish nature would lead us to expect.

This all-round character of Spanish love explains why it is at the same time deeply carnal yet strangely chaste. The mutual gift of the body is but the natural manifestation in the realm of matter of the most intimate relations established by the blending of the individual "passions," i.e. the two individual life-streams turned by love into one. No intellectual or ethical elements come to disturb the free flow of a passion which feels itself in so direct a contact with life's own sources. No social elements come to complicate or alter its primitive laws. The two sexes keep to their original and natural roles; the assertive and possessive man, the self-denying and self-giving woman. However wilful, capable, and energetic—and Spanish women often are all three—women accept as a matter of course, nay, as a matter of nature, the supremacy of the male. There is in all this nothing but instinctive fidelity to natural laws. Thus love, in Spain, is often found to act with that implacable strength which made of it an awe-inspiring myth in antiquity.

Spanish folk-songs show the power of love over the people of passion, and the popular vocabulary is significant in this connexion. The language has discarded the words *amor* and *amar*, somewhat too literary for its taste, and substituted for them the forcible *querer*, so loaded with the forces of tense will. *Querer*, to will somebody, has an all-round meaning—it aims at full ownership and would spurn with contempt the merely physical possession. The strength and power of the passion of love is one of the features which gives its flavour and originality to Spanish life. Lives are made and unmade by it. *Perdición* is no rhetorical word in Spanish folk-lore.

We know that envy is the specific Spanish vice. In the realm of love, envy becomes jealousy. Love is jealous in Spain. Not merely because it fears to lose the beloved, but still more, perhaps, because it cannot bear the idea that any portion of her beauty should be diverted from its own true owner. The beloved becomes part of the lover with such intensity that any movement on her part, the inner tendency of which points away from the lover, is felt by him as an unbearable tearing-asunder of his own being.

But such diseases of love belong to its feverish period. Love of man and woman, if a genuine, simple, natural, and spontaneous passion as we know it to be in Spain, is bound to evolve from the satisfaction of sex to that of parenthood. Such is the evolution of Spanish love. The beloved gradually merges into the mother; the lover into the father. The children become the true centre and interest of love. It is a striking fact, often observed in Spain, that even irregular *liaisons*, born under a purely erotic impulse, gradually become homes peopled with children, as if they had begun with a priest's benediction at the parish church.

2

Love in France is, like everything else, dispassionate. Hence, it loses the primitive warmth which alone can weld together the heterogeneous elements with which nature composes it. The clear rationalistic bent of the French mind tends also to deprive it of much of its spiritual glow. Thus it is that French love may not unfairly be understood as a series of variations on the theme of pleasure. It is a typical fact that *s'aimer* in French has a most precise, nay, concrete, meaning.[1]

The two main elements which compose it are the body and the intellect. The first is the willing instrument of the second. But the intellect leads and regulates French love with all the qualities of French conscious mastery and coolness. This leadership is recognizable in the three main characteristics of French love; its control over passion; its freedom from ethical fetters; its hedonistic tendency.

It is a master of its own passion, that is, it allows its passion full play while keeping it well in hand. French love is reasonable, and does not lose its head. An association of two persons for the purpose of amorous pleasure, not a furnace in which two beings melt into one. The two persons remain sufficiently themselves to enjoy their relationship. Let us recall here the observations made on the French attitude towards passions in general. The reasonable person watches the play of his love as that of a familiar dog, knowing that he can always bring it to submissive obedience almost instantaneously.

In such an attitude there is, of course, that mastery over the passions which is to be expected in the intellectualistic character if only because, by a process which we analysed in its place, the irrational elements of passion—which are the most unruly—are weakened or eliminated by the deadly light of the intellect. But the cool calm of the Frenchman in love comes also from his freedom from ethical fetters. The passions, we know, are for him perfectly legitimate manifestations of human life. So are the pleasures of the body. The all-embracing, or rather, the all-comprehending intellect admits as legitimate all actions, all ways but those which run counter to the predominant French requirement—truth. Truth, that urge for truth which is the mainspring in the French soul, strengthens this frank and open attitude in matters of sex. In French psychology, no "lid," no "censor," no repression. Everything is

1. Still more so, *vouloir* when applied to love. *Je te veux* is purely physical, while *Te quiero* expresses a synthetic passion.

above-board and matter of course. Hence no sentimentalism. An intimacy which, in other types of humanity, would imply a permanent connexion may mean in France no more than a passing nod.

Thus simplified and clarified, French love is free to evolve along a frankly hedonistic line. Leader of the world in the refinement of pleasure, France has by no means neglected her duties as such in the cultivation of the gardens of love.

In the collective sphere, all these tendencies harmonize happily with the tendency towards moral tolerance which we have noted in French social life. Superficial observers believe French society to be effete because it is tolerant. But the fact is that, since "nothing is either good or bad but thinking makes it so," liberties which would prove a grave social corruption in other countries are in France but healthy signs of life.

There is, moreover, an undoubted connexion between love, vanity, and the collective form of vanity known as glory (in the military sense of the word). Not in vain is the cock, the French symbol, both an amorous and a bellicose animal. The matter has been put in a nutshell by the author of four lines of doggerel which deserve a pinch of immortality:

> Je suis de St. Étienne (Loire),
> Où l'on fabrique tour à tour
> Les fusils, instruments de gloire,
> Et les rubans, objets d'amour.[2]

This line of approach may help us to understand why the French should be singularly free from jealousy. Their attitude in the matter differs from that of the Spaniard as their vanity differs from Spanish pride. Montesquieu it was, I think, who said that pride prevented the Spaniard from working, and vanity made the Frenchman work. Similarly, pride makes the Spaniard suffer agony in the throes of jealousy, while vanity

2. I come from St. Étienne (Loire),
   Where they make alternately
   Rifles, instruments of glory,
   And hair ribbons, emblems of love.

saves the Frenchman from attaching too much importance to the feelings of the woman who turns away from him. For, if love is manly pleasure, spoilt pleasure is not worth troubling about. Hence it is that these matters, in France, should evolve naturally towards reasonable solutions.

3

In so far as it is a passion, love, individual love, is bound to be considered by the man of action as something of a nuisance. And, in fact, the community being possessed of this opinion protects its young men against the nuisance by turning their vitality towards sports. Race, climate, and the athletic education of the English youth retard in them by many years the manifestations of sexual emotion, which appear so early in most continental countries. When they appear, the community frowns at them unmistakably, and even calls them names—such as *calf love*.

Thus from its very inception love lives in England under the close supervision of the community. Repression follows; the world of emotions rooted in sex becomes an underworld. It has a respectable manifestation: sentimentalism; and an escape: all that vast area of vaguely-defined lands with an unhealthy damp and warm climate which goes by the name of *romance*.

Pretence and unreality hover about English love from its early days, while self-discipline exerts itself as an important force on the side of reality. This mixture of real and unreal elements is perhaps the atmosphere necessary for the growth of some of the peculiarly English love flora; for instance, the frequent friendships between men and women—from the truly genuine, in which the sexual element is really absent, to the extreme cases in which the friendship in question is but the sublimation of a sexual attraction which dares not come out into the open.

England is thus the ideal field for the psycho-analyst. Through social pressure the passions lose caste. Driven under, lacking air, they develop more strongly if more morbidly. As an alternative, the passions lose vitality altogether and lead to types in which sex plays an unimportant role, or even no role at all. England is undoubtedly the country which can show the greatest number of unsexed men and women. In most of these cases, the central activity of life has been absorbed by some public interest. The wider group—the nation—has again proved victorious over the smaller ones—the family and the individual.

This domination of love by social and ethical influences carries with it considerable advantages for the community. Energy which in other countries is—from the collective point of view—wasted in love experiences is kept within the channels which lead to the mill of the community. Health and vigour are the reward of the individual's restraint; yet, as the devil, since treated as such, reacts accordingly, signs are not lacking of the unhealthy interest in sex which such healthy restraints tend to foster. A typical example will be found in a comparison between English and French illustrated periodicals. French ones treat sex as an open affair, even as a joke, but, though dwelling on it to the point of monotony, they are not obsessed by it. English illustrated periodicals are, with some honourable exceptions, obsessed by it, and serve it under all sorts of disguises—art, sport, society—which may dress it however scantily with a few trappings of respectability.

B. PATRIOTISM

I

Patriotism is love of country. As a passion it is powerfully felt by the Spaniard, particularly since (the country living in each of its individual components) love of country involves self-love. Patriotism in the Spaniard is, therefore, apt to take an egotistical form.

Inasmuch as it represents a social force, i.e. a spring of action, patriotism in the Spaniard shows all the features of action in the man of passion. It is therefore controlled by subjective standards.

Hence it is that in Spain the patriotic passion makes the

country subservient to the individual rather than the individual to the country. There develops thus between the individual and the country a relationship not unlike that between the lover and the beloved, i.e. one of possession through "annexation." The country is part of the passion-world of the individual. This explains the vivacity of patriotic reactions in the individual Spaniard when the sensitive spot of his country is touched.

It accounts also for the singular ineffectiveness of Spanish patriotism in the sphere of action. In the political and municipal atmosphere, patriotism is not, in Spain, so effective a force as in other countries. This is another cause which contributes to create that curious disproportion which we have already observed between the value of Spain as a whole and that of individual Spaniards. On the other hand, the prevalence of subjective standards in patriotism saves the Spaniard from that exaggerated devotion which allows misguided patriots to sin against more general laws for the sake of their country. The passionate and individual character of Spanish patriotism is undoubtedly the best explanation of the fact that it is easier to make a Spaniard die for his country than live for it.

2

French patriotism is not so much an idea, fed by passion, as a passion born of an idea. If the hypothesis of Frenchmen, constituted as we know them, yet citizens of a small and obscure country, were self-consistent, French patriotism would lose most of its contents. The driving force of patriotism in France is not in or behind the Frenchman, but in front of him—it is not, in fact, a driving but a drawing force. The country for him is a vision; an intellectual vision, Victor Hugo's "beau spectacle à ravir la pensée."

By such a glorious vision the Frenchman must be drawn; neither policies nor passions would suffice to make him surrender his personality to the wider collective Being. And this vision, as we have observed when commenting on French historical development, is illuminated by two sources of light:

the prestige of French intellect and the glory of French arms.

There is a curious spectacular feeling in the French sense of military glory. Power is not what attracts the Frenchman in all these epochs of his military past. What attracts him is the sight of pageant, the *light* which it irradiates, for light is ultimately the true element of the French spirit.

Similarly with the prestige of French thought. What pleases the French in it is the universality of France as the intellectual fatherland of all men. The man who wrote, "Every man has two countries: his own and France," struck a perennial fountain of pleasure for all Frenchmen to enjoy, though, by the same stroke, he made the Frenchman the only man with but one fatherland. Let us admire this fine hospitality by which Frenchmen open the gates of their country wide to admit all the world. It is a fresh proof of the intellectual character of their patriotism, as free from the possessive passion of the Spaniard as from the racial limitations which the group-sense imposes on English patriotism.

3

For English patriotism is almost purely racial and instinctive. Imagination and passion have little to do with it. It is a force acting within each individual, making of him a member of an harmonious body—the country.

The language reflects the instinctive, the unimaginative character of this patriotism in its lack of an original adequate word. What the French call *Patrie* and the Germans *Vaterland* is best expressed in English by *King and Country*. It is as if the Englishman, unable to get away from the concrete, took from his immediate surroundings two tangible things, King and Country, and made them the respective symbols of the two elements of the idea to be expressed: King, the soul, Country, the body, of the collective being.

But, though instinctive, English patriotism is far from being weak. One might even say that it is just because it is instinctive that it is so strong and so efficient. This racial impulse which beats in every heart of the race with the same rhythm is the most vigorous link, the true unity which groups the whole race together in action.

The patriotism of a people of action, it is turned towards action and efficiency. It is not drawn or led by a vision, but more surely still, almost infallibly, it acts from within in the service of the whole. The patriotism of a people spontaneously organized as a team, it has the limits of the team, i.e. it stops at the frontiers of the race. Here, none of that universality which we were able to observe in France. When Captain Scott, alone at the South Pole in the presence of his Maker, died so like a man, he wrote on the last page of his diary that he would die as an Englishman. In this solemn scene can be dramatically summed up the greatness and the limitations of English patriotism.

C. RELIGION

Religion may be a passion; it may be considered as a way of understanding our experience of life; or it may act as the mainspring and inspiration of our own behaviour in this present life. Types of religion will vary according to whether one or other of these three elements predominates. It is easy to forecast that religion, without, of course, losing its complex character, is dominated respectively by passion, by intellectual influences, and by ethical tendencies in each of the three peoples concerned.

I

In Spain religion is above all an individual passion, just like love, jealousy, hatred, or ambition. It consists in a relation between the individual and his Creator. In its more popular forms it partakes of that sense of the concrete which we know to be a Spanish characteristic, and which tends to bring down to earth the forms or objects of worship in order to visualize them better. The worship of images or advocations of the Virgin and of the Saints is thus, in the sphere of religion, a feature not unlike the affection bestowed by a lover on the portrait of the beloved or on objects belonging to her. But further still, there is in the religious sense of the Spaniard a kind of "annexation" of the worshipped beings which incorporates them into the daily life of the worshipper. Numerous Spanish popular songs witness to these reincarnations of holy beings through a kind of legend or mythology which, leaving aside, of course, theological and cosmogonic differences, resembles the pagan belief in its attractive creative virtue. Just as the Pagan peopled the wood with nymphs and satyrs, so the Spanish peasant girl sings of the Virgin washing the Baby's linen and spreading it on the rosemary to dry:

> La Virgen lava pañales
> A la sombra de un romero;
> Y los pajaritos cantan
> Y el agua se va riendo.

Inasmuch as this passion which connects the creature with the Creator takes perforce a filial form, the feeling of a common Source or Father fosters in the Spaniard a sense of fraternity; a sense rather than a feeling, for the Spaniard, though given to passion, is not particularly given to feeling. There is in feeling an element of "awareness" too akin to self-consciousness (though different from it) to be found in great strength in the Spanish character. That men are brothers is to the Spaniard a fact placed too deep down in him, one of those primal data of nature which one does not so much accept as bring into the world at birth. Fraternity, therefore, is apt to be taken for granted, and to be matter of course and even cold; it is compatible with indifference and even with cruelty. Yet it is, perhaps, the most important factor in Spanish life, and may even be observed at work, in a curious efficient sympathy towards the fallen, the persecuted by the law, or the victims of their own folly.

Here again we touch Spanish individualism. In a conflict between the individual and the community, the religious reaction of the Spanish soul tends to the side of the individual. Sin, fault, crime are felt rather as valuable sources of human experience enriching the individual than as injuries inflicted on the community.

Ultimately, and apart from other more topical causes to be found in history manuals, these considerations suffice to explain Spain's attachment to Catholicism. Of the dogmatic religions it is the one which can be best adapted to Spanish national characteristics.

The Spanish contribution to Catholicism is wholly consonant with these characteristics. Its outstanding features are the Counter-Reformation, the Company of Jesus, and the Mystics.[3] We find in the Counter-Reformation and in the Company of Jesus (in a sense a part of it) the earnestness, the soldier-like austerity of a religious passion which holds the men it possesses like an absolute and uncompromising mistress. Rome, weakened and corrupted by her brilliant if vicious life, is purified by these stern Spaniards [4] who come to Trent in order to insist on reform from within, and carry the day. As to the Mystics, they are to Spanish religion what great poets are to literature. In them the religious passion of Spain reaches towards greatest heights. Spanish mystics are not intellectual as French and German mystics are apt to be. Even the most scholarly amongst them, such as St. John of the Cross, live their religion as an experience of human passion.

2

The main fact about the religious life of France is that it is both a Catholic country and a sceptical country, nay *the* sceptical country.

It will be seen that these two forms of religious thought cor-

3. What about the Inquisition? It is doubtful whether the Inquisition can be considered as a typical Spanish institution, except in so far as it worked as an instrument of Spanish religious unity. The sinister reputation which it has earned it fully deserves—but not alone. The system whereby so-called justice was administered all over Europe in its time was wholly "Inquisitorial" in its methods, while less disinterested in its aims.

4. As if to illustrate that other Spanish characteristic, the wealth of contradictory features, Rome reached its maximum licence and corruption under the Spanish family of the Borjas, known by their Italianized name of the Borgias—a family which—paradox within paradox—gave to the world in the same century that noble figure Saint Francis Borja.

respond to the activities of the French intellect: the constructive and the analytical.

The analytical mind acts like an acid which corrodes and finally dissolves belief. Nowhere is it possible to find masterpieces of unbelief to rival those which we owe to Voltaire or Anatole France. We may even say, just as Shakespeare is unthinkable outside of England, and St. Theresa unthinkable outside of Spain, Voltaire is unthinkable outside of France. He is more than a Frenchman; he is the Frenchman, in that he could not be anything else.

Still, Voltaire, under his analytical mind, has a sufficient proportion of constructive tendencies to be a deist. True, his God is more of an idea than of a religious experience. God is, in Voltaire's own words, "The watchmaker of this watch"—the world. But a little farther, we are to find that typical French epigram: "God is a very convenient word in philosophy"; and farther still we find Anatole France dying after a long life of refined enjoyment with a declaration of unbelief on his thin, smiling lips: "Je ne crois à rien." This Voltarian type is frequent in France, particularly amongst the peasants and the scientifically educated middle classes. It corresponds to the first stage of the French mind, that which sees and analyses the world and tends therefore to overlook the irrational elements in it.

But the intellect of the French nation is not merely analytical. It is also constructive. The constructive mind of France is not all Catholic. By no means. Most of the great names of French constructive thought have in one way or another overstepped the strict lines of the Catholic dogma. But the attachment of a considerable proportion of the French nation to the Catholic faith is best explained by the attraction of a well-built, well-centralized system of thought and of universal government on a people specialized in intellectual order. The representative man in this connexion would be Bossuet. But, in every epoch of France as we know it, we may observe a strong intellectual tradition as the backbone of the religious order of the country. A history of religion would be in France mostly composed of a history of religious ideas. True, France has her mystic strain which flourishes in Madame Guyon. True, Pascal was a French-man. But how intellectual the mysticism of Madame Guyon when compared, for instance, with Spanish mysticism; and as to Pascal, how dialectical his Christianity as explained in that argumentative book characteristically called *Pensées*.

3

Meanwhile religion in England is frankly concerned with the things of this world. To the positive Englishman, used to im-mediate action, the postponement of the aims of religion to a distant and hazy future must be instinctively abhorrent. "Here and now" is his motto, in religion as in everything else. It is true that he does not neglect the other world—if time and tide permit. A clergyman it was, unless it was a minister, who wrote a book on "How to make the best of both worlds," but it is easier to smile at this programme than to live up to it. The Englishman tries his best to fulfil this difficult task. His natural bent leads him to begin with the world in which he is living at present.

Hence the strong ethical character of English religion. Reli-gious bodies take a powerful interest in collective tasks. Begin-ning with those closest to religious interests, such as charity and teaching, they gradually extend their sphere of action to well-nigh every social and collective activity. This religious growth, so similar to, and so intimately connected with, the English tendency to self-government, manifests itself in a wealth of institutions, such as the Y.M.C.A. and the Salvation Army, the social value of which could hardly be exaggerated.

It should be noted that these institutions tend to circumvent sin; to prevent men and women from falling; and therefore to deprive them of moral experience. In so doing they act instinc-tively as agents of the community, saving individuals from their own selves in order to preserve them in better use for the service of the nation.[5] Charity, then, rather than fraternity,

5. The double column of Charity Appeals published by *The Times*, in itself an eloquent sign of the admirable vitality of English public gen-erosity, is headed by the following significant statement:

"H.R.H. THE PRINCE OF WALES, in a speech broadcast from the Albert Hall is the true virtue of English religion; charity, undoubtedly more efficient and positive than fraternity, as a social force, and as an element of co-operation, yet looking downwards, while fraternity looks level ahead.

The religious life of England presents one of those paradoxes with which complex reality stimulates our thought. The superabundance of English sects and forms of worship would seem at first sight to betray an undue intellectual interest strong enough to keep alive differences of opinion, as well as an undue lack of sense of co-operation. The existence of these two tendencies, moving like eddies against the main current of English character, must not be denied.[6] Yet even these exceptions help in their way to confirm the general rule. They witness in a twofold way to the strong sense of co-operation of the British nation: first, because all this religious activity grouped in England's minor sects corresponds to what in other countries would be purely isolated individuals who, having dropped out of the Church, remain at home quietly worshipping in their own individual manner, without feeling the need of forming a congregation; secondly, because, in spite of the differences of opinion which divide them, these sects think of nothing but unity, as the continuous efforts of the churches towards union show. But the language provides the most final revelation of the true attitude of the general mind to such differences of religious opinion by referring to these multitudinous sects as *denominations*.

Thus the sense of unity acts under and against the intellectual eddies which divide English religious life on its surface. This sense of unity is, we know, limited to the frontiers of the race. Religion, that most universal of passions, is not universal in England. The people of action has its own Church. It wants to

---

on 10 July 1926, stated: '*Great Britain is a country in which voluntary causes have always flourished, and it is very desirable to foster the spirit of public service on which they are based, because that spirit is one of our best assets as a nation.*' "

6. Due account should be taken, however, of the strong proportion of Iberian elements (Welsh and Scotch) to be found in Nonconformity.

ensure fair play even in heaven. All over the world this people, whose action is so universal, erects as witnesses to its insular passions English churches and English churchyards, and thus, sailing on English coffins, it lands at last on an Eternity which is but another Dominion beyond the Seas of Death.

Conclusion

WHEN DUE ALLOWANCE IS MADE FOR THE ELUSIVE COMPLEXITIES of life, the survey of the several manifestations of life in three prominent European peoples substantiates the view that there is such a thing as national character. England, France, and Spain have been found to represent in the main three definite types or characters.

We have endeavoured to show how each of these three peoples brings to history a point of view, a turn of mind of its own. In a sense this variety of the human race, even in so small a compass as this little western cape of the Asiatic Peninsula which we know as Europe, explains the variety of history itself. Surely the order in which the hegemonies of Spain, France, and England succeed each other is not purely fortuitous. Spain was the leading country when the world strove between two spiritual principles—unity versus variety—and when the wealth at stake was of the kind which lives in men's souls; France becames the leader of a world turned intellectual and classical by the Renaissance, engaged in the investigation of the ideas which were to serve for the building of modern society; England followed suit when the French cycle closed with the French Revolution, and, the problem of liberty solved, the world turned towards the conquest of things, trade becoming its main activity and a life of ease, leisure, and mutual trust its immediate aim. For every period of history mankind found its national protagonist and representative nation.

There is an impressive natural order in the distribution of psychological and geographical features in Europe. Gradually seceding from Asia by the tapering plains of Russia and Central Europe, it points towards America three definite nations, like three fingers—England, France, Spain. Similarly, in character, Russia is still a boundless plain. Her people, so rich in spiritual gifts, is curiously inapt for action, and is as boundless and formless in its mind as the plains it inhabits. Germany, powerful in brain and will, is still fluid, always moving along in a feeling of "becoming"—no longer formless in all directions like the Russian spiritual sea, but, if limited at the sides and banked like a river, yet fluid and vague along the direction of its progress. Europe does not take definite forms until it reaches these three westernmost peoples pointing towards America—England, France, Spain.

England, France, and Spain have made America. Spain, the people of passion, discovered it. Faith, vision, and inefficiency led to the sublime and absurd adventure which events unexpectedly justified, and even glorified, before an astounded world. The people of passion gave itself to its creation. It poured its life into it. The people of action and the people of thought came later. In the struggle that ensued the people of action, as was to be expected, won, directly at first, and then in its offspring. In the economic organization of America—both north and south—the active hand of the Englishman and of the Anglo-Saxon American is to be seen everywhere. Finally the people of thought exerted on the new continent the influence nearest to its own heart. France intellectualized America. If we compare a South-American with a Spaniard, or a North-American with an Englishman, one of the most striking differences in both cases will be found to be a greater attraction towards Paris, a greater readiness to seek and to absorb French civilization and thought. England, France, and Spain are the three points of Europe through which the European spirit, like an electric fluid, flows towards the West.

This fact should help to dispel many a dismal prejudice born of our age. We live in an era dominated by national worship. The idea of nationality, born in relatively recent times, has sunk rapidly into the several peoples of mankind and become a religion, with all the power for elevating men's souls to sacrifice, but, alas, with all the tendencies towards narrowness, bigotry, and even cruelty which dogmatic religions evinced in the past. For the wary eye, this religion of the God-Nation has already evolved forms of national worship amounting to a rite. Through this process the nation is rapidly becoming an irresponsible divinity. The intelligent and critical devotion of old becomes insufficient; an absolute abnegation, a surrender of will and brain is asked of the worshipper when the nation is at stake.[1] Let us not paint the picture too black. Things have not

1. On the day on which this was written the *Manchester Guardian* reported a speech delivered in the English Parliament by Mr. John Buchan on the dealings which led to the parliamentary union between England and Scotland. The speech as reported contains the following sentence: "He admitted there might have been a little money passing, but it was almost too small to dignify it with the name of bribery, and when a nation was at the cross-roads there was sure to be a little dirty work (Laughter)." *Manchester Guardian*, 21 July 1927.

yet come quite to that pass, but they are moving fast that way.[2]

The world of men tends thus to evolve from a world of individuals, God-made souls, towards a kind of Olympus of Nation-Gods. The League of Nations itself, though it ultimately may, and must, provide the remedy for the evil, does at first but increase it by adding a new vigour to each nation through the self-consciousness fostered in it by collective life. Nations meet and discuss in Geneva as nations, and thereby acquire a deeper sense of their existence, a greater sense of their importance. Nationalism, born obscurely in the Middle Ages, come to its maturity in the nineteenth century, and to its explosive crisis in the World War, becomes the most important spiritual force of our own times, and thrives even by that which at first sight might appear to be its antidote. Geneva is the sacred town on which the new Olympus is rising. Poor men that we are, we crawl dejected amidst national Gods, carrying our frail destinies in our hands, exposed to their awful whims and passions.

Is it strange then that this age should evince a tendency to judge men according to their capacity for creating great strong national Gods? "See"—they seem to say—"our national God is greater and stronger than yours. He can do far more good—or evil—in the world. His power can stretch ever so far beyond our territory, and no other national God dare raise his voice when our own has spoken. *Therefore we are better men than you.*" Great publicists, whose word is printed in all languages and read all over the world, preach the gospel of efficiency, that is to say of the capacity for creating a big national God, and thus are men progressing along a freely chosen road which leads to slavery.

For the transition is all too easy and the danger obvious. While human individuals, in all but a few dismal spots in the

2. These remarks were already written when the remarkable *Essays on Nationalism* by Professor Hayes of Columbia University came into my hands. Having read his chapter on "Nationalism as a Religion," I fear that my views on the subject are too moderate, and that the evil is much greater than I imagined.

world, have forgotten the days of cannibalism, these collective human beings, the Gods we call nations, can devour each other. The big ones, that is, can devour the small. To be sure, there are ways and ways of doing it. There was a time, not so long ago, when it was done openly. The world has become more fastidious, and nowadays reasons must be given to appease the qualms of the squeamish. A favourite one is that the nation attacked is not in a position to govern itself. This argument amounts to the one given above—i.e. the people in question is unable to produce a strong (even if small) nation-God.

But why? Why should capacity for creating a well-ordered nation be the standard to be adopted amongst men? Is there no other way of understanding life than that which leads to strong and well-ordered communities? We have seen how three prominent peoples, chosen within a small area of the world, differ profoundly in this respect. Is it too much to say that the splendid success of England as a community is due as much to English defects as to English gifts? Are we not certain now that the shortcomings of France and Spain, as communities, are due as much to French and Spanish qualities as to French and Spanish faults? Further still, between the nation and the individual there would seem to be a certain psychological osmosis or mutual infiltration, so that it may well be that certain qualities of the individual result from his delegating the corresponding defects to the character of the group. Are we sure that the individual sense of co-operation is not paid for by a national tendency *not* to co-operate? Can we affirm that individual self-denial is not compensated for by national egoism? Our knowledge of these matters is still in its infancy. All we know is that we do not know enough to pass judgement on others for the crime of differing from us.

Relativity is the word. Our judgements in matters of national character and aptitude (even if we attain political impartiality) are bound to be coloured by our own character. There is no firm, no immovable ground from which to measure the movements of other peoples' souls. That which they neglect, we cultivate. That which they cultivate, we neglect. But Man as seen by God is surely more complete than any of our types, since it includes them all. Ultimately, national psychologies are but lived world-philosophies, lived *Weltanschauungen*. How can we choose between them save from the basis and with the standards of our own?

England's world-philosophy is that of the will. The Englishman lives in action. He is busy. He moves. For relaxation and rest he moves again, passing from business to sport. He mixes with people and things. He is sociable and social. He is even gregarious. He sees himself in his community. He does not mind being poor since his community is rich. He can put up with a mediocre house in a mediocre street of a mediocre town, since he is a member of the British Empire. His pride is in the nation, and so the nation goes well, whether he does or not. He understands liberty as non-interference with his choice of social activities. All he wants is to be allowed "to do his bit." His pilgrimage in life he sees as the accumulation of these "bits." His being finds itself in action, grows in co-operation, and fulfils itself in the community. Complex in all his functions, thinking with his instincts, acting with his mind, he naturally attains the supreme virtue of the man of action—wisdom.

France's world-philosophy is that of the mind. The Frenchman wants to understand reality. Living for him consists in the development of his intellect and of the five avenues which lead to it—his senses. Refinement and enjoyment are his ultimate categories, and of the two, perhaps the second is the only one really *ultimate*. The vision of a mind-satisfying community guides him in his collective life, and order in his social prerequisite. Liberty for him is above all liberty of thought, and as long as he can think freely (which, of course, includes expressing his thought in freedom), he is happy as a citizen. He is not gregarious, but his enjoyment is not complete outside a well-ordered society, in which the purely relative qualities which the mind cultivates may be kept polished by constant friction, and offer their smooth surface to the light in the intellect. His heart is cool, but his mind is generously open and universal, and he is an equalitarian by mental conviction. His nature leads him to clarify and analyse his functions. He thinks with his head, and his main virtue is that of the man of thought —reason.

Spain's world-philosophy is above all static and passive. While others travel on the road of progress the Spaniard stays, perhaps with the subconscious feeling that the others are travelling towards the very state he has attained by intuition. "All is one and the same" is his intimate creed. Nothing lives for him that does not live in him. He does not seek events; he does not aim at deflecting towards him the river of life. The predominating, nay the only factor, is the individual. It is his soul which lives—the rest are either forms and illusions, or parts and passions of his soul. The Spaniard is therefore the very reverse of gregarious. If he seeks company, it is in order to feel the edges of his personality against that of other personalities, so that in society it is not the community he seeks out but other individuals: hence that hard feeling in Spanish gatherings, that impression they give as if they were a field of sharp flint-stones. His main interest is in life itself as it comes, felt as a passion in him, and thus he can attain the supreme virtue of the man of passion—serenity.

Let us imagine that the English convert the whole world to their philosophy, and that, moreover, they persuade the world to adjust itself to their ways. What would be the result? The earth would become an immense tennis-golf-cricket-swimming club, with elegant and simple clothes, mediocre food, excellent roads, magnificent sanitation, and impeccable police. Sundays a little dull perhaps, but first-rate week-ends, and not too strenuous weeks in between. Good humour, a sprinkling of wit, and even at times cleverness, though in moderation, and worn, so to say, with tactful decency. Greek known, but half forgotten; Latin on the visible horizon; an extensive reading of bad novels, and some conversation about those recognized as good ones. In all, a pleasurable world for the well-to-do, and therefore for the others, whose main pleasure would be to look at them. Plenty of physical movement, but moral adventures reserved for the few. Men would learn the experience of things rather than that of their own selves.

Should the French succeed in shaping the world to their liking it would go like clockwork, according to schedule. All would speak French like Mirabeau and write it like Racine. Wit and cleverness would shine upon the world like strings of diamonds, and every minute of life would be a drop of exquisite pleasure for man to enjoy. There would be Titians in cookery and Tintorettos in the art of the butler. Nature would keep her secrets just long enough for man to enjoy their discovery, and Truth would show herself as generous in the matter of clothes as a lady of birth at the sea-shores of the Riviera. All men would be able to predict eclipses and to understand Einstein at a first reading. A salon would be a kind of paradise in which all women would be Aphrodites and all men Platos. Now and then a first-rate fight for a principle, irrespective of the eventual application thereof. All things permitted, though in moderation, but no more than a reasonable importance granted to the experience thus acquired.

Should the world wish to take Spain for its model, it would considerably abate the speed and efficiency of its mechanical activities. There would be less co-operation, but less to cooperate about; less order, less technique, less grinding of individuals in the social mill. The general level of life would tend to be simpler and more primitive. There would be more leisure, if less comfortably spent. Man would be more inclined to let things go by, as they did centuries ago, and would accept with equal serenity events generally held as good and events generally held as bad. The world of things would be less active and the world of men less smooth, so that physical movements would be slower and scarcer, and moral movements more violent and frequent. There would be more depth and less surface; more fundamentals and fewer accessories. Men would live life more and be less lived by it. They would toss up and down the social hillocks, shaken by fickle fortune as single individuals with loose social ties and little weight, and the experience thus gained would be more that of the soul than the experience of things.

In the name of what could we wish to impoverish the world by reducing these three types to one? The ideal of a world-regulated community is but a mirage. We do not know for certain by what standards to define it. An attempt was once made to lay down such standards in the United States of America on the occasion of the oft-repeated request of the Philippine Islands for independence—a request which the Government of the United States of America does not wish to grant until the Philippines are in a position to govern themselves as a well-organized community. It was explained that a well-organized community meant a community capable of raising loans at a normal rate of interest. This definition would narrow down the meaning of the word *interesting* to that of *interest bearing*. However justified that may be in Wall Street, it might be less appreciated—let us not say in Benares—but even in Harvard.

The fact is, the conception of a well-organized community implies criteria—well organized for what? from the point of view of whom?—which in their turn depend on national character and on world character, therefore, on time.

Moreover, even if a common criterion were found, it is surely wrong to consider the community as an aim in itself. The community at most may be accepted as an immediate aim towards the ultimate aim, which is the individual. This admitted, we might then consider the different national characters of the world—the three characters here studied being the three typical examples of them—as different ways of rearing individual souls. And it is obvious that there is no possibility of choosing the best between them, for in these matters there is no standard of better and best.

Nor if there were, would it be possible or desirable to effect a choice? For what would be our means? Conquest? It is as dangerous to the national character of the conqueror as it is ineffective for assimilating the national character of the conquered. Education? You may train a pony into an excellent horse, but you will never educate it into a hound. What then?

The obvious answer is that the admirable variety of national characters is one of the manifestations of the wealth of Creation, and that, as such, men owe it to the Creator to respect it as a manifestation and to themselves to enjoy it as a spectacle and a gift.

An Afterword on Language and National Character

LANGUAGE IS BOTH THE OFFSPRING AND THE SIRE OF NATIONAL character, a biological absurdity but a fact of life.* The acceptance of this, however, requires that you believe both in language and in national character. It is said that two ghosts once wandering about forlorn and perhaps bored in a derelict castle came upon each other and sat down for a chat, in the course of which one of them asked the other: "Do you believe in human beings?" So it is with learned men. There are amongst them

* Written for the 1969 edition.

some who ask "Do you believe in languages?" and others who ask "Do you believe in national character?"

At bottom, these might well turn out to be the same question. For the man who doubts that there are such things as languages does not of course deny that Chinese and English exist as separate systems of communication; what he denies is that they derive from, are manifestations of, two different forms of the human spirit, since for him they are just two different ways into which communication has evolved in different zones of time and space through a uniform law of response to stimulus.

So please note: both the Englishman who starts a grocery and proudly paints over his gate JOHN SMITH, GROCER, and the Frenchman who in a similar situation derives a Cartesian satisfaction from the sight of a sign which reads ALIMENTATION GÉNÉRALE are to be considered as merely heirs to a Pavlovian dog salivating at the sound of the bell which used, alas, to announce his food before the eminent doctor tricked him into mere salivation for its own sake—and that of nonsense.

As for national character, let it be known that it is a mere myth. People will imagine that Frenchmen are *this* way and Englishmen *that* way only to discover that within fifty years this *this* and this *that* have interchanged their allegiances and the positions are reversed. So what else can we do but turn to statistics? For this myth of national character is built, you should know, on generalizations made with no respect whatsoever for the guarantees expected from anyone applying an inductive method. And so on and so forth. And this so on and so forth is so full of promise and potency that rather than seek light on the Russian character in the novels of Dostoevsky, seekers after truth there have been who thought it better to study the repercussions on the Russian psychology of the way in which Russian mothers bind the waistbands round the bellies of their babies. But don't you go and believe that such things would prove the existence of a Russian character. That would be a generalization.

Now the odd thing about all this is that *generalization* is a favourite word in the United States—and a dirty word at that.

If you want to hurt an American professor try to utter what a Frenchman would call "une idée générale," *l'alimentation générale*, for instance. He would be hurt, and in a twofold way: first, because you would be trying to induce or reason from the particular to the general, which no decent American would ever do. Turnips, onions, cauliflower, yes; *alimentation générale*, no. And second, because you would land yourself in an abstract idea, and that is tantamount to a blasphemy for a pragmatist—which all Americans are, I would add, if this were not in itself a generalization. Do they hate error so much that they are afraid of letting it in through generalizing, i.e. through opening too wide the gates of their thoughts? By no means. For they let error in just as easily when closing their gates so as to let squeeze through only the most concrete and obvious facts. Thus, this plain, pragmatic, concrete sign: DRUG STORE, to describe a shop in which you can buy every possible thing you can think of—even drugs.

It may be hard for the pragmatists to realize that other types of mind seldom generalize. What appears to the pragmatist as a generalization is often in fact a snapshot of intuition, a flash of insight which, at one stroke, reveals the shape of the whole landscape. The surveyor came, measured length and angles for days, and drew up a perfect map of it. Then came the painter, measured nothing, looked at everything, and lo, the landscape was alive. The contrast is similar to that between knowing and understanding. You may know everything and understand nothing; and vice versa. Most of us get along with a fair mixture of both. But the dogmatic academic who grumbles "generalization" every time he is confronted with a dash of intuition usually belongs to the type who knows far more than he understands. There is an old Gallegan proverb which sums it up admirably:

O que mais mira menos ve.

(The more one looks the less he sees.)

The beauty of it all is that, confronting the existence of national characters, the Americans who deny by word, affirm by deed. It is, in fact, a feature of the American character to keep as close as possible to direct experience and to refuse to divert the eye from the ball of fact and let it wander in the sky of ideas. For so doing they are by no means to be blamed, since, leaving aside that to blame them for being pragmatic would amount to blaming them for being born in Brooklyn or Pasadena, their pragmatism has proved most fertile for them and for the world—just as fertile as the French faculty and taste for *idées générales* has been for the French. So, we shall consider the American refusal to admit to the existence of national character as a proof of the existence of national character, and we get on with our work.

National character is a fact of nature. It matters little that some people deny its existence: there are many persons, some of them highly intelligent, who are colour blind; and Victor Hugo was deaf to music, though there is fine music in his poems. If national characters change, it shows that they exist; and if they exist, they are bound to change. But they will change each within a particular equation defining each of them, so to speak. The Thames at Oxford is a very different river from the Thames at Henley or at Greenwich; yet it is the same river, and certainly not La Seine.

All this should be obvious—as well as that the most direct outcome of a national character is the language in which it utters itself. After all, the most immediate, the most intimate sign of life is breath, and breath is the raw material of language. When we have heard a person speak, we know—well, perhaps we do not know, but we guess—most about his character. We guess, because we experience it. Through the years and the centuries, a people is bound to shape its language so as faithfully to correspond to its spirit. When the spirit changes, the language changes. The fact that nowadays English is shared by two peoples as different and as dynamic as the British and the American is exerting a considerable influence on its vocabulary, its grammar, and its taste.

Of the many differences between the British and the American forms of the English language one has always struck me as most remarkable: the British say *lift* and the Americans *elevator*; but the British speak of an *elevating* thought when the Americans would say an *uplifting* thought. Now, the English language is most apt, perhaps the aptest in the world, for expressing physical movements and qualities. Such words as *smooth, swift, waft, sharp, grit, slither, twist* are unsurpassable utterances of what they represent. *Stop* is so perfect that it has become universal, or should we rather say, in a more English form, world-wide. Nor should we think that this is all an accident of fortune, as do those good people who fondly imagine that if the apple had fallen on *their* heads it would have been *they* who would have discovered the law of gravitation. No. The neat aptness of the English language to express motion and matter is due simply to the fact that it is *motion* that *matters* most for the English, and *matter* that *moves* them most to action. So they watch it with their mind's eye.

Consider this very word *stop* I have just mentioned, made up of the system *st* which *st*ands for *st*ability and that *p* which closes the lips to all traffic. Compare it with *star*, made up of *st* for *st*ability and that *r* which stands for vibration, and the open *a* for the circular irradiating movement of light—a perfect verbal image. And compare this again with *stir*, where the consonantal hints are identical with those in *star*, while the vowel, open and luminous in star, has become obscure, so that instead of light the impression conveyed is one of turbulence; and keep on comparing with *stick, stack,* and *stock*, where the *r* of vibration has vanished to be replaced by that hard *ck*. And you will measure the depth, the concrete, divinatory depth of the English intuition for matter and movement.

In contrast, the English language is awkward whenever it tries to express ideas, or anything that happens in the mind. It is not natural for the Englishman to deal with things of the mind. Do not misunderstand me. I am not saying that the English are incapable of or ungifted for dealing with ideas. They are indeed so capable and gifted that they reached the forefront of our Western civilization in the realm of the sciences and the letters and the arts even before they attained it in the sphere of political and economic power. But, outstanding though they are in the activities of the mind, they do not undertake them willingly, and are even somewhat shy about it all, as if thinking were a foible the less spoken about the better. Instead of "I think," the Englishman prefers to say "I feel," and he is probably right, since the sun of thought generally rises in these latitudes amongst mists of feeling.

And so you will find that the English of motion and movement is made of athletic words, alive with speed, power, and beauty, ready for a sprint; while the English of thought is made of donnish vocables coming solemnly out of a monumental dictionary, clad in heavy, moth-ball-smelling robes as if ready for an Oxford Encaenia procession.

Now we can return to the comparison of *lift* with *elevator* and *elevating* with *uplifting*, and we can see why the British use the Latin word for the thought that raises your mind, and the Saxon word for the cabin that raises your body: because, for them, dealing with the body is natural while dealing with the mind is bookish. The former happens in nature, on the grass or over the fences; the latter, in a study, library, or church —places where one meets Aristotle and Cicero. The mind is something earnest, to be revered and talked about in Latin or in words that savour of it.

While for the Americans, the thing to be respected, if not revered, is the machine, the gadget. You should not trivialize an apparatus which takes you up sixty stories, conquering the force of gravity by sheer ingenuity. Furthermore, for many Americans, English is a language learnt at school and in books, and therefore tends to be bookish, to be learnt first through the bookish sector of its vocabulary; and so, the physical movement is granted the more solemn and dignified word, *elevator*, leaving the Saxon word *uplifting* for the Sunday church language. Why? Because the feeling of raising the mind is but sluggish in the average active, business-like American, and he has to spur himself into it (he would probably say *to kick* himself into it) by using the Saxon, swift, executive word.

There may be other reasons. The Englishman is an introvert and an adept at under-expression; the American is an extrovert and fond of over-uttering himself. The English will speak of *the government policy*; Americans will have nothing less than *the government policies*. No Englishman would ever have been able to invent, no Englishman would indeed ever have felt like saying "I feel like a million dollars." For the Englishman, therefore, the Saxon side of his language is like a retreat where he speaks as little as possible, with as few words and as short as he can make them, and to that end he will cut off either their tail, as in *bike* for *bicycle*, or their head, as in *bus* for *omnibus*; while the American finds in the Latin side of English the long wavy words he needs to express himself with the eloquence his extrovert vitality demands. And as he speaks more of matter and movement than of mind and thought, he takes Latin words over to his favourite field. Hence *lift* becomes *elevator*, and *peer* becomes *senator*, and *county councils* become *legislatures*, and the *House of Commons* the *House of Representatives*.

Words are like flowers rooted in the soil of the national character. Even when a French word seems to correspond fittingly to an English word, it does not *feel* the same for those who live in the familiarity of both languages. Nothing is truer than that one lives as many lives as one knows languages. Every word that is said carries with it its own atmosphere of national connotations, harmonics, sidelights and aromas, which for the most part are lost in translation. We thus can see in translation a kind of transplantation. Will the roots take on in the new soil? Will the plant in the new soil wilt and die or flourish and give forth colour and aroma? We are all familiar with those pathetic dead flowers in some lines of translated works.

Furthermore, every nation has its own peculiar way of using its words. The English, for instance, use words as tools; and that is why they wait till the last moment to decide whether a word will be used as a noun, an adjective, a verb, or an adverb —or even an expletive. And so, in English, words are apt to be peeled in the course of time until they have shed every prefix or suffix which would—well, which would *fix* beforehand the class to which they belong for the time being. The word must do for every purpose and must fit into any sentence the speaker may require. This brings forward the efficient, utilitarian, pragmatic nature of the English national character.

But the English are also an eminently social nation. Every Englishman is inserted into a group the rules of which, even if unwritten and uncodified, he instinctively knows and respects. So his sentences are like societies within which his words will take on the value and meaning that the society of the sentence will grant them; just as he himself (unlike, say, the Spaniard, who is very much the man he is no matter the group he happens to be in at the time) gathers most of his value and meaning from the society to which he belongs.

That is why in English the accent of the sentence is more important than that of the word and determines its meaning. The same sentence will do for a number of meanings, which will depend on the intention of the speaker. English thereby gains a subtlety entirely due to the conventional and social colour those who speak it are able to impart to everything that is said.

For the French, a word is like a diagram of the idea or object the speaker has in mind. This feature reveals at once the predominance of *l'esprit de géométrie* in the genius of the French people. Compared to Spanish, which is a language in the round, and full of colour—painted sculpture, in fact—French is a two-dimensional and black-and-white language. Its words are like projections of the objects they represent, drawings for the engineer or the architect, clear and abstract. The partitive article, moreover, emphasizes this abstraction. The doctor will not say to his patient "You've got some intestinal catarrh," but "Vous faites de l'entérite," just as he would say "Vous faites de la philosophie." Both philosophy and bowel trouble become abstract categories.[1]

The good photographer does not order his model about: "Sit up. Look this way. Head a bit more down." He just hangs

1. Compare: *Swing-wing aircraft* becomes *avion à géométrie variable*.

about, his camera on the ready, and snaps his victim when the real self comes through, unexpectedly. So we may hope to snap a national character if we watch the language until we see it giving the character away. Choice is revealing. Choice is the use of liberty; and what more clearly could reveal our character than the use we make of our liberty?

We can catch languages in the act of choosing when we compare the words each of them selects as metaphors for the same fact of nature. For, confronting the same nature, some will react in one way, some in another; and the difference may be significant and characteristic. Here is a soft fruit—apricot, peach, plum. That hard core inside, how do the several languages call it? *Stone*, say the English, picking up the image from the inanimate world of matter. *Hueso*, "bone," say the Spaniards, borrowing from the animal world. And the French say *noyau*, a purely abstract notion which they find in the intellect. Do you suspect me of some kind of trickery in conspiracy with chance? Here is a fish; the pieces of its skeleton which we have to separate carefully on our plates lest we have to struggle with them desperately in our mouths, how do we name them? *Bones*, say the English, making no bones about it, since they are bones. *Espinas*, "thorns," say the Spaniards, more poetically. And the French, *arètes*, just as if the fish were a cube or a dodecahedron. The English, by the way, haven't even bothered to coin a word for *arète*: "a line of meeting of two planes forming a dihedral angle," says the French-English dictionary. Could you wish for more geometry in the French, who find it even in fish, or for less in the English, who don't even bother to put it in their dictionary?

These examples are a guide to the workings of the minds of the peoples concerned. In them we see the English and the Spaniards remaining attached to the tangible side of nature, while the French reveal their capacity to see within nature the inner laws of the human mind.

The dominant English vowel is a non-descript, foggy, undelineated, and above all uncommitted sound which wanders freely over the aeiou—again, a sign of that pragmatism which waits until the last minute and does not cross the bridge until it comes to it. The predominance of this synthetical vowel might explain the maddening juggling with the plain, straightforward, fundamental vowel-sounds the English have shamelessly indulged in. *A* becomes *e, e* becomes *i, i* becomes *ai, o* becomes *ou,* and *u* becomes *iu*—John Bull in the China-shop of vowels. Not a single one remains intact. I know of no other language in which more disorder has been introduced more unnecessarily. Why? It is a fascinating question to which one dares offer little more definite than mere conjectures. The first that comes to mind arises from an observation: the Englishman is indefinite as to his vowels but definite as to his consonants. Now, by and large, we may take the vowels as utterances of the will and the self, and the consonants as utterances of the world and its resistance to our will. The Englishman would then express his awareness of the fixity of the material world and of the elasticity and adaptability of his will to meet this resisting reality.

In contrast with the indefiniteness of the English vowel, the French language is dominated by the second of the Latin vowels, *e. Pater* becomes *père;* and *asparagus, asperge.* I have elsewhere explained this fact as the expression of French moderation and sense of measure—no, *mesure.* Do you feel the difference in the taste of the word? (Incidentally, those who deny the existence of national characters might try to explain how three peoples—the French, the Italian, and the Spanish—managed to evolve three such different languages out of the same Latin, three languages in each of which a different key-vowel dominates in perfect harmony with each of the three national characters concerned.) That *e,* the middle or half-open vowel, so typical of the French, does not merely express their sense of measure. It also corresponds to the flattening of the object on its being projected onto the drawing board so as to form the word, the geometrical representation which is characteristic of the diagrammatic and abstract genius of France.

For the Englishman words may be tools, and for the Frenchman drawings on the board or blueprints of the objects they represent, but for the Spaniard they are projectiles. They are not said but thrust. And, of course, they possess weight, volume, and colour. That is why Spanish is the most expressive of languages; and in particular, if you feel like swearing, you should not waste your hot breath in words of any other language. Here we have, of course, lost sight of *la mesure*, and, in fact, the Spaniard, whose language abounds in a's and o's, the full-breath vowels, feels the utmost contempt for any state of mind that can be expressed with the moderate letter *e*, which he proves by setting this letter aside to signify disdain and ridicule. *Viejecito* means a nice little old man. *Vejete* means a ridiculous, contemptuous little fellow. Examples are so abundant that the intention behind this Spanish use of the favourite French *e* cannot be doubted.

It was in the early fifties that I pointed to the significance in terms of national character to be attributed to the omnipresence of the letter *i* in Italian. It turns up even twice in the very name of the country and language. I then wrote of "the keen, steely foil of the Italian intellect." In an endeavour to concentrate national character into one single symbol, I defined the Englishman as the man-island, the Frenchman as the man-crystal, the German as the man-river, the Spaniard as the man-castle, and the Italian as the man-stiletto. This was at least ten years before the stiletto heels of ladies' shoes became fashionable. You all know where they came from.

Shall we speak of the contrast between the men who say *add* and those who say *hinzufügen*? The German language is the most heavily consonant-ridden in Europe. It is thereby—and also because of its rich play between short and long syllables— one of the most musical, perhaps the one which most closely resembles the sonorities of the organ and even of the full orchestra. It is the fitting language for a people of musicians and philosophers, whose inner world flows with the formlessness of rivers.

Here is a case parallel to that of the three so-called Latin

peoples who, out of the same Low Latin, evolved three languages as different as French, Italian, Spanish. Both English
and German are Germanic languages with a fair amount of
Latin words thrown in; but while Latin English is the language
of the bookish intellectuals, Latin German is of little significance, for all Germans speak rather a language of abstractions
than a language of things. In this they resemble the French; and
it is no exaggeration to say that while considered from the
point of view of their bodies, German goes with English and
French with Spanish, considered from the point of view of the
spirit which animates them, German goes with French and
English with Spanish. For German and French are abstract and
slaves to their grammars, while English and Spanish are concrete and free from grammatical fetters. What the Spaniard
would reproach to the Englishman is his chaotic spelling. This
at any rate seems to have been the opinion of that Spaniard who
said to one of his countrymen: "Imagine how chaotic, that they
have a poet they spell Shakespeare and they pronounce Scho-
penhauer."

Again, why this chaos? It does not occur in any other language. It is, of course, a fact that the English revel in lack of
logic (with the single exception of accountancy) and detest
anything that has to do with preconceived systems, and that
they love after-thoughts and even second thoughts; that no
decent English house would do without at least two different
levels in every storey, so that its dwellers keep stepping up and
down and even risking their lives if the postman knocks im-
periously at 7 A.M.; and that they shun looking too closely into
such things as etymology, so they will add a g to *sovereignty*
just because the sovereign reigns and because it looks more like
royalty as there have been so many kings named George. But
surely, even all these disarming idiosyncrasies are not sufficient
to have fostered so chaotic a chaos.

The chief cause of the trouble may still be the uncreated,
inchoate, maid-of-all-purposes, universal vowel-cloud of the
English language, uoiea or aeiou, ever ready to shape itself into

any sort of dragon or weasel the occasion—or the speaker—may require. We recall the Yorkshireman who, when asked whether one should say "aheether" or "eether," replied: "You can say oother."

The story shows that in this free country every man can pronounce his English as he jolly well wishes; or in other words, that the King's English no longer belongs to the Crown, but that its sovereignty has passed to the King's subjects—which, by the way, might make it easier for them to get rid of that absurd g, unless it makes it harder if the subjects refuse to have anybody touch their sovereignty, g and all. It also suggests another cause of the chaotic state of English spelling, since no matter the spelling, your Englishman will pronounce his words his own way. I once knew a man in Oxford—he was not an Oxford man, or at any rate not an Oxford don—who never said *pounds*, but *peunds*. Well, why not? *Peunds* is after all not more chaotic than *pounds*.

It also suggests that since every Englishman will pronounce English his own way, and since most Englishmen are class-men, the way one pronounces a given word will tend to vary in two ways: in space, from class to class; and in time, from generation to generation. For the written text, which fixes the pronunciation of other languages and keeps it close to the spelling, has no such virtue in England. This in its turn provides us with another clue for the chaos of English spelling. In the days in which few people could read and fewer still cared to read, spelling was fairly free in every country and language, and that is how languages evolved and reached their separate beings; but with the spreading of the printed word, spelling was fixed in every country. Not, however, in England; for the Englishman did not see why he should be bound to a logical use of the letters as units of sound, and thus he allowed class and individual vagaries and caprices to play ducks and drakes with the live form of his words as opposed to their dead or printed forms. Hence the divergence in pronunciation observable between the English of England and that of the United States whenever the word strays from its printed form, as for instance in *Berkeley* and *clerk*, which the Americans pronounce as they are printed, while the English gargle their *er*'s into *ar*'s. This gargling is probably a class sign, not necessarily an aristocratic one, but perhaps rather an academic class sign. By far the best gargles can be heard at Oxford, where they express the satisfaction the speaker feels in being himself and not you, so that he must first relish his own breath at the back of his throat before he parts with it for your benefit.

Poor Bernard Shaw, whose idealism often was but a form of that hardly veiled way of digging at the mere Englishman which no Irishman can resist, left an impressive amount of money to foster the invention of a new alphabet, roomy enough to house all these English vagaries. He overlooked that these vagaries are almost all oddities not of spelling but of pronunciation, which, no matter what alphabet is used, are bound to evolve on and on away from any fixed new spelling that might be built on a new system of letters. Indeed, it is easy to prophesy that, presented with a dozen or so more letters to play with, the Englishman would lose no time in developing a far more chaotic chaos than that which he enjoys at present.

What has all this to do with that pragmatic, positive feature supposed to be so prominent in the English character? Far more than meets the eye. For the pragmatic, positive Englishman is unperturbed by contradictions, and he takes his class where he finds it, and accepts its standards, indeed cultivates them; and so, a kind of eddy of his spirit seems to be flowing in a direction just opposite that of the main-stream. Similar eddies are to be found in the French language and character. For instance, even though we have recognized in French a language of reason and clarity, of precision and exactitude, French could not have become the language of diplomacy had it failed to reveal such a genius for expressing with the utmost precision the most flagrant inexactitudes. Thus, a *note verbale* is, as everybody knows, a written document; and an *ambassadeur extraordinaire et ministre plénipotentiaire* is a perfectly ordinary envoy and a short-tethered civil servant. There are other inexactitudes which one does not mind swallowing, such as *hors-d'œuvres*, and others again even more flagrant in fields into which we had better not enter, such as *gorge* and *soutien-gorge*.

But this inexactitude is exact in its intention. It amounts to a transformation in geometry, whereby a figure becomes an entirely different one, and yet through rules of such precision that the one can be deduced from the other by any person at any time. This means that the French are exact even in their inexactitudes, just as the English are pragmatic and positive even in their fancies and vagaries. This parallelism finds its perfect illustration in the communiqués or hand-outs of Franco-British diplomatic meetings, when the perfectly French exact inexactitude perfectly fits that wonderful, better-than-natural English with its occasional patches of fog, of course in the right places.

As you would expect, the elasticity indispensable to diplomatic texts is attained in different ways on either side of the Channel. In England it is accomplished by sheer indecision as to the meaning of sentences and even of words, such an indecision as to permit endless discussions on the intention of the original writer, not excluding the possibility that his intention was to be unintelligible, or even that he faithfully wrote down the opaqueness of his own thought at the time, whereupon his chiefs, on realizing that it was unintelligible, thought it a good thing. The French, on the other hand, prefer to provide such elasticity by means of verbal hinges or gadgets. In my League of Nations days we had discovered four such hinges, whose well-oiled working we (I believe, rightly) thought to be the hidden reason for the smooth success of the institution. These four hinges were: *notamment, autant que possible, le cas échéant,* and *en principe.*

Any of them was potent enough to neutralize the most recalcitrant opponent of a text we had proposed, of course through a delegate. The United Nations is sure to have evolved a whole arsenal of these verbal gadgets, for they have a much bigger budget, and the Americans, though as pragmatic as, and even more positive than, the British, do not equal their cousins, and in part ancestors, in elasticity of meaning and nebulosity of language. Nebulous and gaseous in England, the English language turns liquid and flowing in America—possibly one, among several others, of the signs of the Germanic element in the composition of her citizens. There is a grand example of this which deserves to be left waving in all its majesty at the end of this essay: what English sea captain would have dared to speak of his Red Duster as Old Glory?